REFLECTIONS ON HANGING

ARTHUR KOESTLER

REFLECTIONS
ON HANGING

With a Preface by
EDMOND CAHN
Professor of Law, New York University

And an Afterword by
SYDNEY SILVERMAN
Member of the British House of Commons

The Light of Lights
Looks always on the motive, not the deed,
The Shadow of Shadows on the deed alone.

W. B. YEATS

THE MACMILLAN COMPANY, New York

1957

LIBRARY OF CONGRESS CATALOG CARD NUMBER: 57-9545

To the Memory of
ROY CALVERT

ACKNOWLEDGEMENTS

MY GRATEFUL acknowledgements are due in the first place to the editors of *Hansard*'s "Parliamentary Debates," from 1808 to the present; next, to the Parliamentary Select Committee on Capital Punishment of 1929–30 and the Royal Commission on Capital Punishment of 1949–53. These two monumental documents I regarded as the Old and the New Testament of my text, with the Select Committee Report of 1819 and the Royal Commission Report of 1866 playing the part of the Apocrypha. With one exception, their admirable and moderate recommendations were never implemented, the governments who appointed them having taken the view of the Pasha in a novel by Mr. P. H. Newby: "Monsieur Perry is a fanatic. I can see that he is the sort of man who prepares a report and then thinks it ought to be carried out." Next in documentary value come Leon Radzinowicz's *History of English Criminal Law* and Messrs. G. Gardiner's and N. Curtis-Raleigh's pioneer work on *The Judicial Attitude to Penal Reform*. I am indebted to Mr. C. H. Rolph for his advice on procedure at identification parades, and to Mrs. Cynthia Paterson Jefferies for her patient help with the manuscript and proofs.

PREFACE FOR AMERICANS

In my judgment, this is the ideal book on capital punishment for an American reader. For one thing, it comes from the incandescent pen of Arthur Koestler, whom the London *Times Literary Supplement* described recently as "political tutor to his generation." For another, the Afterword by Sydney Silverman, M.P., recounting the strange adventures of the Silverman abolition bill in the British Parliament, brings the narrative to date and makes it uniquely comprehensive. Though these excellences are quite enough, there is something additional for American readers. By concentrating on capital punishment as inflicted overseas in England, Mr. Koestler gives us an unprecedented opportunity to see the issue objectively and without passion, rationally and without sentimentality.

Here is the pith of the matter. In 1764, when Cesare Beccaria first assailed the death penalty in his *On Crimes and Punishments,* he appealed to men's intelligence, practical wisdom, and political judgment. He believed that the case against capital punishment was entirely safe in the forum of reason. That, of course, was why his theme succeeded as well as it did with philosophers and even with despots in an Age of Reason. For decades, capital punishment fell back in continual retreat before the Enlightenment. And when, in later times, the process was reversed and the death penalty reinstalled in this or that state, we can readily identify the specific wave of popular passion which flooded and overwhelmed the discipline of reason. If emotion and feeling were the only propelling force in public affairs, there would be no prospect of abolishing capital punishment, for hatred of hangings would be matched by hatred of murders, and sympathy for the plight of the convict by sympathy for the victim and the victim's family.

Reason—indispensable though it be—will not respond to the snap of an author's fingers. It is hard to induce people to examine their own institutions objectively. Various ways have been tried.

One way is to present an imaginary republic or utopia; another is to depict one's native country as it might appear in the eyes of fictional visitors from a remote and completely different culture. The principal difficulty with these devices is that readers who appreciate the point may find only entertainment in it. Consequently, utopias are more likely to make good literature and conversation than good law.

I think *Reflections on Hanging* offers a nearly perfect solution, at least for Americans. When Mr. Koestler denounces the social attitudes of English judges, we can read without antecedent bias, however we might smile or scowl if he were discussing American judges. When he commends or criticizes a Home Secretary in connection with granting or refusing a reprieve, the chances are we can judge the incident fairly and with detachment. The political parties he mentions are not ours. His murder trials are held at a calm distance from our homes.

Yet on every page, we are engaged in judging ourselves, for whatever is not literally in America is nevertheless about America. Who will forget that our political ancestors brought their main concepts and institutions along with them from England? Who of us can eradicate the pictures of lawyers, judges, courts, and jails which memory lifts from the pages of English novelists and dramatists? Granted that there are some differences between English and American courts as well as resemblances; they are just such differences and resemblances as one would expect to find within a family.

Judging the Judges

In this book, you are about to meet some harsh comments on British judges and their support of capital punishment. When you come to passages of the kind, I hope your only question will be whether the criticisms are sincere and reasonable. Though in England and in the United States there are certain judges who would like to be considered immune from criticism, their attitude is neither sound political democracy nor valid public law. On the one hand, judges are entitled to perform their functions absolutely free of pressures, influences, and outside clamor. On the other hand, any action in the name of and by authority of the public is necessarily subject to the public's comment and appraisal. The principle applies to judges. As Lord Atkin said in a judgment of the Privy Council:

Justice is not a cloistered virtue: she must be allowed to suffer the scrutiny and respectful, even though outspoken, comments of ordinary men.[1]

Speaking for the United States Supreme Court, Justice Hugo L. Black stated the American view:

The assumption that respect for the judiciary can be won by shielding judges from published criticism wrongly appraises the character of American public opinion. For it is a prized American privilege to speak one's mind, although not always with perfect good taste, on all public institutions. And an enforced silence, however limited, solely in the name of preserving the dignity of the bench, would probably engender resentment, suspicion, and contempt much more than it would enhance respect.[2]

No man who is unwilling to be judged can be fit to judge. In this, the best judges of both countries concur.

Are We More Righteous Than the English?

There are various ways to create the impression that, in America, capital punishment is not really so obnoxious. For example, you may have heard it argued that, unlike the English, our penal laws generally distinguish "degrees" of murder. First-degree murder involves capital punishment but second-degree murder does not. Though the statutes say that one of the tests of first-degree murder is "premeditation and deliberation," American courts and juries have often made a travesty of the requirement. A few years ago, the United States Supreme Court (5 to 3) affirmed a first-degree murder conviction of a Negro janitor who was subnormal mentally and had a psychopathic personality.[3] This janitor, having been told that a woman librarian had complained of his work, got into a fierce argument with her and, when she called him a "black nigger," struck her. Her screams sent him into a wild panic. To stop them, he hit her with a piece of wood and, when that broke, stabbed her with his pocket knife. On his confession, the verdict was mur-

[1] Ambard v. Attorney-General [1936] A.C. 322, 335.
[2] Bridges v. California, 314 U.S. 252, 270 (1941).
[3] Fisher v. United States, 328 U.S. 463 (1946).

der in the first degree and the sentence was death. So much for what the judges and juries may accept as adequate proof of "premeditation and deliberation."

This case came to the United States Supreme Court from the federal courts in the District of Columbia. Not long after, the judges in that small yet important jurisdiction apparently decided that their test of criminal responsibility had not kept pace with modern psychiatric progress. They were deeply discontented with the old M'Naghten test, imported by American courts from England. The test, which Mr. Koestler criticizes so keenly in Chapter IV, is based on the mental capacity of the accused to distinguish right from wrong and to tell that the act he was committing was wrong. In 1954 the District of Columbia court adopted a new test, holding that if the unlawful act was the product of a mental disease or defect, the accused could not be convicted.[4] Some criminologists have hailed the change; others have attacked it severely, because it throws the whole question of criminal responsibility into the lap of the jury without providing standards or guides to decision. One thing is certain: No matter how we amend or restate the legal test of criminal responsibility, we shall never feel sure that we are not sending mentally defective, diseased, or irresponsible persons to the electric chair. A poor legal test of responsibility can aggravate the wrongs of capital punishment, but a satisfactory test cannot remove them.[5]

There is one more purported palliative to mention. Mr. Koestler relates some gruesome incidents of technical incompetence on the part of English hangmen, resulting in devastating cruelties. In a number of American states, hanging has been replaced by electrocution. Yet blunders still occur. A few years past, the United States Supreme Court (5 to 4) held that it was not "cruel or unusual punishment" for the State of Louisiana to "electrocute" a convicted murderer a second time, the current having been insufficient to

[4] Durham v. United States, 214 F.2d 862 (D.C. Cir. 1954). See 1955 *Annual Survey of American Law* 135-7.

[5] For information on lesser palliatives, see *Report of Royal Commission on Capital Punishment* (1953) at 182. The American experience with the death penalty is the subject of an excellent symposium, edited by Professor Thorsten Sellin, in 284 *The Annals of The American Academy of Political and Social Science* (Nov. 1952).

extinguish life on the first attempt.[6] In short, the social question is capital punishment itself, not the modernity of the particular gadget that inflicts it. Gibbets and electric chairs and gas chambers are all the same *sub specie humanitatis*.

In one respect, we Americans do have a slim justification for optimism which the English seem to lack. Unlike English judges, American judges have not presented a solid phalanx to defend capital punishment. Justice Benjamin N. Cardozo, our paragon of moral ideals on the bench, said, a generation ago:

I have faith . . . that a century or less from now, our descendants will look back upon the penal system of today with the same surprise and horror that fill our own minds when we are told that only about a century ago one hundred and sixty crimes were visited under English law with the punishment of death, and that in 1801 a child of thirteen was hanged at Tyburn for the larceny of a spoon. Dark chapters are these in the history of law. We think of them with a shudder, and say to ourselves that we have risen to heights of mercy and of reason far removed from such enormities. The future may judge us less leniently than we choose to judge ourselves. Perhaps the whole business of the retention of the death penalty will seem to the next generation, as it seems to many even now, an anachronism too discordant to be suffered, mocking with grim reproach all our clamorous professions of the sanctity of life.[7]

Recently Judge Jerome Frank, champion of humane justice, insisted that we ought to put an end to the "grim reproach."

At Any Rate, Are We No Worse Than the English?

A historical comparison would be inconclusive, for we began rather well and continued poorly. During the era when we were forming a nation of our own, the horizons seemed to glow with new hopes. On this side of the Atlantic as in Europe, intellectual leaders responded ardently to the Enlightenment. Beccaria's *On Crimes and Punishments* (1764) became popular with John Adams, Thomas Jefferson, James Madison, Dr. Benjamin Rush (pioneer in

---

[6] Louisiana v. Resweber, 329 U.S. 459 (1947).

[7] "What Medicine Can Do for Law" in *Selected Writings* 381 (M. E. Hall, ed., 1947).

medical science and signer of the Declaration of Independence),
and William Bradford (Attorney General of Pennsylvania and
later of the United States). In point of fact, the American movement to abolish capital punishment began a couple of months before the opening of the Constitutional Convention, for on March
9, 1787 Dr. Benjamin Rush read a paper against the death penalty
to a select meeting in Benjamin Franklin's home. Since that date,
the movement has marked some fine victories and suffered some
disconcerting setbacks. Its history varies from penal code to penal
code in forty-eight states, the District of Columbia, and the Federal
Government. A minority of the states—usually between one-fourth
and one-third at a given time—have abstained from using the death
penalty; among these, Maine can claim temporal priority and
Michigan the most continuous and consistent policy. Nevertheless,
even after allowance made for differences in population, the executions taking place annually in the United States are many more
than the corresponding totals of capital punishment in England.

How, then, may one decide whether we are worse than the English on the score of capital punishment? What can we take for the
criterion of comparison? Here again, I think, Cesare Beccaria has
furnished us with a guide. It is not to be found in *On Crimes and
Punishments,* the book from which Dr. Benjamin Rush and the
other early disciples derived their reasoning. In chapter after chapter of his famous book, Beccaria was engaged in attacking one or
another form of excessive and disproportionate punishment. Since
hanging was a specific instance of excessive punishment, he denounced it. The death penalty should be abandoned, he said, because it infringed natural law and the social compact, because it
was unnecessarily severe, because it brutalized the state, because it
barbarized the citizenry, and because it was more likely to inspire
than prevent crimes of violence. These were Beccaria's contentions
then and for the rest of his life.

Twenty-eight years later, Beccaria seems suddenly to have discovered that he had been taking much for granted. He had been
assuming (had he not?) that whenever capital punishment was inflicted, it was inflicted on the right person! All his arguments
amounted to contending that the right person, the responsible
criminal, had received the wrong punishment. But suppose, as he
had observed so many times during the twenty-eight years, the

person executed was not responsible for the crime. Suppose either he had nothing to do with the crime, as in a case of mistaken identity, or, though he had participated physically in some way, he was not morally or legally "responsible." Then—Beccaria recognized for the first time—capital punishment is not merely another instance of excessive penalty; it belongs in a class entirely of its own because it alone is irrevocable and irreparable.[8]

Here we have a workable criterion of comparison. In his new wisdom of 1792, Beccaria insisted that trials at law never achieve a completely certain outcome, that at very best they reach what we call "moral certainty," and that the chance of error constitutes, of itself, a sufficient reason to abolish capital punishment. Death was irreversible in Beccaria's day; it is still irreversible.

This proposition may strike a reader in his moral solar plexus. For even if he can feel uninvolved and indifferent when the "right" man is executed, how can he live in company with the thought that it may not be the "right" man? If courts are susceptible to error, then the officials in his own state may be putting innocent people

---

[8] This new idea of Beccaria's emerged in his report for a commission on the penal system of Austrian Lombardy (1792). The report appears as an appendix in Cesare Cantù, *Beccaria e il Diritto Penale* 369 (Florence: G. Barbera 1862). The most probable source of Beccaria's new insight was—of all men—Maximilien Robespierre!

The relation between Robespierre and capital punishment constitutes one of history's most edifying moral dramas. No man ever opposed the penalty more earnestly. A few years before the Revolution, he resigned his office as criminal judge rather than pronounce the sentence of death. As late as 1791, when the short-lived Legislative Assembly of the Revolution debated the question of abolishing capital punishment, Robespierre uttered this brilliant appeal, which apparently came to Beccaria's notice:

"Hear the voice of justice and of reason! It cries that human judgments are never certain enough that society can inflict death on a man condemned by other men, themselves subject to error. Even if you could imagine the most perfect judicial system, if you could find the most honorable and enlightened judges, you would still leave room for error or bias. Why deny yourselves the means of repairing them? Why condemn yourselves to being unable to extend a rescuing hand to oppressed innocence? Of what use are sterile regrets, illusory reparations that you may accord to vain shadows and insensible ashes?"—Charles Lucas, *Receuil des débats* 85 (Paris: Béchet 1831).

Then came the crisis and the turn. In December 1792 Robespierre ruthlessly demanded the execution of Louis XVI, whether guilty or innocent, as a political measure to preserve the peace and safety of the nation. The demand prevailed. Robespierre had destroyed part of himself. The ensuing events were called "The Terror."

to death under the laws. The lot of irreversible mistake may fall on any of us, even on him—the formerly indifferent reader. It is an interesting thought. With it before us, we can attempt a practical comparison—perhaps an uncomfortably practical one—between the American system and the English. We need only ask: By and large, is there a greater chance of convicting and executing the "wrong" person in England or the United States?

The question is inexorable and our opportunities to temporize are over. All informed American lawyers know that, by and large, there can be only one truthful answer. The general inferiority of criminal justice in the United States has been notorious for generations. Despite minor reforms and advances here and there, our penal administration stands indicted as grossly deficient when measured against minimum standards. Let me list some of the main counts.

An Indictment Filed Against American Criminal Procedure

Count I.   Race prejudices and hatreds have often vitiated the administration of criminal justice, have influenced and intimidated jurymen and public officials, and have made conviction of the innocent highly possible.

As I am addressing American readers, I need not elaborate this count.

Count II.   Even in the absence of racial conflict, criminal proceedings often lead to false results because of our excitability and propensity to haste and violence.

This count, also, can find its own confirmation in the experience of the average American citizen. We are still disconcertingly close to the impetuous methods of frontier justice. Our impulses are often too quick for our discretion; they convince us against our sober sense; they blind us to rational evidence.

Impulse and excitement led American courts and juries to so many wrongful convictions that at length the law's mask of infallibility wore through and had to be discarded. In 1938, Congress enacted that any prisoner who had been unjustly convicted and imprisoned by the United States might file a claim against the government for damages, not exceeding $5,000.[9] There is similar

[9] 28 U.S.C. § 1495, § 2513.

legislation in several of our states. It constitutes public and official acknowledgement—if any were needed—that at times justice does miscarry and innocent persons are convicted and imprisoned. To make reparation to the imprisoned innocent is splendidly right; but what can we say to conscience if we have put the innocent beyond the possibility of receiving reparation?

Count III.   Most American newspapers handle crime news so unfairly and sensationally that they deprive the accused of an impartial jury.

If they lived in England, the majority of American newspaper editors and crime reporters would be sent to jail for interfering with the administration of justice and depriving accused persons of a fair trial. How the members of a panel of jurymen can claim to be unbiased in a typical American murder case is quite a mystery; illiteracy might protect some of them from the pre-judgments of the press, but surely they cannot all pretend to complete illiteracy. Here is the setting in a representative example of quite recent date:

Murder and mystery, society, sex and suspense were combined in this case in such a manner as to intrigue and captivate the public fancy to a degree perhaps unparalleled in recent annals. Throughout the preindict-ment investigation, the subsequent legal skirmishes and the nine-week trial, circulation-conscious editors catered to the insatiable interest of the American public in the bizarre. Special seating facilities for reporters and columnists representing local papers and all major news services were installed in the courtroom. Special rooms in the Criminal Courts Building were equipped for broadcasters and telecasters. In this atmosphere of a "Roman holiday" for the news media, Sam Sheppard stood trial for his life.[10]

You have just read the first paragraph of an opinion of the Supreme Court of Ohio. Are you not disposed to infer that the court was about to set aside the conviction, rebuke the trial judge, and, at very least, reverse the ruling by which he had refused to grant a change of venue? If these are your inferences, I fear you are unfamiliar with the standards obtaining in many American courts.[11] As a matter of fact, the Supreme Court of Ohio affirmed the

[10] State v. Sheppard, 165 Ohio St. 293 (1956). The United States Supreme Court declined to consider the case. 352 U.S. 910 (1956).

[11] Testifying before the Royal Commission on Capital Punishment in 1950, Justice Felix Frankfurter of the United States Supreme Court said:

conviction of Sam Sheppard. True, the evidence against him was entirely circumstantial and partly inconsistent; true, the trial judge had committed several errors of law; true, the jurymen had violated a state statute by communicating with their families during their consideration of the case. Yet after all, the verdict was merely murder in the second degree, and even Sheppard could not deny that someone or other had brutally killed his wife.

As we see, English judges are not the only ones who could profit from the attention of Arthur Koestler's pen.

Count IV. A verdict of guilt may result less from the evidence than from the prosecutor's political ambitions, the "third degree" and other brutal police methods, and the intricate technicalities of local procedure.

The facts in support of this count are humiliatingly familiar. Fired by political ambition, a district attorney may recklessly prosecute the wrong man, whip up popular hatred against the accused, suppress truthful evidence that might lead to acquittal, and even (in rare but terrible instances) proffer testimony that he knows to be false and perjurious. Nor is this all. At least since 1893, when Governor John Peter Altgeld of Illinois ruined his career by freeing three prisoners convicted—as he believed, falsely and unfairly—for participating in the Haymarket Massacre, the majority of executives and parole boards have been excessively sensitive to newspaper clamor. The very passions that induce an erroneous conviction can prevent the exercise of executive clemency.[12] If a president or gov-

---

"I am strongly against capital punishment for reasons that are not related to concern for the murderer or the risk of convicting the innocent, and for reasons and considerations that might not be applicable to your country at all. When life is at hazard in a trial, it sensationalises the whole thing almost unwittingly; the effect on juries, the Bar, the public, the judiciary, I regard as very bad. I think scientifically the claim of deterrence is not worth much. Whatever proof there may be in my judgment does not outweigh the social loss due to the inherent sensationalism of a trial for life. I am speaking about my country, not yours. Any opinion I may give is subject to one's bias on the question of capital punishment; so, naturally, I view every system that mitigates the imposition of capital punishment with favour. . . . I myself would abolish it."—Frankfurter, *Of Law and Men* 81 (1956). Though this is, in some respects, a very strange statement, it points correctly to the evil effects of sensationalism.

[12] "He who desires to inflict rational punishment does not retaliate for a past wrong which cannot be undone; he has regard to the future, and is desirous that the man who is punished, and he who sees him punished, may be deterred from doing wrong again. He punishes for the sake of prevention." Plato, *Protagoras* 324 (Jowett trans.).

ernor hears a substantial public group baying for blood, he may take precautions to see that the blood they get is not his.

Amid a surfeit of examples, let me mention only the case of James Smith, trapped and enmeshed in the technicalities of Pennsylvania procedure.[13] Smith was a schizophrenic who had been adjudged insane by a New York Court and had begged to be committed to a naval hospital because, according to his own statement, he was afraid he might kill someone. From 1941 when he was nineteen until 1948 when he did kill someone, he had not been at large for any period longer than nine months. His years had been spent in various prisons and state hospitals. When he was arraigned in the Pennsylvania court and charged with the killing, Smith was "over-reached" [14] into pleading guilty to the capital offense of murder in the first degree. Thus he was never permitted to prove his mental state to a jury. As he was impecunious, his lawyer asked the court to provide a psychiatrist to advise and assist in defending him. The Pennsylvania judge declined this request, and decided that Smith was legally sane. The basis of the judge's decision was the testimony of a court psychiatrist who had gone to the prison and talked with Smith all of an hour. The atrocity became complete a couple of years later when the court psychiatrist was himself committed to an institution because he had "an incurable mental disease which had deprived him of any judgment or insight." The United States Supreme Court (6 to 3) affirmed the conviction.

How can a case like this penetrate so far into a labyrinth of horrors? Surely, at some point or other, the prosecutor can find a way to retrace his steps and take the situation back to the light of social sanity. When, on the contrary, we see the shutting and sealing of door after door that might have led to a civilized outcome, we may appreciate why Justice William O. Douglas commented in a recent public address:

During that time [of sitting on the Supreme Court] it has seemed to me that the quality of prosecutors has markedly declined. . . . Sometimes they

---

[13] Smith v. Baldi, 344 U.S. 561 (1953).

[14] I quote this seemingly scandalous characterization from Chief Judge Biggs's splendid dissent in the Court of Appeals. 192 F.2d 540, 549. For lack of space, my summary omits several very disturbing circumstances recounted by Chief Judge Biggs.

treated the courtroom not as a place of dignity, detached from the community, but as a place to unleash the fury of public passion.[15]

Of course, our state and federal governments do not lack prosecutors and judges of the highest professional caliber and most scrupulous official behavior. Some of them exemplify the very finest and noblest ethical qualities. Owing, I believe, to the statesmanlike capacities that our American system of constitutional review requires of our jurists, the best among them seem, at least during this century, to excel England's best contemporary judges in wisdom and intellectual vigor. But control over trials and the death penalty is not confined to the hands of our best; it resides also with the many officials and judges who are insensitive and mediocre, not to mention the minority who are cynical, ruthless, and corrupt. . . .

These are four principal counts in the indictment of our penal justice, demonstrating how readily it may slip into error and send the "wrong" person to the scaffold. Surely the counts are awesome enough to trouble a man's imagination, afflict his conscience, and make him pay heed when Judge Jerome Frank says:

Were human judgment about guilt infallible, still a death sentence would be immoral because no man may morally play God. But such a thesis need not be considered, for it assumes the impossible. Experience teaches the fallibility of court decisions. The courts have held many an innocent man guilty. How dare any society take the chance of ordering the judicial homicide of an innocent man? [16]

I would have us take Judge Frank's phrase very seriously. If, instead of presuming to "play God," we should determine to pursue His ways in humility and reverence, then we would never consent that the law destroy our fellows, His creatures, whose breath—as it were—flows to them from Him. All our learning and experience teaches that the most confident of human judgments are inherently fallible; the judgments of courts in every country are quite fallible;

---

[15] Douglas, "A Challenge to the Bar," 28 *Notre Dame Lawyer* 497, 503 (1953).
[16] Statement furnished to me by Judge Frank expressly for this preface.

and the judgments of many American courts are far more fallible than they need be.

Criticism and Patriotism

As *Reflections on Hanging* demonstrates in every chapter, there are many good reasons—some of them merely persuasive, some ethically peremptory—for abolishing the death penalty. The fact that prosecutors, judges, psychiatrists, juries, and executives are so fallible is not the only reason; perhaps other considerations will appear, and deserve to appear, loftier or more dignified. But at least the inveterate fallibility of penal administration constitutes a *sufficient* reason. If it stood entirely alone, it would be powerful enough to enlist rational and patriotic readers in the struggle against capital punishment.

Rational, yes, but also patriotic, for this book which Arthur Koestler has written is a work of intense patriotism. Of course, Koestler's kind of patriotism may not appeal to citizens who sit at ease in their fancied security and, like carved ivory monkeys, decide to hear no evil, see no evil, speak no evil concerning the inherited laws and hoary customs and unlettered prejudices of their nation. Let them sit there on the shelf. The patriotism I mean is no synonym for looking smug and shutting one's mind. It consists rather in prizing what one's country might become if it would live according to its best aspirations and potentialities.

This is why a genuine patriot will never overlook a cruel practice or condone a social injustice on the ground that it happens to obtain at home. On the contrary, to him an injustice seems the more repulsive for arising at home and marring the image of his land and people. When his own state inflicts a wrong, the burden of responsibility becomes peculiarly his, at least in some part. He bears the guilt, the duty to repair as far as possible, and, above all, the duty to prevent.

We who live as free citizens in a democratic society are responsible for capital punishment imposed by our law. Every day the penal codes draw their validity from our name, the executions are ordered by our authority, and the rope or electric current or lethal gas is

bought with our tax money. There is no one else: it is we who ar-
range, through hired deputies, for pulling the lever or pressing the
button.

As the moral responsibility is ours, so too is the political power
to object and prevent. If we resolve that capital punishment is not
civilized enough for America, we can unite and abolish it. The task
requires only dedication and courage. Who, living under these
skies, dares not hope? America may yet fulfill its earliest vision and
every state become worthy of the just, the understanding, and the
compassionate.

EDMOND CAHN

New York University

PREFACE

IN 1937, DURING the Civil War in Spain, I spent three months under sentence of death as a suspected spy, witnessing the executions of my fellow prisoners and awaiting my own. These three months left me with a vested interest in capital punishment—rather like "half-hanged Smith", who was cut down after fifteen minutes and lived on. Each time a man's or a woman's neck is broken in this peaceful country, memory starts to fester like a badly healed wound. I shall never achieve real peace of mind until hanging is abolished.

I have stated my bias. It colours the arguments in the book; it does not affect the facts in it, and most of its content is factual. My intention was to write it in a cool and detached manner, but it came to naught; indignation and pity kept seeping in. This is perhaps just as well, for capital punishment is not merely a problem of statistics and expediency, but also of morality and feeling. Fair pleading requires that one's facts and figures should be right, that one should not distort or quote out of context; it does not exclude having one's heart and spleen in it.

Some of the learned friends who helped with the material for this book, warned me against offending certain venerable prejudices and traditional susceptibilities concerning judges and juries, the notion of a fair trial, the handling of the prerogative of mercy, and so on. I have disregarded their warnings because appeasement never pays, and because I believe that the case for abolition has been weakened by lack of outspokenness. Others advised silence regarding the physiological facts about executions, past and present. That amounts to saying that the Queen of Spain has no legs and the hanged man has no neck. We hang on an average one person each month; if this thing is done in the name of the people, they have a right to know what is being done.

The reason why, twenty years ago, I made the acquaintance of the condemned cell was the hopeful belief in the salvation of mankind by a world revolution; this book aims, more modestly, at saving thirteen wretches a year the pain and terror of going through the same experience. Apart from that, there is also a larger issue involved, for the gallows is not merely a machine of death, but the oldest and most obscene symbol of that tendency in mankind which drives it towards moral self-destruction.

A. K.

LONDON.
October 3rd, 1955.

CONTENTS

Part I

*TRADITION
AND
PREJUDICE*

THE HERITAGE OF THE PAST

The charge is prepar'd; the lawyers meet;
The Judges all rang'd (a terrible show!).
JOHN GAY: *The Beggar's Opera.*

1. The Jack-in-the-Box

GREAT BRITAIN is that peculiar country in Europe where people drive on the left side of the road, measure in inches and yards, and hang people by the neck until dead. To most Britons it never occurs that there may be something odd about this custom. Every nation takes its traditions for granted, and hanging is as much part of the British tradition as counting in shillings and pence. Generations of children have squeaked with delight at the appearance of the puppet hangman in the Punch and Judy show. Four executioners are included in the *Dictionary of National Biography;* Jack Ketch, Calcraft, and "William Boilman" * were as popular figures in their time as film-stars are today. There seems to be a jolliness about the procedure as if the victim twitching at the end of the rope were not a real person but a dummy burnt on Guy Fawkes' Day. The present hangman, Pierrepoint, runs a public house called "Help the Poor Struggler"; his former assistant, Allenby, ran one called "The Rope and the Anchor"; [1] and the present Lord Chief Justice delighted a Royal Academy banquet with the story of a judge who, after passing sentence of death on three men, was welcomed by a band playing the Eton Boating Song's refrain: "We'll all swing together." This was printed in an amiable "Profile" of Lord Goddard in *The Observer,*[2] which continued:

There is a story of his boyhood, which even though it be apocryphal, may illustrate the Goddard legend. When he first went to Marlborough, it was apparently a school custom to make every new boy sing or recite

---

* Nickname for the executioner, derived, according to Macaulay, from the custom of publicly boiling the entrails of traitors after they were disembowelled alive.

in his dormitory. Called upon to sing, the future Lord Chief Justice is said to have surprised the other boys by chanting in a piping voice: "You will be taken from here to a place of execution and hanged by the neck until you be dead. And may the Lord have mercy on your soul."

It all goes to show that hanging has, for Britons, a kind of macabre cosiness, like a slightly off-colour family joke, which only foreigners, abolitionists and other humorless creatures are unable to share. On November 2nd, 1950, Mr. Albert Pierrepoint was called to testify as a witness before the Royal Commission on Capital Punishment. He was asked how many people he had hanged in his career as an executioner, and answered: "Some hundreds." [3]

Q. Have you had any awkward moments?—*A.* No, I have only seen one in all my career.

Q. What happened?—*A.* He was rough. It was unfortunate; he was not an Englishman, he was a spy, and he kicked up rough.

Q. He went for you?—*A.* Not only for me, he went for everybody. [4]

The acting Under-Sheriff for the County of London, Mr. H. N. Gedge, was also examined by the Commission on the unpleasant character who had kicked up rough, and confirmed Mr. Pierrepoint's view:

Yes. He was a foreigner, and I personally have noticed that English people take their punishment better than foreigners. . . . He just dived at the Executioner with his head, and then he just fought with everything he had. [5]

There you are. Hanging is quite all right for Englishmen; they actually seem to like it; it is only the foreigners who cause trouble. The outsider appreciates neither the clean fun, nor the solemn ritualistic aspect of the procedure, nor the venerable tradition behind it. The Lord Chief Justice, asked by the same Royal Commissioners whether he was in favour of retaining the black cap, answered:

I think so. It is traditional, and I do not see any reason for interfering with a tradition which has existed over hundreds of years, unless there is some good reason for doing it. . . . The reason why the judge wears a black cap when passing sentence of death, I believe, is simply that the covering of the head, in ancient times, was regarded as a sign of mourning, and that is why it is done. [6]

Mr. Pierrepoint expressed equally strong views about the traditional aspects of the process:

Q. I imagine that people must talk to you about your duties?—*A.* Yes, but I refuse to speak about it. It is something I think should be secret. . . . It is sacred to me, really.[7]

One could hardly imagine a greater contrast in rank and dignity between two servants of the public; a fact which makes the similarity of their views on certain points the more remarkable. Thus, Lord Goddard was asked his views on the suggestion that women ought no longer to be hanged; he answered: "I do not understand that point of view at all." [8] Mr. Pierrepoint was asked whether there was anything particularly unpleasant in the execution of a woman. Mr. Pierrepoint said there wasn't.

Q. Do you find your duties very trying, or have you got accustomed to them?—*A.* I am accustomed to it now.
Q. You do not turn a hair?—*A.* No.[9]

Lord Goddard was not asked how many people he had sentenced to hang, nor whether he turned a hair; but he was asked whether he thought that fewer people ought to be sentenced to death, or that fewer ought to be reprieved. He answered that too many were reprieved.[10] He was asked whether he thought it proper that a man, certified insane, should be hanged. He said he thought it was perfectly proper.

Q. Even though he was insane, and presumably . . . not in a fit state to make his peace with God?—*A.* He could make his peace with God, I think, quite well.[11]
Q. Another suggestion that has been made is that, whenever the jury makes a recommendation to mercy, the Home Secretary should have to carry it out?—*A.* That, I think, would be most disastrous.[12]

I have no personal animosity against Lord Chief Justice Rayner Goddard; but as the highest judge in the realm, he is the symbol of authority, and his opinions, which I shall have frequent occasion to quote, carry immense weight in the debate about hanging. The views which he holds are not accidental; they are a very consistent expression of the attitude shared by all who favour the continuation of capital punishment. Their arguments, and the philosophy behind their arguments, have remained unchanged over the last two hundred years, as the pages which follow will show. They can only be properly understood in the light of past history.

The scaffold and the executioner are memories of the past in all Western European democracies except France. The death-penalty has also been abolished in several North American States, in virtually the whole of Central and South America, and in a number of Asiatic and Australian states; making altogether thirty-six countries, the major portion of the civilized world.

The British are a proverbially disciplined and law-abiding people—more so than the average of abolitionist nations, which include hot-tempered Latin Americans and Germans who had been exposed to the brutalizing influence of the Nazi régime. Yet the defenders of capital punishment claim that the British nation, unlike others, cannot afford to dispense with the services of the hangman as protector and avenger of society. They say that the example of other nations proves nothing, because conditions in this country are "different"; foreigners may be deterred from crime by the threat of long-term imprisonment, the British criminal can only be deterred by the gallows. This paradoxical belief is so deeply rooted in the pro-hanging party that they do not even see it as a paradox. Many of them hate the idea of hanging and admit that the practice is repellent and evil, yet they believe it to be a necessary evil. This belief in the irreplaceable deterrent value of the death-penalty has been proved to be a superstition by the long and patient inquiries of the Parliamentary Select Committee of 1930 and the Royal Commission on Capital Punishment of 1948; yet it pops up again and again. Like all superstitions, it has the nature of a Jack-in-the-box; however often you hit it over the head with facts and statistics, it will solemnly pop up again, because the hidden spring inside it is the unconscious and irrational power of traditional beliefs. Hence all arguments are wasted unless we go back to the origins of that tradition, and unearth the elements in the past which exert such a strong influence on our present beliefs.

Let us go back, then, to the days of the Tyburn tree. It will be an excursion into a strangely neglected and little-known chapter of English history, which is very curious indeed—a forensic wonderland where the March Hare wears a wig and Malice wades through gore.

2. The "Bloody Code"

It will be convenient to proceed in two steps: to describe the unique method of dealing with crime which prevailed in this country around A.D. 1800, and then go even further back to explain how that situation came about.

At the beginning of the nineteenth century the criminal law of this country was commonly known as the Bloody Code. It was unique in the world inasmuch as it listed between 220 and 230 offences to be punished by death, from the stealing of turnips to associating with gipsies, to damaging a fishpond, to writing threatening letters, to impersonating out-pensioners at Greenwich Hospital, to being found armed or disguised in a forest, park or rabbit warren, to cutting down a tree, to poaching, forging, picking pockets, shoplifting, and so on, through 220-odd items. The exact number of capital offences was not even known to the best legal authorities.[13] Besides, each statute was so broadly framed that "the actual scope of the death-penalty was often as much as three or four times as extensive as the number of capital provisions would seem to indicate".[14]

Let us remember that we are not talking of the Dark Ages, but of the beginning of the nineteenth century, up to Queen Victoria's reign, when everywhere in the civilized world offences against property were being removed from the list of capital crimes. In 1810, Sir Samuel Romilly said in the House of Lords that "there was no country on the face of the earth in which there had been so many different offences according to law to be punished with death as in England".[15] Twenty years later Sir Robert Peel complained to the House of Commons: "It is impossible to conceal from ourselves that capital punishments are more frequent and the criminal law more severe on the whole in this country than in any country in the world." [16] And the greatest nineteenth-century authority at law, Sir James Stephen, talked of "the clumsiest, most reckless, and most cruel legislation that ever disgraced a civilized country". [17]

This state of affairs was the more puzzling as in some other respects British civilization was ahead of the rest of the world. Foreign visitors were impressed by the exemplary fairness of British courts—and horrified by the savage penalties they inflicted. They were amazed to find the highways dotted with gibbets, creaking and groaning with the bodies of criminals. The gallows and the gibbet were such common objects in the English countryside that in early guidebooks they were used as landmarks for the traveller; for instance:

By the Gallows and Three Windmills enter the suburbs of York. . . . You pass through Hare Street . . . and at 13'4 part for Epping Forest, with the gallows to the left. . . . You pass Penmeris Hall, and at 250'4

Hilldraught Mill, both on the left, and ascend a small hill with a gibbet on the right. . . . You leave Frampton, Wilberton and Sherbeck, all on the right, and by a gibbet on the left, over a stone bridge.[18]

Between London and East Grinstead alone, three gallows stood at different points on the highway, in addition to several gibbets where the dead criminal's body was suspended in chains "till his corpse rot". Sometimes a criminal was "hung in chains" alive, and died only after several days. Sometimes the corpse was drenched in tar to make it last longer. Sometimes the skeleton was left hanging after decay of the body was completed. The last gibbeting took place in 1832 in Saffron Lane, near Leicester, when the body of James Cook, a bookbinder, was suspended thirty-three feet high, his head shaved and tarred, but had to be taken down after a fortnight to stop the merrymaking of the Sunday crowds.[19]

"Hanging days" were, during the eighteenth and up to half-way through the nineteenth century, the equivalent of national holidays, only more frequent. We read, for instance, that in George III's reign, working hours for the poor "were inordinately long, and there were very few holidays except just at Easter, Whitsuntide and Christmas, and on the eight 'Hanging Days' at Tyburn".[20]

According to Lord Templewood, there were about one hundred public executions a year in London and Middlesex alone:

"This constant round of spectacles had much the same effect on industrial production as mid-week races and football matches at the present day. It was, for example, common in London for coach-makers, tailors, shoemakers, and other craftsmen who were engaged to complete orders within a given time, to remind their customers: 'That will be a hanging-day, and the men will not be at work.' " [21]

Yet we must remember that in 1800 the total population of England and Wales was only just over eight million (as opposed to forty-five million today).

The cherished symbol of the hanging tradition was the "Tyburn Tree". The scenes that took place at the public executions were more than a national disgrace, they were outbursts of a collective madness, a kind of mediaeval St. Vitus's dance. Its distant echoes are still discernible when the notice of a hanging is posted at the prison gates. The crowds assembled to watch at Tyburn (the present Marble Arch) sometimes numbered a hundred thousand and more. An early chronicler gave this description of the scene:

All the Way, from *Newgate* to *Tyburn,* is one continued Fair, for Whores and Rogues of the meaner Sort. Here the most abandon'd Rakehells may light on Women as shameless: Here Trollops, all in Rags, may pick up Sweethearts of the same Politeness. . . . Nothing is more entertaining to them, than the dead Carcasses of Dogs and Cats, or, for want of them, Rags, and all Trompery that is capable of imbibing Dirt. These, well trempled in Filth, and, if possible, of the worst sort, are, by the Ring-leaders, flung as high and as far as a strong Arm can carry them, and commonly directed where the Throng is the thickest.[22]

In the provincial towns, it was the same. A clergyman from Shrewsbury testified before the Select Committee of 1856 on the first public execution he had witnessed, the hanging of Josiah Misters in 1841:

The town was converted for the day into a fair. The country people flocked in their holiday dresses, and the whole town was a scene of drunkenness and debauchery of every kind. . . . A very large number of children were present: children and females constituted the larger proportion of the attendance.[23]

The nineteenth century marched on, and some European countries had already abolished capital punishment altogether, others let it fall into abeyance; yet in England public hangings, although they were now transferred to places near the prison gates, remained a kind of officially sanctioned Witches' Sabbath. As late as 1864, this is how *The Times* described the crowd assembled to watch Mueller's hanging:

. . . sharpers, thieves, gamblers, betting men, the outsiders of the boxing ring, bricklayers, labourers, dock workmen, with rakings of cheap singing halls and billiard rooms, the fast young men of London. . . . Before the slight slow vibrations of the body had well ended, robbery and violence, loud laughing, oaths, fighting, obscene conduct and still more filthy language reigned round the gallows far and near. Such too the scene remained with little change or respite till the old hangman (Calcraft) slunk again along the drop amid hisses and sneering inquiries of what he had had to drink that morning. After failing once to cut the rope he made a second attempt more successfully, and the body of Mueller disappeared from view.[24]

Stampedes and fights of all against all were frequent occurrences; in 1807 the crowd of forty thousand became so crazed at the execution of Holloway and Haggerty that nearly a hundred dead and dying were lying in the street when the show was over.[25]

Not only the lower classes were affected by the national perversion. For distinguished onlookers grandstands were erected as at contemporary football games; balconies and windows in the vicinity were let at fabulous prices; ladies of the aristocracy, wearing black Venetian masks, queued to pay last visits to the condemned man in his cell; fobs and dandies travelled all over the country to see a good hanging. The Governor of Newgate Prison habitually entertained onlookers of distinction, after an execution, for breakfast:

And if there were no more than six or seven of them hanged, his guests would return grumbling and disappointed to breakfast, complaining that "there were hardly any fellows hanged this morning". His good-looking daughter, who did the honours at table, admitted, however, that few did much justice to the fare. The first call of the inexperienced was for brandy, and the only person with a good appetite for the broiled kidneys, a celebrated dish of hers, was the chaplain. After breakfast was over the whole party adjourned to see the "cutting down".[26]

Yet this was the age of romantic sensibility, when women swooned on the slightest provocation, and bearded men shed happy tears in each other's arms.

The victims were hanged singly or in batches of twelve, sixteen and up to twenty. Frequently the prisoners were drunk, and the executioner too:

This day Will Summers and Tipping were executed here for housebreaking. At the tree, the hangman was intoxicated with liquor, and supposing that there were three for execution, was going to put one of the ropes round the parson's neck, as he stood in the cart, and was with much difficulty prevented by the gaoler from so doing.

Until fairly recent times, the executioner was usually a reprieved criminal, "such as John Price, who was ultimately hanged himself, being, it is said, actually arrested in the process of performing his duty".[27]

Whether drunk or not, the public hysteria frequently caused the hangman to lose his nerve and bungle his job. The volumes of the *Newgate Calendar* abound in examples of people who had to be hanged twice, and even three times. In some cases the victim was revived by bleeding at his heels and then hanged again; in others the hangman and his assistants had to add their weight by hanging on to the victim's legs; in others his body was mangled or his head partly or entirely torn off. On several occasions the Royal reprieve arrived when the victim was already suspended, and he or she was then cut down. In one case, that of "half-hanged Smith", "he had hung near fifteen minutes . . . and being conveyed to a house in the neighbourhood, he soon recovered in consequence of bleeding and other proper applications".[28]

These horrors continued through the nineteenth century. The whole process was carried out in such uncertain, haphazard and barbaric ways that not only were victims found to be alive fifteen minutes and more after the onset of strangling, but there are also authenticated cases of people reviving in the dissecting hall. Others were resuscitated by their friends after cutting down, by immersing the victim in hot water, bleeding, massaging the limbs, etc.[29]

It is unavoidable, in discussing capital punishment, to go into these ghoulish technicalities in order to make people realize what exactly we are talking about. For these are not entirely matters of the distant past. Official hypocrisy, taking advantage of the fact that executions are no longer public, pretends that modernized hanging is a nice and smooth affair which is always carried out "expeditiously and without a hitch". But the hanging of the Nuremberg war criminals in 1946 was as terribly bungled, and the hanging of Mrs. Thompson in 1923 was a butchery as revolting, as any reported in the *Newgate Calendar*. Her executioner attempted suicide a short time later, and the prison chaplain stated that "the impulse to rush in and save her by force was almost too strong for him". Yet Government spokesmen tell us that all executions are smooth and nice, and Government spokesmen are honourable men.

Even more degrading, if possible, than the execution itself were the scenes which took place immediately after it. Mothers took their children up to the scaffold to have the hand of the corpse applied to them, for this was considered to have a curative effect; chips of the gibbet were carried off as a remedy for toothache. Then the body-snatchers went into action:

As soon as the poor creatures were half dead I was much surprised before such a number of peace officers to see the populace fall to hauling and pulling the carcasses with so much earnestness as to occasion several warm encounters and broken heads. These, I was told, were the friends of the persons executed, or such as, for the sake of tumult, chose to appear so, and some persons sent by private surgeons to obtain bodies for dissection.[30]

The spirit of the whole thing, and its elevating moral effect, were summed up in the famous *Ballad of Sam Hall*. I owe the relatively expurgated version that follows to the courtesy of Mr. Monty Carew of the "Players' Theatre", which revived this memorial of the Tyburn tree in the nineteen-thirties.

THE BODY OF SAM HALL

(Anonymous around 1800)

Oh my name it is Sam Hall, Samuel Hall,
Oh my name it is Sam Hall, Samuel Hall,
Oh my name it is Sam Hall and I hate you one and all;
You're a gang of muckers all—Damn your eyes!

Oh they say I killed a man, so they said,
Oh they say I killed a man, so they said,
For I hit him on the head with a bloody great lump of lead.
Oh I left him there for dead—Damn 'is eyes!

Oh they put me into quod, into quod,
Oh they put me into quod, into quod,
Oh they put me into quod all for killing of that sod,
They did—so 'elp me God—Damn their eyes!

Oh the parson 'e did come, 'e did come,
Oh the parson 'e did come, 'e did come,
Oh the parson 'e did come and 'e looked so bloody glum,
And he talked of Kingdom Come—Damn his eyes!

So hup the steps I go, very slow,
So hup the steps I go, very slow,
So hup the steps I go and you muckers down below
Are standing in a row—Damn your eyes!

I sees Molly in the crowd, in the crowd,
I sees Molly in the crowd, in the crowd,
I sees Molly in the crowd, so I hollered out aloud
"Now ain't you bleedin' proud—Damn your eyes!"

And now I 'ears the bell, 'ears the bell,
And now I 'ears the bell, 'ears the bell.
And it is my funeral knell, and I'll meet you all in Hell
And I 'opes you frizzle well—Damn your eyes!

Amid all this distress and degradation there is only an occasional fleeting moment when the dignity of man asserts itself. Such a moment occurred when George Manley delivered his last speech to the crowd assembled at the gallows on which he was to be hanged at Wicklow, Ireland, in August, 1738:

My friends, you assemble to see—what? A man leap into the abyss of death! You see what I am—I'm a little fellow. My Redeemer knows that murder was far from my heart, and what I did was through rage and passion, being provoked by the deceased. You'll say I've killed a man. Marlborough killed his thousands, and Alexander his millions. I'm a little murderer and must be hanged. Marlborough and Alexander plundered countries; they were great men. I ran in debt with the ale-wife. I must be hanged. How many men were lost in Italy, and upon the Rhine, during the last war for settling a king in Poland. Both sides could not be in the right! They are great men; but I killed a solitary man.[31]

The *Newgate Calendar* says that no particulars have survived either of Manley or the circumstances of his crime. Yet, this strangely powerful and dignified speech came, not from a learned judge or counsel, but from a man convicted of murder.

There was little discrimination of sex or age. Women convicted of high or petty treason (i.e. murdering a husband) were not drawn and quartered, only burnt alive. Children were not liable to the death-penalty if under seven years, and fully liable over fourteen; between seven and fourteen they could be and were hanged if there was "strong evidence of malice" because malice was held "to supply age".[32] Here are a few cases:

In 1748, William York, a boy of ten, was sentenced to death for murder. Chief Justice Willis postponed the execution to find out whether it was proper to hang the child. All the judges concurred that it was. Their ruling deserves to be quoted because it epitomizes the judges' blind belief, throughout the centuries, in the unique and irreplaceable deterrent effect of the death-penalty. The judges ruled that the child—

is certainly a proper subject for capital punishment, and ought to suffer; for it would be a very dangerous consequence to have it thought that children may commit such atrocious crimes with impunity. There are many crimes of the most heinous nature . . . which children are very capable of committing; and which they may in some circumstances be under strong temptation to commit; and therefore, though the taking away the life of a boy of ten years old may savour of cruelty, yet as the example of this boy's punishment may be *a means of deterring other children from the like offenses;* and as the sparing of this boy, merely on account of his age, will probably have a quite contrary tendency, in justice to the publick, the law ought to take its course.[33] (Italics mine.)

In 1800 another boy of ten was sentenced to death for "secreting notes" at the Chelmsford Post Office. The judge, in a letter to Lord Auckland, explained as follows the reasons why he had refused commutation of the sentence:

All the circumstances attending the transaction manifested art and contrivance beyond his years, and I therefore refused the application of his Counsel to respite the Judgment on the ground of his tender years, being satisfied that he knew perfectly what he was doing. But still, he is an absolute Child, now only between ten and eleven, and wearing a bib, or what your old Nurse (my friend) will know better by the name of a Pinafore. . . . To pacify the feelings of a most crowded court, who all expressed their horror of such a Child being hanged, after stating the necessity of the prosecution and *the infinite danger of its going abroad into the world that a Child might commit such a crime with impunity,* when it was clear that he knew what he was doing, I hinted something slightly of its still being in the Power of the Crown to interpose in every case that was open to Clemency.[34] (Italics mine.)

That was in 1800. Let us compare this with Lord Goddard's summing up to the jury in the case of Craig, sixteen, and Bentley, nineteen. It will be remembered that Craig, at sixteen, could not read and that Bentley was a Grade 4 mental deficient; and that both had been nurtured on gangster films and horror comics to which they were addicted:

Now let us put out of our minds in this case any question of films, or comics, or literature of that kind. These things are prayed in aid nowadays when young prisoners are in the dock, and they have very little to do with the case. These two young men—boys or whatever you like to call them—are both of an age which makes them responsible to the law. They are over fourteen, and it is surely idle to pretend these days that a boy of sixteen doesn't know the wickedness of taking out a revolver of that description and a pocketful of ammunition, and firing when he is on an unlawful expedition. . . .[35]

The Lord Chief Justice remained equally true to tradition when, in the 1948 debate, he successfully opposed raising the age limit for liability to suffer capital punishment from eighteen years to twenty-one years. According to British law, a person under twenty-one is not considered sufficiently responsible to sign a legal contract or to make a will; but he is sufficiently responsible to be hanged without signing a will.

Sentences of death were passed on children as late as 1833—when a boy of nine was sentenced to hang for pushing a stick through a cracked shop-window and pulling out printer's colour to the value of tuppence, but was respited owing to public protest.[36] Samuel Rogers relates in his *Table Talk* that he saw "a cartload of young girls, in dresses of various colours, on their way to be executed at Tyburn". And Greville describes the trial of several young boys who were sentenced to death "to their excessive amazement" and broke into tears. He laconically remarks: "Never did I see boys cry so."

In 1801, Andrew Brenning, aged thirteen, was publicly hanged for breaking into a house and stealing a spoon. In 1808 a girl aged *seven* was publicly hanged at Lynn.[37] In 1831, a boy of nine was publicly hanged at Chelmsford for having set fire to a house, and another aged thirteen at Maidstone.[38] Three years later the Lord Chancellor, Lord Eldon, in opposing any mitigation of the law, had the temerity to state that "he had been His Majesty's adviser for twenty-five years and so far as his knowledge extended, mercy had never been refused in any instance where it ought not to have been withheld".[39]

Similar statements about mercy "never being refused" where there is a "scintilla of doubt" were made in the 1948 debate on capital punishment, and on later occasions after Bentley, Evans, Rowland, etc. had been hanged.

Let me repeat: we are not talking about the Dark Ages, but about the Period of Enlightenment, when all over Europe criminal legislation was rapidly being humanized. Influenced by the teachings of Beccaria, Montesquieu and Voltaire, capital punishment was abolished in Austria for the first time as far back as 1781 by Joseph II.[40]

His brother, the Grand Duke of Tuscany, followed suit in 1786 [41] and promulgated a penal code which proclaimed the readaptation of offenders to normal life as the main object of all punishment. The French National Assembly debated complete abolition in 1791, and arrived at a compromise solution which reduced the number of capital offences from 115 to 32.[42] Catherine the Great of Russia issued in 1767 her famous "Instruction" [43] which abolished capital punishment, and declared that: "It is Moderation which rules a People and not Excess of Severity." *

In Sweden, after the criminal reform of 1779, on the average only 10 people were executed per year.[44] In Prussia, under Frederick II, on the average less than 15 people were executed per year; between 1775 and 1778, altogether 46 people were executed and among these only 2 for offences against property (robbery in the street).[45]

During the same period (1775 to 1778) 149 people were hanged in London and Middlesex alone; [46] no statistics are available for the whole country, but the total must have amounted to a multiple of that figure. Detailed statistics are available for 1785,[47] in which year there were 97 executions in London and Middlesex, out of which only one for murder and the remaining 96 for offences against property. The murder rate in England was in fact *lower* than in most European countries.

This shocking contrast between England and the Continent was mainly due to the fact that hanging was regarded by the Bloody Code as a cure-all for every offence, from stealing a handkerchief upward. Yet these comparisons refer to the eighteenth century only. During the first third of the nineteenth, in the period between the Napoleonic Wars and the beginning of Victoria's reign, the contrast is even more staggering. The oldest democracy in Europe, which had never suffered the brutalizing effects of foreign invasion, became distinguished, in Sir James Stephen's words, by "the most reckless and most cruel legislation that ever disgraced a civilized country".

How did this fantastic situation come about? The answer can only be traced in its outlines, but it is of the greatest relevance to the present situation.

* Though the new penal code which the "Instruction" ordered to be drawn up was not promulgated, the "Instruction" itself revolutionized Russian penology and was typical of the spirit of the time.

3. Historic Origin of the Bloody Code

The situation round 1800 was not a heritage of the dark past, but the result of a deliberate turning-back of the clock. Three main causes seem to have been at work to make English criminal law during the eighteenth century develop in a direction opposite to that of the rest of the world:

(a) England's lead in the Industrial Revolution;

(b) the Englishman's dislike of authority, which prevented the creation of an effective police force;

(c) the peculiarity of English Common Law, which led to the emergence of a class of men with the authority of oracles, opposed to any departure from precedent and to any concession to the moving times.

Mediaeval Common Law imposed the death-penalty only on a few grave offences, such as murder, treason, arson and rape. Under the Tudors and Stuarts the law became more rigorous, but at the beginning of the eighteenth century there were as yet no more than fifty capital offences. At the beginning of the nineteenth, there were nearly five times as many. The development of the Bloody Code was simultaneous with, and largely caused by, the Industrial Revolution, which transformed the nation as thoroughly as if it had been put through a cement-mixing machine. It gave England the lead in the western world, but at the same time produced social evils whose distant echoes are still felt in our day.

"The terrible pace at which the world now jolts and clanks along was set in our island where, first, invention was harnessed to organized capital. For fifty years that great change was left uncontrolled by the community which it was transforming." [48] Towns were growing like hideous, squalid mushrooms, without any machinery of administration, local government and public security. The ancient order of society was disintegrating, but nobody had any experience or any clear idea how to cope with the resulting social chaos, and particularly with the new town proletariat of wage-earners, uprooted from their rural existence, transformed into a race of shiftless slum-dwellers. The spreading of extreme poverty with its concomitants of prostitution, child labour, drunkenness and lawlessness, coincided with an unprecedented accumulation of wealth as an additional incentive to crime. All foreign visitors agreed that never before had the world seen such riches and splendour as displayed in London residences and shops—nor so many pickpockets, burglars and highwaymen. "One is forced to travel even at noon as if one was going to battle", Horace Walpole wrote in 1752. It was this general feeling of insecurity, often verging on panic, which led to the enactment, by the dozen, of capital statutes, making any offence from poaching and stealing from the value of one shilling upward punishable by death. And each statute branched out like a tree to cover any similar or related offences.

This process went on for over a hundred years, and was only brought to an end when Robert Peel, in 1829, created the modern police force. Had that been done a century earlier, the whole shame and terror could have been avoided. The reason why it was not done was, paradoxically, the Englishman's love of freedom, and his dislike of regimentation: the fear that a regular police force, once established, would be used to curtail his individual and political freedom.

"They have an admirable Police at Paris, but they pay for it dear enough. I had rather half a dozen people's throats should be cut in Ratcliffe Highway every three or four years than be subject to domiciliary visits, spies, and all the rest of Fouché's contrivances", John William Ward wrote as late as 1811. Even Sir Samuel Romilly, the leader of the penal reform movement, shared this view in his youth. "However great and inordinate the powers with which the Officers of such Police might be armed", he wrote, "they would in the end be found insufficient. Those very powers, rendering the persons who possessed them the objects of suspicion, and perhaps of public detestation, would make other and still more extraordinary powers necessary, till all the precautions, all the restraints, and all the severities of the most jealous tyranny were one by one established." [49]

Faced by the choice between the cop and the hangman, England chose the hangman. He was a familiar figure from the past; the cop was a new-fangled innovation of foreign countries, and a much too dangerous experiment. As all other curiosities in this chapter, I mention this not for curiosity's sake, but because it is directly relevant to the controversy of our day. The last-ditch stand of the defenders of capital punishment is made precisely on the same issue which started the whole disaster: to wit, that if hanging were abolished, the police would have to carry arms to cope with the emboldened criminal. We shall see later on that in some of the countries which abolished capital punishment, the police carried arms both before abolition and afterwards, in others carried no arms before abolition or after; and that there is no reason to believe that there would be any necessity for change in this country. But the point that interests us here is, once more, the powerful unconscious influence of tradition: up to this day, the idea of allowing cops to wear a revolver is more abhorrent to the Englishman's sensibilities than the continuance of hanging.

The panicky character of the emergency legislation of the eighteenth century is strikingly illustrated by the so-called "Waltham Black Act". It set the example and the pace of the whole development. In 1722, the Hampshire landowners were worried by a band of poachers who went around with their faces blackened to make recognition more difficult. They were following yet another and even more ancient tradition: that of the Roberdsmen, the followers of Robert, or Robin, Hood. The gentlemen of Hampshire appealed to Parliament, not knowing that they were going to make British history; and Parliament enacted a statute "for the more effectual punishing wicked and evil disposed Persons going armed in Disguise, and doing Injuries and Violence to the Persons and Properties of His Majesty's Subjects, and for the more speedy bringing of Offenders to Justice".

The Roberdsmen vanished from Hampshire, but the Waltham Black Act came to stay. It was enacted to meet a local and temporary emergency for a limited period of three years; and it stayed for 101 years, till 1823; and all the time it was ramifying. For it was so vaguely and generally worded that the judges could apply it to an unlimited range of offenders and offences, each time creating a precedent on which further convictions could be based. Altogether, the Waltham Black Act, by budding and ramification, created over three hundred and fifty new capital crimes. These referred to: persons either armed and having their faces blackened; or armed and otherwise disguised; or being merely otherwise disguised; or being *neither blackened nor disguised;* or principals in the second degree; or accessories after the act. The offences included: offences against red or fallow deer, thefts of hares, connies and fish, destroying the heads of fishponds, cutting down "a tree planted in any avenue, garden, orchard or plantation for ornament, shelter or profit", offences against cattle, setting anything on fire, shooting at any person, sending a letter demanding money if unsigned or signed by a fictitious name, and so on and so forth through 350-odd items.

A similar fate of growth by ramification befell the statute relating to "Larceny in dwelling houses and shops". It originally referred only to burglary, but eventually covered any theft over twelvepence without the previously essential element of breaking in. One of the earliest reformers, Eden, wrote in 1771 that except for members of the legal profession "there are not ten subjects in England" who knew on what niceties or counts of the Larceny Law they could be hanged. Yet it was not repealed until 1833.

These barbarous laws were passed by Parliament "without debate, enquiry, examination, evidence, or any general interest".[50] Buxton describes a member of the House of Commons who, while writing a letter in the Committee Room:

—at one corner observed a gentleman seated at a table, and seemingly asleep, to whom a clerk was reading a piece of parchment, which looked like an act of parliament. Sir William was continually interrupted by a kind of chorus, with which every paragraph concluded: "Shall suffer death without benefit of clergy." At length Sir William said, "What may this heinous offence be which you are visiting with so terrible a penalty?"—"Why, Sir," replied the legislator, "we country gentlemen have suffered much by depredations in our turnips,—we have at length determined to put a period to this practice; and my good friend the minister has been so obliging as to allow me to make it death without benefit of clergy." [51]

I have tried to trace the origins of this madness which cast the shadow of the gallows over every hamlet, forest and borough of the land. But madness and panic last, as a rule, only a short time. This was the age when Beccaria's, Voltaire's and Montesquieu's teachings fell everywhere on fertile ground, except in England; and in England itself there were Jeremy Bentham, the Mills, Eden and Howard, Romilly, Selborne and other enlightened men, conscious of the national shame, who fought it with the power of the word and the pen. What, then, was the cause, and which were the forces that kept the madness going and resisted all attempts to stop it, all measures of reform, until the mid-nineteenth century? The answer is simple: the judges of England.

4. The Oracles

In the fifteenth and sixteenth centuries, most European countries adopted written codes based on the Roman Law, in replacement of their old customary "common law" or "folk-law". Two hundred years later, a second wave of codification swept over Europe in the wake of the *Code Napoléon*. England alone has adhered to this day to common law, defined by Blackstone as "not set down in any written statute or ordinance, but depending on immemorial usage for support".[52] The validity and application of these usages is to be determined by the judges—"the depositories of the law, the living oracles, who must decide in all cases of doubt, and who are bound by oath to decide according to the law of the land".[53] Their judgments are preserved as records, and "it is an established rule to abide by former precedents. . . . The extraordinary deference paid to precedents is the source of the most striking peculiarities of the English Common Law." [54]

The benefits of the Common Law as a bulwark of the Britons' political and personal freedom were enormous, and are an essential part of English history. One of the minor advantages derived from the refusal to accept Roman Law and/or Canon Law was that England alone never introduced torture as a method for extracting confessions—drawing and quartering, and pressing to death, were aggravated forms of execution, not methods of making the prisoner confess.* Continental law was *inquisitorial,* English law *accusatory;* it admitted of no pressure being exercised on the accused. Hence the superiority of English judicial procedure in giving the accused a fair trial, acknowledged all over the Continent.

But these benefits were heavily paid for. Dislike of regimentation by the police was a major cause for the prevalence of the hangman; dislike of law by code and statute left English legislation at the mercy of the wigged oracles, who, since precedent must be their only guidance, by the very nature of their calling had their minds riveted on the past. They not only administered the law; they made it. "In

---

* This is not strictly true of pressing to death (*Peine forte et dure*), but the point is technical and unimportant.

earlier times unquestionably the judges regarded the Common Law as supreme and unchangeable by any authority other than themselves. . . . Today judges . . . observe Bacon's monition that their office is . . . to declare the law and not to make it. But in practice the judges undoubtedly legislate, if only by the extension of old rules to new sets of circumstances or even by laying down a new rule where there is no precedent." [55]

It was the judges who interpreted the Waltham Black Act in such a way that it finally branched into over 350 capital offences; under whose guidance Parliament enacted more and more capital statutes which they could interpret and expand; and who fought tooth and nail against the repeal of any of them. The word of the Law Lords and the King's Bench carried, and still carries, decisive weight in influencing Government and Parliament, the leaders of the Church and public opinion; and it was, and is to this day, always thrown in against any attempt at making the law more humane—and thereby more effective. These are rather sweeping statements; let us proceed with the evidence. It will be seen to be directly relevant to the situation in our day.

In 1813, when Romilly's Bill for the abolition of the death-penalty for shoplifting was for the third time defeated by the House of Lords (see below), the later Chief Justice Common Pleas, Lord Wynford, stated the judges' attitude in an unusually frank manner. The text of his speech was *Nolumus leges Angliae mutari*—"We do not wish the laws of England to be changed". The shoplifting act which reformers wished to abolish, he said, had been passed in Cromwell's day, "in the best period of our history, and there was no reason for hazarding an experiment". He would vote for the bill if it could be shown that a single individual had suffered under the existing law, but the humanity of judges was proverbial.[56] This, at a time when children from the age of seven upward were being publicly strangled.

The motto "We do not wish the laws of England to be changed" referred, however, only to mitigations, not to aggravations, of the law. There is no known example of a protest coming from the judges against adding new capital offences to the statute, and a considerable number of death statutes were moved by themselves. It was a one-way process, which made every aggravation of the law irreversible.

Needless to say, there always existed humane judges who, in individual cases where the harshness of the law was too obvious, concurred with the jury, and often with the prosecution, in letting the poor wretch off. But as a body, the judges of England have, as far as historical evidence goes, at every crucial juncture exerted their influence in favour of maximum severity as against any humanitarian reform. This influence was and is exerted in different ways: (a) directly in the House of Lords through the Lord Chancellor, Lord Chief Justice, Master of the Rolls and the Lords of Appeal in Ordinary; (b) indirectly through the weight of their authority in the House of Commons, with the leaders of the Church, and with the public; (c) through the shaping of the law by creating precedent. The most striking and mischievous example of the last point is the M'Naghten rules.*

5. *The Revolt of Public Opinion*

The decisive struggle for the repeal of the absurd and shameful Bloody Code took place between 1808, when Romilly brought in his first Reform Bill, and Queen Victoria's ascent to the throne in 1837. At the beginning of this legal Thirty Years' War, the number of capital statutes was 220-odd; at its end, they were reduced to fifteen.

During its first phase, the movement for reform was led by Samuel Romilly, with little direct success; he committed suicide in 1818. If Romilly was St. George, the dragon had two heads: Chief Justice Lord Ellenborough and Lord Chancellor Lord Eldon. Supported by their learned brethren of the King's Bench, by part of the Bishops' Bench and by some noble fossils in the House of Lords, they opposed every reform of the statutes on the same grounds on which capital punishment has always been defended and is being defended today: that it is the only effective deterrent, that no alternative punishment is equally effective, that mitigation of the law is a dangerous experiment which would lead to an increase in crime, and that public opinion won't stand for it.

The stubborn determination of the diehards and hang-hards may be gathered from a single example: Romilly's Bill to abolish the death-penalty for shoplifting to the value of five shillings and over,

* See Chapter IV.

was passed by the Commons and defeated by the Lords no less than six times: in 1810, 1811, 1813, 1816, 1818 and 1820. It was only passed, long after Romilly's death, in 1832. In the first House of Lords Debate on the bill, on May 30th, 1810, Chief Justice Lord Ellenborough made two speeches which, later on, became almost as famous as Nelson's "Kiss me, Hardy":

I trust your lordships will pause before you assent to an experiment pregnant with danger to the security of property, and before you repeal a statute which has so long been held necessary for public security. I am convinced with the rest of the Judges, public expediency requires there should be no remission of the terror denounced against this description of offenders. Such will be the consequence of the repeal of this statute that I am certain depredations to an unlimited extent would immediately be committed. . . .

My Lords, if we suffer this Bill to pass, we shall not know where to stand; we shall not know whether we are upon our heads or our feet. . . .

Repeal this law and see the contrast—no man can trust himself for an hour out of doors without the most alarming apprehensions, that, on his return, every vestige of his property will be swept off by the hardened robber.[57]

A century and a half later, in the House of Lords debate on the suspension of capital punishment for a trial period of five years, their Lordships, one after the other, unblushingly conjured up the same bogey. E.g., Viscount Simon:

We have no right . . . to risk an experiment which may put in jeopardy innocent human lives. . . . women who at this hour fear, as they never feared before, the knock at the door after it is dark.[58]

Romilly did not live to see his shoplifting Bill through, nor the end of the Waltham Black Act. He only succeeded in his lifetime in getting three capital statutes repealed: those relating to pickpocketing, "soldiers or mariners wandering without a pass", and "stealing from bleaching grounds".

Romilly committed suicide, a defeated man, a few days after his wife's death, in November 1818. He was sixty-one when he died, one of the greatest Englishmen of his time, whose name has been unjustly forgotten. His opponent, Ellenborough, survived him only by a month; the circumstances of his death were as symbolic as Romilly's. In 1817, William Hone, a friend of Cruikshank and Charles Lamb, was tried for blasphemy before Ellenborough. "Ellenborough directed the jury to find a verdict of guilty, and their acquittal of the prisoner is generally said to have hastened his death." [59] It was a fitting end to the great duel over the future of English justice.

By the time of Romilly's death, the eventual triumph of the reform movement was already assured, but he did not know it. His Bill about "stealing from bleaching grounds" was passed without opposition, because 150 proprietors of bleaching establishments and calico printers sent two remarkable petitions to the House of Commons, demanding that stealing from their establishments should cease to be a capital offence, because juries refused to convict the thieves. The petitions were dated 1811, and were the beginning of a most astonishing development. A spate of similar petitions followed, among them a petition of the Corporation of London, a petition of the bankers from 214 cities and towns, and a petition from the jurors of London, all on the same lines: that the archaic severity of the law made its enforcement impossible, and thus destroyed its deterrent effect; and that in the interest of public safety, milder punishments should be imposed.[60]

Soon the House of Commons' tables were groaning under the influx of similar petitions; in 1819, there were more than twelve thousand of them.[61] Under their weight Parliament was at last forced to act: one year after Romilly's and Ellenborough's death, the Select Committee of 1819 was appointed. The reasons behind this step were summed up as follows by a member of the House:

If we look, Sir, to the motives which led to this great and important decision, we must in the first place, ascribe it to the previous verdict of a tribunal, to which even the omnipotence of Parliament ought to bow; I mean the verdict of the public opinion, which has loudly and unequivocally pronounced upon the penal code, as it stands in the Statute Book, a sentence of indignant condemnation.[62]

The decision to appoint "a Committee of Inquiry into the Criminal Laws" was carried by a majority of nineteen against the Government. Its report is a document of permanent value, and an outstanding accomplishment. Its two appendices contain the first statistical returns on crime and punishment in England, and the changes in criminal statutes embracing three centuries; it established a scientific basis for criminology, unparalleled in the past or in any other country. It is the first of a series of similar documents: the Royal Commission Report of 1866, the Select Committee Report of 1930 and the Royal Commission Report of 1953, which, in their ensemble, represent a unique and monumental achievement of scholarly research. By their clarity of style and masterly handling of a most complex and unwieldy material, they deserve to rank as classics of English literature.

Characteristically, the Select Committee of 1819 refused to hear the judges' opinion. Their witnesses were picked from various social classes and professional groups, including shopkeepers and tradesmen, merchants and manufacturers, insurance brokers and bankers, magistrates and magistrates' clerks, prison chaplains and gaol-keepers. They refused to hear the judges on the delicate pretext that "as they could not with propriety censure what they might soon be obliged to enforce, they could scarcely be considered as at liberty to deliver an unbiased opinion", and that "as they only see the exterior of criminal proceedings after they are brought into a court they are by their stations and duties placed at a great distance". More than a century later, the Select Committee of 1930 also declined to ask the judges' opinion.

The 1819 Committee's recommendations were moderate: maintenance of the death-penalty for certain offences against personal property, repeal of obsolete statutes, amendment of others. But even these proposals were once again rejected by the oracles. Lord Eldon objected to the repeal of the main provisions of the Waltham Black Act—and triumphantly prevailed. In 1820, after the publication of the Committee's report, Romilly's famous Bill for the abolition of the death-penalty for shoplifting to the value of five shillings was introduced for the sixth time—and had again to be withdrawn when the law officers declared that they would oppose it. The House of Lords, in deference to the oracles, continued to act "as a floodgate against the tide of legislation which is now rolling so impetuously through the House of Commons".[63] Twelve years later, in 1832, Ellenborough's successor, Chief Justice Lord Tenterden, still valiantly stood out against the abolition of the death-penalty for sheep- and horse-stealing on the familiar grounds that "we have at present in this country no substitute for the punishment of death".[64]

The resistance began to break down only when Peel came to the Home Office and created the modern police force in 1829. Ten years later, capital offences were at long last reduced to the number of fifteen; and in 1861 to four (murder, treason, arson in dockyards and piracy). That is where the matter rests until this day.

6. From Ellenborough to Goddard

In the 1948 House of Lords debate on capital punishment, the successors to the posts of Ellenborough and Eldon, Lord Chancellor Jowitt and Lord Chief Justice Goddard, made some interesting remarks on the subject I have been discussing. Lord Goddard said:

It is a common reproach against Judges (though I believe it is absolutely groundless) that they are—the word generally used—reactionary, and are always on the side of severity. It is not so. It is an idea that I think has been fostered by the historical fact that a great predecessor in my office, Lord Ellenborough, in the early days of the last century, was a bitter opponent of the reforms then suggested to make a great number of offences which were then capital, non-capital. I suppose that, to a large extent, he reflected the opinion of his time, and perhaps sufficient credit is not given to him, because at least he erred in good company. If your Lordships refer to the *Parliamentary Debates* of those days, you will find that nearly the whole of the Bench of Bishops supported him.[65]

Lord Goddard was defending capital punishment for murder in 1948 on the grounds (among others) that public opinion was in favour of it, and the passage referring to his "great predecessor" implied that Ellenborough was equally right in defending capital punishment for shoplifting, etc., because public opinion was in favour of it. The historic truth is, as we saw, the opposite. Ellenborough did not reflect the opinion of his time, but was defeated by it. Public opinion was reflected in the juries' refusals to convict, which put the Bloody Code out of action; in the flood of petitions, from the calico printers to the jurors, bankers, the Corporation of London; and lastly, by the Commons, who passed repeal Bill after repeal Bill which the Lords rejected—as they rejected in 1948 the Commons' abolition Bill. The events of Ellenborough's time were summed up in a contemporary article in *The Edinburgh Review* of March, 1824:

Common sense requires an obvious improvement: an Opposition member brings it forward, and is overpowered by sarcasms, invectives, and majorities. But public opinion decides at once in its favour, and gradually diminishes the majority, in each succeeding year, till the scale is turned.

Let us return to the 1948 debate. After Lord Goddard had praised Ellenborough, the Lord Chancellor, Lord Jowitt, seconded him with the following reflections:

I think he [Lord Goddard] showed in that speech that Judges are not the inhuman creatures they are sometimes supposed to be. . . . The old gibe about Lord Ellenborough is really not sufficient ground on which to say for ever afterwards "You may completely disregard what the Judges think". . . . When I think of some of the great Judges since Ellenborough's time, *I think, for instance, of Lord Romilly*—and who has done more to restrict and limit the death penalty than Romilly?—and of many other names which will occur to any educated person. And I should like to think that our Judges today are in the same great line.[66] (My italics.)

The italics are mine; the confusion is the learned judge's. Romilly was never a judge, but a ferocious enemy of the judges. He was not a Lord,* he was not "since Ellenborough's time"; he died before Ellenborough. Translated into political terms, the passage would read as follows:

"It is untrue that the Conservative party was opposed to nationalization. When I think of some of the great Tories, Sir Nye Bevan, for instance, who favoured nationalization, and of many other names which will occur to any educated person . . ." etc.

It is worth noting that during the whole House of Lords debate, nobody remarked on Lord Jowitt's mistake. We shall meet with more examples of the amazing ignorance of social history among the learned oracles; it is a characteristic feature of their mentally inbred world and their concomitant estrangement from reality.

It is sometimes said that Ellenborough and Eldon were isolated cases. Lord Jowitt, for instance, made another attempt at vindicating the role of the judges in history which was not much happier than the first—this time naming Erskine and Brougham as judges on the side of the angels, though Erskine never was a judge and Brougham was at the time still a junior at the bar.[67] The fact that the judges as a body were behind Ellenborough is not a matter of

* Samuel Romilly's second son became a peer in 1866, but since he had nothing to do with reforming the criminal law and only became a judge twenty years after the events under discussion, he could not have been meant by Lord Jowitt.

controversy, but of looking up Hansard's Parliamentary reports. In his 1811 speech opposing Romilly's shoplifting Bill, Ellenborough said:

This, my Lords, is not my own opinion, but it is that of the learned judges with whom I have been in the habit of consulting on the punishment of crimes; for they are unanimously agreed that the expediency of justice and public security requires there should not be a revision of capital punishment in this part of the criminal law.[68]

Lord Eldon bore him out:

I must take the liberty to say that, although the opinions of the twelve judges of England would not decide me against my own judgment, I cannot venture to entertain the idea that it becomes me to treat with disrespect the knowledge and wisdom of men so deeply conversant with the laws of the land.[69]

The Chancellor of the Exchequer bore him out by stating that the Bill was "unsupported by the authority of one single judge or magistrate".[70]

The judges' decisive influence upon legislation affecting criminal law was, in fact, taken for granted at the time, and is only denied in our day through ignorance or dishonesty. In 1786, the Lord Chancellor, Lord Loughborough, affirmed that any project aimed at reform of the criminal law should either originate from the judges, or be approved by them before being submitted for consideration by Parliament. The next year, William Pitt reaffirmed this principle.[71] It was never officially challenged; Romilly was the first man to challenge it:

It appears to me a most unconstitutional doctrine, that no important alteration can be made in the law, unless the judges are first consulted on it. If they are to be consulted, of course their opinions are to be followed; and consequently, if they, or if only a majority of them, disapprove of any proposed alteration in the law, it must be abandoned. They would have to be considered . . . like a fourth member of the Legislature, who are to have . . . a power of preventing any proposed measure . . . from passing into a law.[72]

We have seen that both the Select Committee of 1819 and its successor of 1930 refused to hear the judges, because their opposition to any reform was a foregone conclusion.

7. "Hanging Is Not Enough"

The attitude of the judges as a body to aggravated forms of execution was equally consistent. Sir Edward Coke (1552–1634) was perhaps the greatest English lawyer of all times. By his famous dictum that no royal proclamation can change the law, by his defence of the Common Law against the King, the Church and the Admiralty, he did more than any other man to establish the independence and fairness of British legal procedure. But at the same time, Coke's name remains forever associated with the "Godly butchery" of drawing, hanging and quartering, whose continuance he defended by a series of quotations from the Bible, as follows:

For first after a traitor hath had his just trial and is convicted and attainted, he shall have his judgment to be drawn to the place of execution from his prison as being not worthy any more to tread upon the face of the earth whereof he was made: also for that he hath been retrograde to nature, therefore is he drawn backward at a horse-tail. And whereas God hath made the head of man the highest and most supreme part, as being his chief grace and ornament . . . he must be drawn with his head declining downward, and lying so near the ground as may be, being thought unfit to take the benefit of the common air. For which cause also he shall be strangled, being hanged up by the neck between heaven and earth, as deemed unworthy of both, or either; as likewise, that the eyes of men may behold, and their hearts condemn him. Then he is to be cut down alive, and to have his privy parts cut off and burnt before his face as being unworthily begotten, and unfit to leave any generation after him. . . .[73]

He also explained that this form of execution proved "the admirable clemency and moderation of the King" because it did not foresee any additional torture—apart from disembowelling the traitor alive.

This barbarity continued, in somewhat mitigated form, well into the nineteenth century. It was again Romilly who put an end to it. But when he introduced his first "Bill to Alter the Punishment of High Treason" he was accused by the law officers of the Crown of breaking down the bulwarks of the Constitution, and the great Coke's eulogy on drawing and quartering was quoted on that occasion. The Bill was rejected on Colonel Frankland's motion, who denounced it as yet another of "these mischievous attempts to unsettle the public opinion with respect to the enormity of these atrocious offences".[74] The Attorney-General said in the debate that he would not vote for such a punishment if it were newly invented, but since it had the sanction of centuries, he was against changing it. Romilly notes in his memoirs: "so . . . the Bill is lost and the ministers have the glory of having preserved the British law, by which it is ordained that the hearts and the bowels of a man . . . shall be torn out of his body while he is yet alive." [75]

A year later (1814) he reintroduced his Bill. This time, Lords Ellenborough and Eldon felt that the tide was against them, but they succeeded in introducing an amendment to the Bill whereby it remained part of the sentence that the body of the criminal should be cut into quarters. Since this was now to be done only after the criminal had expired, Romilly agreed to what one might call a reasonable compromise with the upholders of tradition, and the Bill was passed.

I have mentioned before that in the case of women convicted of treason, drawing and quartering was considered to be offensive to the modesty of the spectators and therefore replaced by burning them alive. This form of execution was repealed only in 1790, against the strenuous opposition of the Lord Chancellor of the day, Lord Loughborough, who defended the measure on the grounds of its excellent deterrent value:

because although the punishment, as a spectacle, is rather attended with circumstances of horror, likely to make a stronger impression on the beholders than mere hanging, the effect was much the same, as in fact no greater degree of personal pain was sustained, the criminal being always strangled before the flames were suffered to approach the body.[76]

This was palpably untrue since there are several cases on record where the hangman, having his hands scorched, did not complete strangulation. I mention this not for the sake of macabre detail, but because the defence of a savage method of execution on the grounds that "it doesn't really hurt" is another *leitmotif* down to our day. Blackstone, the greatest legal authority after Coke, put up the same defence for drawing and quartering: "There are but few instances, and those accidental or by negligence, of persons being disembowelled till previously deprived of sensation." [77]

The *pillory* was only abolished in 1816. A year previously, Ellenborough had opposed its repeal on the grounds that there was no equally effective alternative punishment for it: it was as old as 1269 and "particularly suited to perjury and fraud".*

As for *transportation* (to Australia) the judges' attitude was particularly interesting. Whenever transportation for life was suggested as an alternative to capital punishment, they found it much too mild. Thus Ellenborough said in 1810 that lifelong transportation was viewed by some prisoners as "a summer's airing by emigration to a warmer climate"; and Lord Wynford, in 1832, said that it had "no longer any terrors attached to it. It was rather an encouragement to crime . . . than a dissuasive from it".[79] But when public opinion demanded that transportation should be abandoned, Earl Grey (former Chief Justice Common Pleas) informed the House of Lords that: "All the judges concerned in the administration of the criminal law except one . . . agreed that the punishment of transportation cannot be safely abandoned." [80] The same contradictory arguments were used in the Lords' debate of 1948 against life-imprisonment as an alternative to hanging: a life-sentence was considered either too cruel or too mild, or presumably both.

The last non-capital punishment particularly favoured by the oracles is *flogging*. In 1938 a "Departmental Committee on Corporal Punishment" (the Atkins Committee) was appointed, which reported:

We are not satisfied that corporal punishment has that exceptionally effective influence as a deterrent which is usually claimed for it by those who advocate it as a penalty for adult offenders.

They also expressly reported that the judges of the King's Bench Division were not only in favour of the retention of corporal punishment, but moreover wished to extend it.

As usual when such Committees are appointed to appease public opinion, the report was put on ice, and nothing happened for ten

---

* In spite of its tradition of seven hundred years, the pillory was not a very reliable form of punishment: "Some prisoners died from the brutality of the crowd; on the other hand the case was quoted in debate of one Dr. Shebbeare, who excited some sympathy, and had an umbrella held over his head by the Sheriff to shelter him from the elements, while a servant supplied him with refreshments. The judges were accordingly in some doubt as to whether, in imposing the punishment, they were sentencing a man to death or to an agreeable afternoon's relaxation." [78]

years. In 1948, the clause in the Criminal Justice Bill abolishing corporal punishment was passed in the House of Commons without a division. But when it came before the House of Lords, the Lord Chief Justice proposed to abolish only the cat-o'-nine-tails, and to retain whipping. The Lords obliged. They had listened with great respect to the Lord Chief Justice's oration on the psychologically beneficial effect of the whipping of convicts "birched by a chief warder who knows his business".[81] It is indeed the most effective method to prevent the reformation of a prisoner by utterly degrading him; and if all goes well, it may cause a prison riot which will lead to more jolly whippings.

The Lord Chief Justice's profound psychological insight into the effects of corporal punishment may also be gathered from the following particular instance. On December 4th, 1952, two brothers, aged seventeen and fourteen, appeared before him on a charge of robbery with violence. Both had been in trouble before, and had been placed on probation three times. Lord Goddard sent the elder to Borstal * and the younger to an approved school. He commented on the case as follows: "It would have done them good if they had had a good larruping. What they want is to have somebody who would give them a thundering good beating and then perhaps they wouldn't do it again. I suppose they were brought up to be treated like little darlings and tucked up in bed at night."

His comments were widely reported in the Press. The Howard League for Penal Reform investigated the case and found that the father of the boys was a former Sergeant-major in the Grenadier Guards who had tried to reform Donald by frequent thrashings, and when the boy was put in a hostel on probation, went out of his way to urge the warden to beat him.[82]

8. The Judges and the Rights of the Accused

Prisoners on a capital charge were not allowed counsel until 1836. In that year the Prisoners' Counsel Bill was introduced and twice defeated before it was passed. Mr. G. Gardiner, Q.C., comments:

Considering that at one sessions two-thirds of the prisoners were under age, some under ten years, it is difficult, as one looks back, to see how it

* Reformatory institution for young criminals.

was expected that these felons, some barely out of the nursery, were expected to conduct their own defence. The reform had nevertheless been opposed in his time by that great criminal judge Sir Michael Foster, and by Coke himself on the curious ground that "evidence ought to be so clear that it cannot be contradicted". Lord Denman C.J., who finally supported the Bill, expressed the opinion that the result of it would be that counsel would be compelled to take a case, which would be unjust to gentlemen who had entered an expensive profession. Sir Eardley Wilmot took a distressingly unconfident view of judicial ability; he was perfectly certain that the Bill would be impracticable if the judge had to sift the chaff from the corn, and "unmystify the speeches of Counsel". No judge in the country "possessed physical and mental power equal to the task".[83]

The Bill was finally passed,

but the judges . . . were able to some extent to prune the measure. At the suggestion of the Chief Justice, King's Bench (Lord Denman) and the Lord Chief Baron of the Exchequer (Lord Abinger) the clause granting the prisoner a right to see the depositions was struck out.[84]

A person charged with a capital offence was not allowed to give evidence on his own behalf on the witness stand until the Criminal Evidence Act came into force in 1898. It had taken fifteen years for this act to pass. Several of the Law Lords fought the measure, and Lord Chief Justice Collins described it as a "great public mischief" because the opportunity given to the judge to put direct question to the prisoner "must sap the prisoner's confidence in the absolute impartiality of the judge". As Mr. Gardiner points out, the argument was the exact reverse of the objection made against allowing the prisoner to be defended by counsel—namely, that counsel was unnecessary because the judge was *not* an impartial arbiter but "the prisoner's best friend".

The judges were equally determined in their opposition to the establishment of a Court of Criminal Appeal—which they succeeded in postponing by a modest seventy years. During this time the question had come before Parliament no less than twenty-eight times.

Before the Court of Criminal Appeal was established in 1907, there existed no body to which prisoners wrongfully sentenced to death could appeal; their only hope was the Royal pardon. The 1866 Royal Commission had considered the question, but the four judges who gave evidence, Lords Cranworth, Bramwell, Martin and

Wensleydale, unanimously opposed it, on the grounds that it would "worry prosecutors", that "a Court of Appeal is not what one may call a natural thing", and because "people in England are never convicted, except, in my judgment, upon the very clearest evidence".[85]

Forty years later, in the 1907 debate, the Lord Chief Justice, Lord Alverstone, still opposed the dangerous innovation to the end because of his "distinct conviction that the proposed change will undermine altogether the responsibility of juries", and because it would be "tried for the first time in criminal law and in my judgment it is fraught with the greatest danger to innocent persons". He emphasized, as Lord Chief Justices traditionally do on such occasions, that "the views I have expressed are entertained by all my brethren in the King's Bench". The Lord Chancellor, Lord Halsbury, duly sided with the Lord Chief Justice, as Eldon had sided with Ellenborough in 1810–18, and Jowitt was to side with Goddard in 1948, angrily exclaiming:

It must be remembered that you are here dealing with experts who have had long experience of what they are talking about . . . I cannot understand why the legislature of this country in the most serious matter of the administration of the criminal law should be affected one way or the other because irresponsible persons think it proper to assume that they have knowledge superior to His Majesty's judges.[86]

The experts then went on to prophesy that the court would have to deal with no less than five thousand appeals every year and would cost the taxpayer "astronomical sums". As it happens, the highest number of appeals in a single year was 710 (in 1910); and the astronomical expense amounted to $36,400 per year.[87]

9. The Doctrine of Maximum Severity

Of course, there were always kind and understanding judges on the lower rungs of the hierarchy. There were exceptions even at the top, such as Lord Brougham (Lord Chancellor 1830–4), and Lord Denman (Chief Justice 1832–50), who sided with the reformers. But at every turning-point in British legal history, from the eighteenth century to this day, the judges always opposed every major reform, could always claim that the unanimity or majority of their brethren from the King's Bench were behind them, and that "their opinion must be paramount".

The responsibility was not theirs alone: there were other forces which lent them support. But the core of resistance against reform, around which the reactionary forces rallied, was the authority of the oracles. Robed with the august symbols of tradition, they lent to the public strangling of ten-year-olds a halo of respectability, and led this gentle nation through two centuries of gore.

The reasons for this development have already been mentioned: the unique character of British Common Law guaranteed the nation personal freedom, and exemplary fair treatment in its courts, at the price of a preposterously savage system of penalties. It led to the emergence of a powerful new class, the medicine-men of the Law, who monopolized the position of a "fourth member of the legislature". Guided by precedent only, under the hypnotic effect of exclusive preoccupation with the past, they were bound to develop a professional deformity, epitomized in the motto *Nolumus leges Angliae mutari*.

When Lord Goddard told the Royal Commissioners that in his opinion fewer people ought to be reprieved, and that it would be "most disastrous" if the jury's recommendation to mercy should have to be carried out by the Home Secretary, he was not guided by personal motives of cruelty. He was faced with a dilemma which is nearly as old as capital punishment, and gave the same answer which its defenders were logically compelled to give every time it arose. The dilemma is this: whenever social progress outpaces the Law, so that its penalties appear disproportionately severe to the public conscience, juries become reluctant to convict, and reprieves, instead of being an exceptional act of mercy, become virtually the rule, so that only a small proportion of the sentences are actually carried out and the threat accordingly loses its deterrent effect. We shall meet with this dilemma again in the next chapter. There are only two ways out of it: either to bring the Law up to date and, by reducing its severity, make "the punishment fit the crime"—or to increase both the terror of the threat, and the rigour of its application.

The first solution was formulated as early as 1764 by the Italian humanist and reformer, Cesare Beccaria, and became the guiding principle of legal reform in Europe during the Age of Enlightenment. Beccaria taught that the only aim of punishment was the protection of society, which could not be achieved by terror, because in the same proportion as punishments become more cruel "human minds harden, adjusting themselves, like fluids, to the level of objects round them". Terror has its own law of diminishing returns; in a century of savage punishments, people are no more frightened by the gallows than under a milder régime they are frightened of prison. Besides, legal barbarity begets common barbarity, "the same spirit of ferocity that guides the hand of the legislature having guided also that of the patricide and assassin".

Beccaria realized that "severity breeds impunity", because men are reluctant to inflict on their fellow-beings the excessive punishments prescribed by inhuman laws. Hence excessive penalties are less effective in preventing crime than moderate penalties, provided that these are inflicted promptly and with certainty. A disproportionately severe law, therefore, is not only morally wrong but also defeats its own utilitarian purpose; whereas a moderate law, graded according to the offence, if administered swiftly, smoothly and with the certitude of inevitability, is both more humane and more effective.

One may call this the principle of the "minimum effective punishment". I have already mentioned the influence which Beccaria's teaching gained all over Europe, from Russia to France, from Sweden to Italy. There was perhaps no single humanist since Erasmus of Rotterdam, who, without being attached to a definite political or religious movement, had such a deep effect on European thought.

One would have imagined that England, with its great democratic and liberal tradition, should have been the country most receptive to the new trend. Yet through more than a century, England swam against the current, and is doing it still. I have mentioned some of the reasons: the upheaval of the Industrial Revolution, and the reluctance to be regimented by police authority. But the main reason was the monopoly of the "fourth legislature" in legal matters. Elsewhere, no such monopoly existed: the laws were codified, the judges doled them out for better or worse, but they had no power to make them. Penal legislation on the Continent reflected the social currents of the time; England alone let herself be guided by an exclusive class of alleged technical experts who, like the mediaeval alchemists, lived in a mysterious world of secret formulae, their minds riveted to the past, impervious to changing conditions, ignorant of the vital developments outside their closed world.

It was not by chance that they were opposed to every proposed reform of the law, threatening Parliament that "every vestige of our property will be swept off by the hardened robber". They knew by instinct and conviction that to give way on any point, meant to admit that the law was not fixed for all time but subject to change —and then their whole rigid and artificial universe would collapse. The change of social conditions leads to recurrent crises in criminal law which can only be solved either by mitigating its rigours, or by ever-increasing terror, adding capital statute to capital statute; they opted for the second alternative, with the results that we have seen.

So far we have discussed the influence of the "fourth legislature" as a body. Taken as individuals, the great judges who made English history display the same common trend of rigid inhumanity. The heroes of common law—the Cromwells, Nelsons and Marlboroughs among the oracles—are Coke, Blackstone, Paley, Ellenborough and Stephen.

The first of them, Sir Edward Coke, who was called "The Common Law Become Flesh", pointed the way by his classic answer to the classic dilemma: "that for as much as many do offend in the hope of pardon, that pardons be very rarely granted." [88] This solution of the deterrence problem remained the guide of the hanghards through four centuries; it has been quoted on endless occasions by learned judges, and echoed by Lord Goddard's testimony before the Royal Commission that "fewer should be reprieved".

The next landmark was Sir William Blackstone (1723–80). His "Commentaries" are used to this day as textbooks for law students. He was a contemporary of Beccaria, Montesquieu and Jeremy Bentham; yet he approved of drawing and quartering, the burning of women, and held that hanging the corpse of the criminal in chains on the gibbet was "a comfortable sight to the relations and friends of the deceased". He was an expert in precedent, but dismally ignorant in other respects:

"He had only the vaguest possible grasp of the elementary conception of law. He evidently regarded the law of gravitation, the law of nature and the law of England as different examples of the same principle." [89]

Countless arguments against reform were subsequently based on a famous passage in the *Commentaries,* which asserts that "it is one of the glories of the English law that . . . punishment is *ascertained* for every offence; and that it is not left in the breast of any judge, nor even of a jury, to alter that judgment". This was written at a time when the "ascertained" punishment for hundreds of offences was death—from murdering the King to stealing a turnip, from the slaying of a child to damaging a rabbit warren.

Archdeacon William Paley (1743–1805) was not a judge, merely a Justice of the Peace, but he was a friend of Lord Ellenborough, and his treatise "On Crimes and Punishments" exercised a powerful influence on the trend of English criminal legislation during a long period. His *Principles of Moral and Political Philosophy,* of which that treatise formed a part, "reigned widely in England for near half a century as the best modern work on ethical science".[90] Romilly's opponents, from Ellenborough downward, relied mainly on Paley's authority. Paley taught that the main consideration in assessing the degree of punishment should not be the magnitude of the crime, but the facility with which it can be committed, and the difficulty of its detection. Consequently, he unreservedly supported capital punishment for petty thieving simply because "the property being more exposed requires the terror of capital punishment to protect it".[91] He also believed in the absolute incorrigibility of all criminals, in the futility of trying to reform them, and that some of them ought to be thrown into dens of wild beasts to perish "in a manner dreadful to the imagination yet concealed from the view". This was the man whose influence "reigned supreme" among the oracles in the next fifty years. The history of English criminal law is a wonderland filled with the braying of learned asses.

Incidentally, the title of Paley's treatise "On Crimes and Punishments" is identical with Beccaria's *Dei Delitti e delle Pene* which was translated into English seven years earlier. Whether Paley chose the same title out of spite or ignorance, cannot be ascertained.

About Ellenborough no more need be said. The last and greatest nineteenth-century oracle was Sir James Stephen (1829–94) whose *General View of the Criminal Law of England* was the first systematic attempt since Blackstone to explain the principles of law and justice in a coherent form. He criticized the "barbarous system" of the past, as the quotation at the beginning of this section shows; yet as far as his own time was concerned, Stephen conformed to the tradition. In 1883, a full sixty years after the death-penalty for forgery was abolished, Stephen demanded that if a man is "determined to live by deceiving and impoverishing others" or "if he is a habitual receiver of stolen goods", he should be put to death; and he continued:

"These views, it is said, are opposed to the doctrine that human life is sacred. I have never been able to understand what the doctrine means or how its truth is alleged to be proved." [92]

That last sober phrase sums up the attitude of this chain of Abominable Snowmen, from Coke to Stephen and beyond. The terror of the French Revolution preserves in retrospect the grandeur of a tragic but essential chapter of history. The terror of the Bloody Code was wanton and purposeless, alien to the character of the nation, imposed on it, not by fanatical Jacobins, but by a conspiracy of wigged fossils. They quoted the Bible to defend drawing and quartering, and they quoted each other's quotations, and became more and more estranged from reality. Solicitors and counsel, prison chaplains and gaolers know criminals as individuals, and know that they are human. The judges only meet the accused in court, as a case, not as a human being. All the great oracles had a blind belief in the gallows as the only deterrent from crime, though the only criminals they had occasion to see were those who had obviously not been deterred. They were like physicians who would justify their favourite cure by the example of patients who have not been cured by it. Yet they must go on believing in their magic deterrent, for if they renounced that belief, they would stand condemned for those they have condemned, before their own conscience.

In his *Lives of the Chief Justices*, Lord Campbell quotes a judge at Stafford Assizes who, having sentenced to death a prisoner for passing on a forged one pound note, exhorted him as follows to prepare for his journey to another world:

And I trust that, through the merits and mediation of our blessed Redeemer, you may there experience that mercy which a due regard to the credit of the paper currency of the country forbids you to hope for here.[93]

The words convey a complete mental picture of the early nineteenth-century oracle under his corkscrew-braided tea doily.

10. Cops and Robbers

Before an impartial tribunal of historians, the judges of the King's Bench would be found guilty of having led the country through all this unnecessary disgrace and self-humiliation. Yet in spite of the unique power of the "fourth legislature", they could not have caused all this mischief without the support they received from the more ignorant, reactionary forces within the nation. Prominent among these were certain sanguine Lords of the Church, from Archdeacon Paley who taught that criminals were unredeemable, to the Bishop of Truro, who in the Lords' debate of 1948 suggested that, instead of abolishing the death-penalty, we should extend its range.[94] This type of illustrious clergyman has always shown great deference to the wisdom of the secular Lords of the Law.

In more recent times, the Police Force has grown into a powerful opponent of the abolition of the death-penalty. This is not unnatural. The police stand in the front line of the war against the criminal. They have to face constant risks at disproportionately low rewards; they have to show great self-restraint in conditions of danger or irksome provocation, and thus develop an instinctive belief that any softening of the law would make their task even harder. Accordingly the police, as a body, has a blind faith in the effectiveness of capital punishment both as an act of retaliation and deterrence, just as brewers believe that guinness is good for you, undisturbed by fact or argument.

A hundred years ago, in July, 1856, a Select Committee was appointed to inquire into "the present mode of carrying into effect capital punishment", the main point of the inquiry being whether executions should continue to be held in public. Among the witnesses was a retired Detective Inspector, Mr. John Haynes. His testimony deserves to be quoted at some length because of its self-contradictions, which provide an interesting insight into this kind of mentality.

Q. Will you state to the Committee what your impression is concerning the effect produced by the present mode of carrying into effect capital punishment?
A. I believe it has a very beneficial effect upon the public generally.
Q. Will you be good enough to state to the Committee what beneficial effects you think are produced upon those who do see executions?

A. I think it tends to prevent the commission of crime.

Q. In what way does it tend to prevent it?

A. However callous parties may be who witness a public execution, I think they cannot help considering the effect of it afterwards. No one likes to be hung like a dog. . . . It is my general impression that the sight has a very decidedly beneficial effect.

Q. Do you think it desirable that the execution should be seen by the public?

A. I do; I am perfectly convinced . . . that the public generally would not be satisfied except the execution were public.

Q. Will you state what you mean by the word "satisfied"; satisfied of what?

A. The impression among many persons is, that if capital punishments were not carried out publicly, some trickery would be played.

Q. Some trickery in the way of allowing the criminal to escape, you mean?

A. Yes; I do not think any plan which could be adopted to execute persons in private would satisfy the public generally.

Q. Suppose a satisfactory plan were suggested to you by which the public could be convinced of the reality of the execution, should you, in that case, think it more desirable that the execution should be in private?

A. Speaking individually, I am decidedly of opinion that it would be much better that executions should take place privately, but I am perfectly satisfied that it would not satisfy the public; and when I speak of the public, I speak of the large mass of the middle class as well as the lower class.

Q. You said that, as far as your own opinion went, you were in favour of executions taking place in private; on what grounds did you say that?

A. Because I think the present plan tends very materially to satisfy a morbid curiosity on the part of the public which ought not to be gratified.

Q. Are you not of opinion, from the kind of scenes which take place at those executions, that a bad rather than a good moral effect is produced . . . ?

A. I do not think that is the case; I do not think the tendency is that way, because I think any one who has a morbid taste of that description would not be injured by the exhibition. . . . Generally speaking, the persons who attend those public executions are not persons who would be likely to commit murder, whatever other offence they might commit. Your Lordships will perhaps allow me to say, that from my experience I believe, as far as moral or religious feeling is concerned, it has but little effect in deterring such persons from committing crimes.

Q. What is it which has but little effect?

A. Knowing that a man is hanged, or having heard from others that a man has been executed.

Q. Is it your opinion that capital punishment itself has very little effect in deterring?

A. Quite the reverse. I believe capital punishment deters very materially
from the commission of crime; and I have not the slightest doubt that if
capital punishment were done away with, scarcely any man's life would be
safe in this country.

Q. In conversing with criminals under sentence, have you found that
they could trace any good effect to the fact of their having seen an execution?

A. No.

Q. What was the length of your experience in the official post which you
mentioned?

A. I was in the police force nearly twenty-five years; I joined as constable,
and went through the different grades, and have now retired upon a pension.[95]

It is a remarkable statement coming from a man who had loyally
served the Police Force for a quarter-century; remarkable, as I
said, because of its contradictions. When off his guard, he reveals
the private conviction of a decent man that the whole spectacle is
revolting, and that it has "but little effect" as a deterrent from
crime; but when subsequently the Chairman tries to pin him down,
he pulls himself together and dutifully repeats the collective doctrine, or collective myth, of the Police Force which he learnt by
rote, "if capital punishment were done away with, scarcely any man's
life would be safe in this country". And since "the public would not
be satisfied" with anything less than a public execution, we just have
to carry on with the practice, however much we privately dislike it,
amen. Detective Inspector Haynes has given a classic expression
of the philosophy of the Police Force, past and present.

Incidentally, executions were carried on in public for another
twelve years after the Select Committee of 1856 had unanimously
recommended their abolition.

Today, a hundred years later, the police as a body as firmly believe
in hanging as a deterrent as they did in Inspector Haynes's day.
Only on one point have they made a concession to the times. They
now admit that "there are certain individuals . . . to whom no
punishment, not even the death penalty, is a deterrent". But, they
say, if capital punishment were abolished, more professional criminals "would take to using violence and carrying weapons; and the

police, who are now unarmed, might be compelled to retaliate".[96]
The Royal Commission remarks: "we received no evidence that
the abolition of capital punishment in other countries had in fact
led to the consequences apprehended by our witnesses"—meaning
the police.[97] The Select Committee expressed its findings twenty
years earlier in more detail: "We have had no evidence put before
us that after the abolition of capital punishment in other countries
there has been any increase in the number of burglars arming themselves or in the carrying of lethal weapons. The social conditions
that lead to burglars carrying firearms in various countries lie outside
the question of the death-penalty. Thus the criminal classes are less
given to the carrying of firearms in Belgium, where they have abolition, than in France where they have capital punishment. The
United States retains capital punishment in most of its vast terri-
tories, and . . . her executions far outnumber ours in proportion
to population. Nevertheless, the carrying of firearms and other
deadly weapons is common in the States. . . ." [98]

11. Two Recent American Surveys

In 1954, hearings were held in Canada by the "Joint Committee
on Capital and Corporal Punishment and Lotteries". In testifying
before that Committee (on April 27, 1954) the President of the Chief
Constables' Association of Canada summed up in precise form the
classic stand of the police on the question of capital punishment.

Our main objection is that abolition would adversely affect the personal
safety of police officers in the daily discharge of their duties. It would be
interesting to know, and if time had permitted I would have tried to
obtain this vital information as to the number of policemen murdered
in the execution of their duty in those parts of the world where capital
punishment has been abolished. I submit that it will be found the number
is much higher than in those countries where the death-penalty is still
in effect, and this point is the main one in our submission that our government should retain capital punishment as a form of security.[99]

This statement inspired two American scholars to embark on a
statistical investigation to test the validity of the police chief's hypothetical submission. They were Professor Thorsten Sellin of the University of Pennsylvania, and Father Donald Campion, S.J. Professor

Sellin, the Secretary General of the International Penal and Penitentiary Commission, mailed elaborate questionnaires to the police departments of all United States cities with more than 10,000 population. On the basis of the answers received it was possible to make a statistical comparison between the killing and wounding of policemen in the six states which have no death-penalty and the eleven states bordering on the abolition states. The results of this extremely elaborate study may be summarised as follows:

In the total of 82 abolition-state cities, during the period 1919–54, the rate of fatal attacks on policemen was 1.2 in 100,000.

In the total of 182 death-penalty-state cities (Chicago excepted) the corresponding rate for the same period was 1.3 in 100,000.

In the group of cities with populations betweeen 30,000 and 60,-000, the abolition cities had a rate of 1.0, the death-penalty cities of 1.1.

In other categories of cities, the comparison gave equally negative results.[100]

As for very large cities, Chicago (death-penalty) was compared with Detroit (abolitionist). The rate of police killings was to be found distinctly smaller in Detroit.[101]

Professor Sellin concludes: "The claim that if data could be secured they would show that more police are killed in abolition states than in capital punishment states is unfounded. On the whole the abolition states, as apparent from the findings of this particular investigation, seem to have fewer killings, but the differences are small. If this is, then, the argument upon which the police is willing to rest its opposition to the abolition of capital punishment it must be concluded that it lacks any factual basis."[102]

The study further revealed that while abolition or retention does not affect the rate of police killings (except for an insignificant advantage to the abolition states), the rate of police killings is proportionate to the general homicide rate. Nor does the number of executions have any detectable influence on the police homicide rate.

Professor Sellin's questionnaire also requested each police department to state its beliefs regarding the deterrent value of the death-penalty. Roughly one-third of the recipients gave an answer. In the death-penalty states 89.8% of the police officers who answered the questionnaire believed in the added protective force of the death-penalty. In the abolition states 74.1% did not believe in it.[103]

Professor Sellin does not comment on this curious result. The psychological explanation seems simple enough: the police in the death-penalty states cling to their traditional beliefs because they have no experience or knowledge of the results of abolition; the police in the abolition states, who know that abolition "made no difference at all", see no reason to perpetuate the horrors of the gas chamber or electric chair.

The companion study by Father Campion led by different methods to the same conclusion. The study concludes "that the data available to us after a survey of half the state police forces of the United States do not lend empirical support to the claim that the existence of the death-penalty in the statutes of a state provides a greater protection to the police than exists in states where that penalty has been abolished." [104]

*　　*　　*

Britain has maintained capital punishment, yet the carrying of deadly weapons by cosh boys and teddy boys has nevertheless increased in the post-war era, mainly under the influence of American films, horror comics and other literature popularizing the life of gangsters. But people who feed on this kind of celluloid and pulp, and pattern their attitude on it, belong to the mentally unbalanced, bragging and exhibitionist type, of Craig and Donald Brown, to whom the capital threat is not a deterrent and often an attraction; who will carry a "rod" to prove to his girl that he is a tough, and then use it in a moment of panic or frenzy. Nothing could be more remote from the mentality of the professional burglar, at whom the police argument is aimed. He knows that to be found in possession of a weapon is a most damning piece of evidence against him, whether he uses it or not. He knows that for a minor burglary he may get away with a "carpet" (three months), but that he will get a "handful" (five years) if under identical circumstances he is found carrying a rod. Thus the capital threat is not a necessity, as the example of the abolitionist countries shows, to prevent professional burglars from carrying firearms; and it often acts as an incentive on the unbalanced, bragging teddy boy who is the most striking new criminal type of the post-war era.

Yet the police, supported by the high court judges, remain unshaken; and their influence on Parliament and the Home Office is greater than that of any trade union. The refusal to reprieve the half-witted boy Bentley, in spite of the horrified protests of public and Parliament, was a bitter and humiliating lesson, but also an eye-opener to many who realized for the first time that, whereas the average British policeman is a decent, gallant and humane individual, the Police Force as an organization, with its *esprit de corps* and its eye-for-eye, tooth-for-tooth mentality, is a different matter.

This brings us to the last point to be mentioned in this chapter: the influence of party politics on the administration of the criminal law. In recent years we had several examples of Home Secretaries from both parties ardently defending capital punishment when in office, and ardently attacking it when in opposition. Before Sir Samuel Hoare, later Lord Templewood, became Home Secretary, he supported the abolition of the death-penalty; when in office, he opposed the abolition of the death-penalty; no sooner out, he supported the abolition of the death-penalty and wrote a most eloquent book about it. The next example is Mr. Chuter Ede, Socialist. Before he became Home Secretary he ardently fought for abolition; when in office he doggedly opposed it; no sooner out, he ardently . . . and so on. The last one, to date, is Major Lloyd George, Conservative. In 1948, before he became Home Secretary, he voted for the abolition of the death-penalty; in 1955, he opposed abolition in the name of the Government; in 1960 he will, wind and weather permitting, again support it.

Now, the Home Secretary does not only express the Government's policy on the question of capital punishment; he also has, next to God Almighty, the ultimate decision whether a particular victim should hang or not. One would imagine that this terrible responsibility would make a person impervious to any outside influence. The example of Bentley makes one doubt whether this is the case.

English law is based on tradition and precedent. I hope that this —necessarily sketchy—excursion into the past may have dispelled some of the unconscious preconceptions which cloud the issue, and will help the reader to consider the problem of capital punishment against its historical background, with an unprejudiced mind.

THE HANGMAN'S PROTECTION

or Capital Punishment as a Deterrent

1

THE ARGUMENTS in defence of capital punishment have remained essentially the same since Lord Ellenborough's days. In the recent Parliamentary debates the Home Secretary, Major Lloyd George, again patiently trotted out the three customary reasons why the Government opposed abolition: that the death-penalty carried a unique deterrent value; that no satisfactory alternative punishment could be designed; and that public opinion was in favour of it.

The second and third points will be discussed in later chapters. At present I am only concerned with the first and main argument. To give it a fair hearing, we must set all humanitarian considerations and charitable feelings aside, and examine the effectiveness of the gallows as a deterrent to potential murderers from a coldly practical, purely utilitarian point of view. This is, of course, a somewhat artificial view, for in reality "effectiveness" can never be the only consideration; even if it were proved that death preceded by torture, or on the wheel, were more effective, we would refuse to act accordingly. However, it will be seen that the theory of hanging as the best deterrent can be refuted on its own purely utilitarian grounds, without calling ethics and charity to aid.

A deterrent must logically refer to a "deterree", if the reader will forgive me for adding a verbal barbarity to the barbarous subject. So the first question is: who are the hypothetical deterrees, who will be prevented from committing murder by the threat of hanging, but not by the threat of long-term imprisonment? The fear of death is no doubt a powerful deterrent; but just how much more powerful is it than the fear of a life sentence?

The gallows obviously failed as a deterrent in all cases where a murder has actually been committed. It is certainly not a deterrent to murderers who commit suicide—and one-third of all murderers do.[1] It is not a deterrent to the insane and mentally deranged; nor to those who have killed in a quarrel, in drunkenness, in a sudden surge of passion—and this type of murder amounts to 80% to 90% of all murders that are committed.[2] It is not a deterrent to the type of person who commits murder because he desires to be hanged; and these cases are not infrequent. It is not a deterrent to the person who firmly believes in his own perfect method—by poison, acid bath, and so on—which, he thinks, will never be found out. Thus the range of hypothetical deterrees who can only be kept under control by the threat of death and nothing short of death, is narrowed down to the professional criminal class. But both the abolitionists and their opponents agree that "murder is not a crime of the criminal classes"; [3] it is a crime of amateurs, not of professionals. None of the points I have mentioned so far is controversial; they are agreed on by both sides, and will be discussed at greater length in Chapter IX, pp. 144–145, "Murderers as a Class".

Who, then, are the deterrees for whose sake this country must preserve capital punishment, as the only European democracy except Eire and France—which, from the judicial point of view, is not very enviable company? What type of criminal, to repeat the question in its precise form, can only be ruled by the threat of hanging, and nothing short of hanging? It is at this point that the issue between abolitionists and their opponents is really joined. The opponents' argument may be summed up as follows. As things stand, the professional criminal rarely commits murder; but if the threat of the gallows were abolished, he would take to murder, and the crime-rate would go up.

This, of course, is an unproved assumption; a hypothesis whose truth could only be tested either (a) by experiment, or (b) by drawing on analogies from past experiences in Britain and abroad. The House of Commons in 1948 voted for the experiment. It said: let us suspend executions for five years, and see what happens. The House of Lords rejected it, after it was informed by the Lord Chief Justice that the twenty Judges of the King's Bench were unanimous in opposing the measure.[4] His main argument against the five-year suspension was that the experiment would be too dangerous; his second argument, that if the dangerous experiment were tried, abolition would come to stay. He used both arguments in the same speech.[5] So much for the experimental method.

2

Now for the second method: by analogy, or precedent. Perhaps the oddest thing about this whole controversy is that the Judges, who live on bread and precedent, never quote a precedent in support of their thesis that abolition leads to an increase in crime. After all, the burden of proof for this assumption lies on them; and since there is a gold-mine of precedent at their disposal of what happened after the abolition of capital punishment for some two hundred and twenty different categories of crime, why do they never, never treat us to a single case? Why do we never hear: you want to repeal the capital statute for murder; look what happened after the repeal of statute 14 Geo. 2, c. 6, s. 1 (1741) (burglary), 7 Will. 4 & 1 Vic.; c. 89, s. 2 (arson), 9 Geo. 4, c. 31, s. 16 (rape), 8 Geo. 1, c. 22 (1921) (forgery)? Why is it that the reformers, these reckless destroyers of the bulwarks of tradition, always rely on history for support, whereas on this particular issue the keepers of tradition act as if the past did not exist?

Yet the present situation is fraught with precedents and echoes of the past. In the ten years 1940–9 the number of murders known to the Police in England and Wales amounted to 1,666 cases; * the number of executions in the same period was 127.[6] Expressed in annual averages, we have 170 murders but only 13 executions. That means that the law as it stands is only found applicable in practice in 7% of all cases; in Scotland even less: only 1 in 35, that is, under 3% of all murderers are actually executed.[7] The law says that murder shall be punished by death; but in about 95 out of 100 cases the law cannot be applied for a variety of reasons which will be discussed in detail later on. And that again means, as in all cases in the past when such glaring discrepancies occurred, that the law has outlived its time and has become an anachronism.

There are, as we saw before, two methods of remedying such a situation. The first is to bring the law up to date; the second, to put the clock of history back. The latter solution was advocated by the Lord Chief Justice in his evidence before the Royal Commission of 1948, when he suggested that fewer people ought to be reprieved and that it was perfectly proper to hang a person who is certified

*Infanticide excluded.

insane, but is not insane according to the M'Naghten Rules of 1843. We have discussed in sufficient detail the disastrous results to which such attempts to put the clock back have led in the course of the eighteenth and early nineteenth centuries.

The opposite method was tried from approximately 1820 onward. The basic reason why it was tried was the same which underlies the present inquiry: the law had become outdated, and therefore largely inapplicable and ineffective. In November, 1830, the Jurors of London presented their remarkable petition to the Commons. It ran:

That in the present state of the law, jurors feel extremely reluctant to convict where the penal consequences of the offence excite a conscientious horror on their minds, lest the rigorous performance of their duties as jurors should make them accessory to judicial murder. Hence, in Courts of Justice, a most necessary and painful struggle is occasioned by the conflict of the feelings of a just humanity with the sense of the obligation of an oath.[8]

The deterrent of the gallows affected the jury more than the criminal; the juries went on strike, as it were. They made it a rule, when a theft of goods worth forty shillings was a capital offence, to assess the value of the goods at thirty-nine shillings; and when, in 1827, the capital offence was raised to five pounds, the juries raised their assessment to four pounds nineteen shillings.[9] Present-day juries, as we shall see, bring in verdicts of "guilty, but insane" in cases where, according to medical evidence and the Judge's direction, the accused must be regarded as sane before the law. "It would be following strict precedent", says Mr. Gardiner in the Law Quarterly, "for the perversity of jurors to be the prelude to reform." [10]

The perversity of the jurors reached such an extent that it led, in 1830, to the famous "Petition of Bankers from 214 cities and towns", urging Parliament to abolish the death-penalty for forgery—not for any sentimental, humanitarian motives, but to protect themselves against the forgers to whom the gallows proved no deterrent. Here is the full text of the petition:

That your petitioners, as bankers, are deeply interested in the protection of property from forgery, and in the infliction of punishment on persons guilty of that crime.

That your petitioners find, by experience, that the infliction of death, or even the possibility of the infliction of death, prevents the prosecution, conviction and punishment of the criminal and thus endangers the property which it is intended to protect.

That your petitioners, therefore, earnestly pray that your honourable House will not withhold from them that protection to their property which they would derive from a more lenient law.[11]

Few of the bankers may have read Beccaria or Jeremy Bentham, and few would probably have subscribed to their philosophy. Yet for reasons of hard-headed expediency, they subscribed to the theory of the "minimum effective penalty". It took Parliament another six years to abolish capital punishment for forgery. The usual warnings were uttered that this measure would lead to the "destruction of trade and commerce"[12] and in Chief Justice Lord Mansfield's opinion the answer to the predicament was that capital sentences for forgery ought always to be carried out.[13] Yet when death for forgery was abolished, the number of commitments for that crime fell from 213 in the three years before repeal to 180 in the three subsequent years.[14]

If the death-penalty were a more effective deterrent than lesser penalties, then its abolition for a given category of crime should be followed by a noticeable increase in the volume of that crime, precisely as the hanging party says. But the facts tell a different story. After the great reform, the crime-rate did not rise; it fell—as everybody except the oracles had expected. And yet the era of reform coincided with one of the most difficult periods in English social history. As if History herself had wanted to make the task of the abolitionists more difficult, the repeal of the death-penalty for offences against property during the 1830's was immediately followed by the "hungry forties". The great experiment of mitigating the rigour of the law could not have been carried out under more unfavourable circumstances. Yet half-way through the experiment, when the number of capital offences had been reduced to fifteen, His Majesty's Commissioners on Criminal Law, 1836, summed up their report as follows:

It has not, in effect, been found that the repeal of Capital Punishment with regard to any particular class of offences has been attended with an increase of the offenders. On the contrary, the evidence and statements to be found in our appendix go far to demonstrate that . . . the absolute number of the offenders has diminished.[15]

And at the conclusion of this most dangerous experiment in the history of English criminal law, Sir Joseph Pease was able to state in the House of Commons that "the continual mitigation of law and of sentences has been accomplished with property quite as secure, and human life quite as sacred".[16]

"Deterrence" is an ugly and abstract word. It means, according to the *Oxford Dictionary,* "discouragement by fear". If the arguments in favour of the gallows as the supreme deterrent were true, then public executions would have the maximum discouraging effect on the criminal. Yet these public exhibitions, intended to prove that "crime does not pay", were known to be the occasion when pickpockets gathered their richest harvest among the crowd. A contemporary author [17] explains why: "The thieves selected the moment when the strangled man was swinging above them as the happiest opportunity, because they knew that everybody's eyes were on that person and all were looking up."

Public executions not only failed to diminish the volume of crime; they often caused an immediate rise in their wake. The hanging of a criminal served, less as a warning, than as an incitement to imitate him. Fauntleroy confessed that the idea of committing forgery came to him while he watched a forger being hanged. A juryman, who found Dr. Dodd guilty of forgery, committed soon afterwards the same crime and was hanged from the same gallows. Cumming was hanged in Edinburgh in 1854 for sexual assault, which immediately led to a wave of similar assaults in the region. In 1855, Heywood was hanged in Liverpool for cutting the throat of a woman; three weeks later, Ferguson was arrested in the same town for the same crime. The list could be continued indefinitely. The evidence was so overwhelming that a Select Committee of the House of Lords was appointed in 1856; it recommended that public executions should be abolished because they did not deter from crime. The Lords would not believe it, and did nothing. Ten years later, the Royal Commission of 1866 inquired into the same question, and came to the same result as the Select Committee. One of the most striking pieces of evidence before the Commissioners was a statement by the prison chaplain in Bristol, the Reverend W. Roberts, that out of 167 persons awaiting execution in that prison, 164 had previously witnessed at least one execution.[18] What would the British Medical

Association say of the value of a patent medicine for the prevention of polio, if it were found in 167 polio cases that 164 had been treated with that medicine?

Two years after the Royal Commission's reports, Parliament decided that executions should henceforth be private. However, if watching with one's own eyes the agony of a person being strangled on the gallows does not deter, it seems logical to assume that an unseen execution in a more gentlemanly manner would deter even less. One may further argue that if the penalty of hanging does not frighten even a pickpocket, it would not frighten a potential murderer, who acts either in momentary passion, or for incomparably higher stakes. Yet these were not the conclusions reached by the lawgivers. They assumed that while watching an execution from a few yards' distance did not act as a deterrent, reading a Home Office communiqué about it did.

The results of the abolition of the death-penalty for crimes against property provide a powerful argument for abolishing it altogether. But in itself, the argument is not conclusive. The fact that abolition of the death-penalty did not increase the volume of cattle-stealing strongly suggests, but does not prove, that abolition of the death-penalty would not increase the volume of murder. That proof can only be initiated by analogy with other crimes; it must be completed by actual precedents for the crime of murder itself.

3

Fortunately, these precedents are available through the experience of the thirty-six states which have abolished capital punishment in the course of the last hundred years. They are listed below.[19] The dates in parentheses indicate the year in which the death-penalty was abolished or abandoned.*

Europe: Austria (1919; reinstated by Hitler; abolished for the second time in 1950), Belgium (1863), Denmark (1933; in abeyance since 1892), Finland (1826), Iceland (1944), Italy (1890, restored by Mussolini in 1931; abolished again in 1944), Luxembourg (1822), The Netherlands (1870), Norway (1905, in abeyance since 1875), Portugal (1867), Sweden (1921, in abeyance

* Several countries behind the Iron Curtain have also abolished capital punishment for non-political offences, but these have not been included in the list.

since 1910), Switzerland (1874 and 1942, see appendix), Turkey (1950), Western Germany (1949).

Latin America: The Argentine (1922), Brazil (1891), Colombia (1910), Costa Rica (1880), Dominican Republic (1924), Equador (1895), Mexico (Mexico City and seven states, 1929 and after), Nicaragua (1893), Panama (1903), Peru ("end of nineteenth century"), Uruguay (1807), Venezuela (1873).

U.S.A.: Michigan (1847), Rhode Island (1852), Wisconsin (1853), Maine (1876), Minnesota (1911), North Dakota (1915).

Other Countries: Queensland (1911), Israel (1948), Nepal (1931), Travancore (1944).

For a detailed discussion, see Appendix I.

The evidence has been studied by criminologists and Departments of Justice all over the world, and summarized with previously unequalled thoroughness by the British Parliamentary Select Committee of 1929–30 and the Royal Commission on Capital Punishment of 1948–53. The report and evidence of the first fills some eight hundred closely printed pages; the report of the second, plus its Minutes of Evidence, nearly fourteen hundred pages of quarto and folio. The conclusion of the Select Committee is summed up as follows:

Our prolonged examination of the situation in foreign countries has increasingly confirmed us in the assurance that capital punishment may be abolished in this country without endangering life or property, or impairing the security of Society.[20]

The conclusions of the Royal Commission were essentially the same, although more cautiously expressed. Their terms of reference prevented them from considering the question whether capital punishment should be abolished or not; they were only allowed to make recommendations concerning changes in the existing capital law. Moreover, their report was unanimous,* whereas the Select Committee report of 1930, as the previous Royal Commission report of 1866, was a majority report. The Commission's final conclusion regarding the expected consequences of abolition (which they managed to smuggle in, though the terms of reference excluded this question) was formulated thus:

* Except for some minority reservations on subjects which are irrelevant to the issue under discussion.

There is no clear evidence of any lasting increase [in the murder-rate following abolition] and there are many offenders on whom the deterrent effect is limited and may often be negligible. It is therefore important to view the question in a just perspective and not to base a penal policy in relation to murder on exaggerated estimates of the uniquely deterrent force of the death-penalty.[21]

They reached this conclusion by taking two types of evidence into account: on the one hand, the crime statistics of foreign countries; on the other, the opinion of the British Police Force, the prison services and the judges. It is to this second, or local evidence that the expression "exaggerated estimates" refers; and in their conclusions the Commissioners make some allowances for it. But in the text of their report, as distinct from their cautious "conclusions", they make their findings unmistakably clear. They dismiss the police's and the judges' contention that abolition would entice burglars to wear firearms: "We received no evidence that the abolition of capital punishment in other countries had in fact led to the consequences apprehended by our witnesses in this country." [22] Their opinion on the general effect of abolition on the crime-rate in foreign countries is equally unambiguous. They analysed the staggeringly extensive material which they had assembled under three headings:

(a) by comparing the homicide statistics of a given country before and after abolition of the death-penalty;
(b) by comparing the homicide statistics of neighbouring countries of a similar social structure, some of which have abolished the death-penalty and some not, over the same period of time;
(c) by analysing the possible influence of the number of executions in a given country in a particular year on the homicide rate in the immediately following period.

Concerning (a), they state: "The general conclusion which we have reached is that there is no clear evidence in any of the figures we have examined that the abolition of capital punishment has led to an increase in the homicide rate, or that its reintroduction has led to a fall." [23]

Concerning (b), their findings are mainly based on comparisons between the homicide curves in closely related states in the U.S.A.; and between New Zealand and the Australian states:

If we take any of these groups we find that the fluctuations in the homicide rate of each of its component members exhibit a striking similarity. We agree with Professor Sellin that the only conclusion which can be drawn from the figures is that there is no clear evidence of any influence of the death-penalty on the homicide rates of these States, and that, "whether the death-penalty is used or not, and whether executions are frequent or not, both death-penalty States and abolition States show rates which suggest that these rates are conditioned by other factors than the death-penalty".[24]

Concerning (c), they state: ". . . about the possible relation between the number of executions in particular years and the incidence of murder in succeeding years . . . we are satisfied that no such relationship can be established." [25]

4

Once more the mountains laboured and a mouse was born. The mountainous statistical survey of the Royal Commission of 1948 merely confirmed the findings of the Select Committee of 1930, which confirmed the findings of all abolitionist countries in the course of the last century for crimes against property: to wit, that abolition has not caused an increase in murder nor stopped the fall of the murder-rate in any European country; and that in the non-European countries, the U.S.A., Australia and New Zealand, the ups and downs of the murder-rate show a striking similarity in states of similar social structure whether the death-penalty is used or not.

The defenders of capital punishment are well aware that the statistical evidence is unanswerable. They do not contest it; they ignore it. When pressed in debate, they invariably fall back on one of two answers: (a) "statistics lie" or "do not prove anything"; (b) that the experience of foreign countries has no bearing on conditions in Britain. Let us examine both answers.

That "statistics don't prove anything" is, of course, nonsense; if it were true, all insurance companies, physicists and engineers would have to go out of business, and the Chancellor of the Exchequer could never present a Budget. Statistics are indispensable in every human activity; and like every tool they can be put to careless and dishonest use. Statistics cannot prove or disprove that smoking "causes" lung cancer; it can prove that the average Englishman is taller than the average Italian. In the first example, the observational range is too small in relation to the number of causative factors involved.* In the second example, the statistician merely states a fact which can be interpreted in various ways; by race, nourishment, climate, and so on.

In discussing the statistics of abolitionist Europe, we have to distinguish with great care between fact and interpretation. The facts are beyond dispute: throughout the twentieth century, abolition was in no European country followed by an increase in the murder-rate, and was in nearly all countries followed by a decrease. These facts can be interpreted in the following manners:

(1) Abolition causes a fall in the murder-rate.

(2) Abolition causes an increase in the murder-rate, but this increase is too small to stop the general downward trend of the murder-rate, which is due to different causes.

(3) Abolition does not perceptibly influence the murder-rate one way or another.

All three interpretations are possible, although the examples of post-war Germany and post-war Italy (see Appendix I) seem to contradict the second hypothesis; but that, of course, is not conclusive. It is at this point that the comparisons between similar states with different legislation come in. They prove that "both death-penalty states and abolition states show rates which suggest that they are conditioned by other factors than the death-penalty. . . . The general picture is the same—a rise in the rates of the early twenties and a downward trend since then." [26]

This eliminates interpretations (1) and (2) and leaves us with (3): that the death-penalty cannot be proved to influence the murder-rate one way or another.

Let me make the point clearer by a familiar example. If the medical profession wants to test the efficiency of a new serum there are, by and large, two methods of doing this. The first is to administer the serum to a number of patients and see how the results compare with the use of older medicines. The substitution of prison sentences in lieu of capital punishment was an experiment of this kind. It showed that it was followed nearly everywhere in Europe by a fall in the

---

* Thus it is possible that people of a certain temperament and constitution are more liable than others both to become heavy smokers and to develop lung cancer, without any causal relationship between the two.

fever chart of crime. This in itself did not prove that the new treatment was the direct *cause* of the improvement, because perhaps the epidemic was on the wane anyway; but it did prove that the new treatment could at least not be sufficiently harmful to impede the fall on the fever chart, whatever the cause of that fall. The second method is used as a check on the first. The new serum is administered to patients in one hospital ward, and the rate of recovery is then compared to that in a second or "control" ward, where treatment is continued on the old lines. If the rate of recovery remains substantially the same in both wards, the British Medical Association will conclude that the new treatment is just as good or bad as the old one, as far as its deterrent effect on the disease goes. The choice will then be decided by other considerations. If the new treatment is less painful or repellent, then only the oldest fogeys of the profession will, just for the hell of it, stick to their ancient method.

To sum up: the experience of the civilized world proves as conclusively as the most rigorously sifted evidence can ever prove, that the gallows is no more effective than other non-lethal deterrents.

But statistics don't bleed; let us always remember the individual sample falling through the trap.

5

So much for the contention that "statistics don't prove anything". The second stock answer of the hang-hards runs: "Foreign experience doesn't prove anything, because foreigners are different". It was said in defence of death for shoplifting when all the rest of Europe had abandoned it; it is repeated today with the same unction. The grain of truth in it is that no nation is like any other nation; thus the example of, say, Switzerland *alone* would be of little value because Switzerland is a more "peaceful" country than England. But the whole point of the statistical approach is that, over a large number of samples, individual differences cancel out, and the general trend common to all is revealed.

Now the evidence concerning abolition embraces thirty-six countries with vastly different populations, and in different periods of development; agricultural and industrial nations, old and new civilizations, countries rich and countries poor, Latin, Anglo-Saxon and

Germanic races, hot-tempered and placid people, countries which became abolitionist after a long period of peace and security, and others, like Germany and Italy, which have only just emerged from war, demoralized by defeat, brutalized by years of totalitarian terror. The convincingness of the proof rests precisely in the fact that, however different the countries and conditions, abolition was nowhere followed by an increase in the crime-rate, or any other noticeable ill-effect.

6

The general reader who is new to this controversy would naturally assume that the opponents of abolition have their own arguments, figures and evidence on the same reasoned and factual level as the abolitionists, and that it would require a good deal of expert knowledge to decide which party is right. This is not the case. The defenders of capital punishment have produced no evidence of their own; nor contested the correctness of the documentary material assembled by Royal Commissions, Select Committees, etc.; nor even tried to put a different interpretation on it. They simply ignore it, as they ignore the experience gained from mitigations of the law in this country's own past. When challenged, they invariably and uniformly trot out the same answers: there is no alternative to capital punishment; statistics don't prove anything; other nations can afford to abolish hanging, but not Britain, because the criminal Englishman (or Welshman or Scotsman) is different from any other criminal in the world; for foreigners prison may be a sufficient deterrent, the English criminal needs the gallows.

Since the Select Committee's report, the Royal Commission has vastly extended the scope of the former's inquiry, and arrived at the same results. The answer of the hang-hards remained the same. It seems hardly believable that in a nation-wide controversy which has now been going on for some twenty-five years, one side should produce, with ant-like diligence, facts, figures and historic precedent, mobilize the whole array of psychiatry and social science, borne out by impartial Royal Commissions —and the other side should content themselves with evasion, stonewalling and the ever repeated nonsense about the unique and indispensable deterrent value of the death-penalty. The legend about the hangman as the protector of society has been refuted and exposed to ridicule on every single past occasion, and yet it popped up again on the next.

This is perhaps the saddest aspect in this whole heart- and neck-breaking business. For it shows that an officially sponsored lie has a thousand lives and takes a thousand lives. It resembles one of the monster squids of deep-sea lore; it spurts ink into your face, while its tentacles strangle the victim in the interest of public welfare.

Part II

THE LAW

REFLECTIONS ON THE HANGING
OF A PIG

or What Is Criminal Responsibility?

IN MANGIN's *L'Homme et la Bête* [1] there is an engraving, entitled: "Infliction of the Death Penalty on a Sow." The sow, dressed in human clothes, legs pinioned, is held down on the scaffold by the executioner, who is fixing the noose round its throat. Facing the sow is the town clerk, reading the sentence from a scroll; at the foot of the scaffold is a jostling crowd. Mothers are lifting up their children to give them a better view; and a stern worthy is pointing his finger at the screaming sow, obviously explaining: "She is only getting what she deserves."

Animals guilty of killing a human being were, in the Middle Ages, and in isolated cases up to the nineteenth century, tried by lawful procedure, defended by counsel, sometimes acquitted, more often sentenced to be hanged, burned, or buried alive. The sow on the engraving had killed a baby, and was hanged in 1386 at Falaise; a horse which had killed a man was hanged at Dijon in 1389; another sow, with a litter of six, was sentenced for the murder of a child at Savigny in 1457, but the baby pigs were reprieved "in lack of positive proof of complicity".

A further capital crime for animals besides homicide (with or without malice aforethought) was sexual intercourse with a human being. In such cases both partners in crime, man and animal, were burned alive together, according to the Lex Carolina. The last recorded case was the burning of Jacques Ferron in 1750 at Vanvres for sodomy with a she-ass; but the animal was acquitted after the Parish Priest and several leading citizens had testified that she was "the victim of violence and had not participated in the crime of her own free will". [2] Capital punishment of animals fell gradually into abeyance in the eighteenth century; the last recorded case is the trial and execution of a dog for having participated in a robbery and murder in Delémont, Switzerland, 1906.[3]

Why do we find the hanging of an animal even more revolting and disgusting than the hanging of a human being? The question deserves some reflection.

Take the word "disgusting" first. Most of us, who are not vegetarians, have no strong feelings of disgust about the painless slaughtering of cattle and the shooting of game; but the idea of executing an animal is disgusting because it appears to us as a purposeless and "artificial" way of ending its life, made even more gruesome by a grotesque ceremony. But hanging a man or a woman is an equally unappetizing and artificial ceremony. Both the murderer and the soldier have a motive to kill, which makes their act more or less spontaneous; in the execution chamber this redeeming aspect of spontaneity is absent, and only the ghastly ceremonial aspect of breaking a neck remains. However, aesthetic revulsion is only a minor point. The real question is why we find capital punishment of animals *intellectually* more revolting than capital punishment of humans.

Let us look at the problem from the point of view of the protection of society. We know that hanging pigs won't deter other pigs from attacking babies left carelessly lying around; properly penning up the pigs is a quite sufficient protection of society. But this answer won't hold good either, because experience proves that executing the human criminal is also no more effective as a deterrent than penning him up; thus once the belief in deterrence falls, hanging a man is just as pointlessly cruel as hanging a horse. Why, then, are we more horrified by the idea of strangling a horse? Because it is a helpless creature? A woman pinioned or strapped to a chair and hoisted to the rope is just as helpless.

We must try another approach. Let us put it this way: "The poor, dumb creature did not know what it was doing, it is not responsible for its acts; and hence the proceedings of the court are an absurd farce." Now at last we seem to be getting somewhere. But are we really? For if you have ever seen the guilty look in your dog's eye after he stole a chop or chewed up your slippers, you know that the jury would have no choice but to find him criminally responsible according to the M'Naghten rule: *that he knew the nature of his act, and knew that it was wrong.*

A pig, of course, is less intelligent than a dog, and may be said to be lacking, comparatively, in moral sense. But feeble-mindedness and lack of moral sense do not abolish criminal responsibility, nor are they sufficient grounds for pleading "guilty but insane". Straffen was mentally defective, yet he was sentenced to death, after Mr. Justice Cassels instructed the jury to bear in mind only the M'Naghten Rules and "*not* that he is feeble-minded, *not* that he has a lack of moral sense".[4] Thus the Prosecution would have no particular difficulty in proving that the sow, according to her dim lights, knew what she was doing, and knew that she was doing something that was not permitted, for as soon as the keeper appeared on the scene she ran away guiltily instead of approaching him as usual in the expectancy of food. We can go even further than that and still remain on solid legal ground: every animal capable of being tamed and domesticated would be found criminally responsible in our Courts —for the simple reason that the process of taming itself is based on establishing in the animal's mind distinctions between what is permitted and what is not. Similarly, discipline in mental homes can only be maintained because all lunatics, except those in the padded cell, are able to distinguish between "right" and "wrong" with reference to the regulations in their wards. As Lord Bramwell remarked some eighty years ago: "The present law lays down such a definition of madness that nobody is hardly ever really mad enough to be within it." [5] It is true that if a feeble-minded creature is hauled up in court, the court may, according to Section 8 of the Mental Deficiency Acts, send him to an institution, or place him under guardianship instead of passing judgment—*except if the offence is punishable by death;* in which case judgment must be passed on the creature.[6]

Hence counsel for the defence of the animal must try another line. Stupidity and lack of moral sense won't get his client off. Nor a plea of "diminished responsibility"; because a creature can have its responsibility diminished in Scotland, but can't have it diminished in England and Wales.

The last hope is to get the charge reduced from murder to manslaughter. In the case of the horse who kicked its master to death, "provocation" might perhaps do the trick, for the horse had been nervous and irritable ever since it was shocked by a blunderbuss in the battle of Cherbourg, and witnesses testified that its nasty master had fired off a firecracker in front of its nose to tease it. So the fool had only to blame himself if the horse went off its head. But that won't do either; firstly because provocation is not a mitigating circumstance if committed by mere word or gesture.* And secondly, because the provocation must be such as to satisfy the jury (a) that it deprived the accused of his self-control, and (b) that *it would also have deprived any other reasonable man (or horse) of self-control.* Thus a creature "who is mentally deficient or mentally abnormal or is 'not of good mental balance' or who is 'unusually excitable or pugnacious' is not entitled to rely on provocation which would not have led an ordinary person to act as he did".[7] This nicety of the law referring to provocation is usually called "the test of the reasonable man". It states expressly that when the jury has to decide whether the provocation was sufficient to deprive a reasonable man of his self-control, they ought *not to* "take into account different degrees of mental ability".[9] That means that the jury, in assessing the effect of provocation, must not consider the living individual before them but an abstract ideal being. This fantastic ruling was approved by the Court of Criminal Appeal (in 1940), and again by the House of Lords (in 1942).[10] Accordingly, the firecracker let off in front of the shell-shocked horse, which made the creature go off its head, does not justify a plea of provocation because a reasonable horse wouldn't have gone off its head; nor calling a refugee from a Nazi concentration camp a filthy Jew, because a reasonable person wouldn't turn a hair.

As a last resort, Counsel might try to argue that the poor horse did not act with "malice aforethought"; if he could prove that, the charge would be reduced from murder to manslaughter. But how could he prove that? For in the phrase "malice aforethought" "neither of the two words is used in its ordinary sense. . . . It is now only an arbitrary symbol. For the malice may have in it nothing really malicious; and need never be really aforethought, except in the sense that every desire must necessarily come before— though perhaps only an instant before—the act which is desired. The word 'aforethought' in the definition has thus become either false or else superfluous." [11]

---

* Except "in circumstances of a most extreme and exceptional character".[8] There has been no recent case in which mere words or gesture have been accepted as sufficient provocation.

And yet this meaningless phrase is still the basic criterion of murder. "The statement of the modern law most commonly cited as authoritative is that given in 1877 by Sir James Stephen in his *Digest of the Criminal Law:* 'Malice aforethought means any one or more of the following states of mind preceding *or coexisting* with the act . . . by which death is caused, and *it may exist where the act is unpremeditated.*' " [12]

The short and long of the matter is: if animals were still prosecuted in our courts, the jury, according to the law as it stands, would have no choice but to bring in a verdict of guilty against the pig, the horse and the cow, and to add a strong recommendation for mercy. Only the dog with rabies would get off, for that dog alone would qualify as "M'Naghten mad".

The absurdity of the law when applied strictly and literally has been known to the legal profession for a long time. In 1874, a Select Committee of the House of Commons reported: "If there is any case in which the law should speak plainly, without sophism or evasion, it is where life is at stake; and it is on this very occasion that the law is most evasive and most sophistical." [13] Seventy-five years have passed since, yet in spite of countless attempts to reform it, the law is substantially the same today as it was a hundred years ago. The most glaring example of its "evasive and sophistical" nature is the famous M'Naghten Rules—which for reasons which will presently become apparent, deserve a chapter to themselves.

THE PRECEDENT WITHOUT PRECEDENT

or The Anti-M'Naghten Rules

In the first fifty years of our century, approximately 20,000 men and women were tried for various offences other than murder. Out of these, altogether twenty-nine were found "guilty but insane"; that is, 0.15%.

During the same half-century, 4,077 people were tried for murder. Of these, 1,013 were discharged or acquitted; of the remaining 3,064 convicted murderers, 1,241 were found "guilty but insane", insane on arraignment or reprieved as insane, making a total of around 40%.[1]

In other words, insanity as a defence is an exception in crimes other than murder, and almost the rule where murder is concerned. In considerably more than half of the murder trials the question of the accused's sanity is debated in court and twice as many murderers are sent to Broadmoor as are actually executed.

Murder, of course, is more closely related to insanity than any other crime. But this fact plays only a minor part in the enormous disparity (40% as opposed to 0.15%) between insanity as a defence in murder and non-murder trials. The true reason for the disparity is that in all offences the punishment of the convicted person is a matter in the discretion of the court—except in capital offences where the penalty of death is rigid and fixed. A burglar or rapist can be sentenced, according to the individual circumstances of the case, to anything from probation to fifteen years prison; when a murderer is convicted, regardless whether he is a cold-blooded poisoner, a mercy-killer or a partner in a suicide pact, the jury only has the choice of finding him either "guilty" or "guilty but insane". There is no other way (except the recommendation for mercy, of which the result is uncertain) of taking individual circumstances into consideration, of saving a man who, in the jury's opinion, clearly should not hang.

Hence the immense importance of the M'Naghten Rules which define insanity; for insanity is the only escape-line for jury and accused, both trapped by the rigid and antiquated law. Moreover, the M'Naghten Rules are virtually a definition of what is meant by "criminal responsibility", and play, therefore, a crucial part in the philosophical, scientific and ethical problems involved in human justice. This latter aspect I shall, however, reserve for the chapter on "Free Will and Determinism".

Thus the M'Naghten Rules embody the delinquent's only hope, his life-line from the gallows to Broadmoor—apart from the Royal mercy, there is no other way out. We saw that two out of three who were found guilty are saved by it. Hence the history of the M'Naghten Rules is essential to the understanding of the problem of capital punishment.

M'Naghten was not a judge; he was a madman. He was a Protestant from Northern Ireland who laboured under the delusion that His Holiness the Pope, the Jesuit Order and the leader of the Tory Party, Sir Robert Peel, were conspiring against him. He accordingly bought a pistol and, one day in 1843, planted himself in Downing Street with the intention of shooting Peel, the Prince of all Evil. Press-photography was not yet invented in those days, and M'Naghten did not know what Peel looked like; so he shot by mistake Mr. Edward Drummond, Peel's secretary, who happened to walk by.

At his trial, eight medical witnesses gave evidence (the term "psychiatry" was not yet invented), all of whom concurred that M'Naghten, owing to his delusion, was deprived of all restraint over his actions. When they had finished, Lord Chief Justice Tindal virtually stopped the case and instructed the jury to bring in a verdict of "not guilty by reason of insanity". M'Naghten was sent to an institution, and then the unprecedented precedent took place.

The case had given rise to much public discussion, and the oracles of the day thought that M'Naghten ought to have been hanged, presumably to deter other lunatics from believing that the Pope and Sir Robert Peel were after their lives. The House of Lords, as usual, obliged. Their lordships drew up a questionnaire

regarding the criminal responsibility of persons suffering from insane delusions. The questionnaire was sent, not to the medical
profession, but to the fifteen High Court Judges. The replies, as
given by fourteen out of the fifteen Judges, constitute the M'Naghten Rules. More properly, they ought to be called the anti-
M'Naghten Rules, because the fourteen Judges concluded that the
eight doctors were mistaken in their diagnosis and that M'Naghten
should have been hanged. This happy improvisation has, like the
Waltham Black Acts, triumphantly survived the storms of a century,
or more precisely, of a hundred and thirteen years to date. The
crucial passages of the Judges' answers are firstly that,

to establish a defence on the ground of insanity, it must be clearly proved
that, at the time of the committing of the act, the party accused was la-
bouring under such a defect of reason, from disease of the mind, *as not
to know the nature and quality of the act he was doing, or, if he did
know it, that he did not know he was doing what was wrong.*

And, secondly, that if a person labours under an insane delusion
"he must be considered in the same situation as to responsibility
as if the facts with respect to which the delusion exists were real."
In other words, M'Naghten ought to have been hanged because,
though he was insane in believing that Peel was persecuting him, he
ought to have been sane enough to refrain from shooting him because he must have known that shooting one's persecutor is not
permitted by law. It will be seen that Lord Goddard, more than a
century later, took exactly the same position in his evidence before
the Royal Commission referring to the case of Ley.
Although the M'Naghten Rules were established way back in the
year when Joseph Smith authorized polygamy for the Mormons,
they represented a regression into a still remoter past. In 1800, a man
called James Hatfield, who suffered from the delusion that the
salvation of the world depended on him, made an attempt on the
life of George III. He was acquitted on the grounds of insanity
after a famous speech for the defence by Lord Erskine, the gist of
which was that a man governed by delusions is insane, and therefore irresponsible, even though reason is not wholly dethroned.
Erskine knew what the oracles will never learn, because it would
disrupt their whole artificial universe: that human nature is, in
its core, governed by emotion and impulse, passion and belief,

covered by a relatively new and precarious crust of reasoning which is liable to crack when the inner pressure becomes too great; and that once the crack has occurred, reason loses its control, regardless whether its ability to distinguish between "right" and "wrong" survives or not. The slang expressions "crackbrain" and "crackpot" convey a clear understanding of the indivisible nature of the human mind, which the law denies by the preposterous assumption that if $x\%$ of the reasoning faculty is destroyed, the remaining $y\%$ continues to function as if nothing had happened, and enables a man to control his impulses as if he were normal.

Erskine's view of insanity which led to the acquittal of Hatfield in 1800, was not always accepted in subsequent cases, yet it was a famous precedent and the acquittal of M'Naghten conformed to it. The anti-M'Naghten Rules, on the other hand, are an unprecedented curiosity in the history of Common Law because they were a judgment given in an *abstract and fictional, not in an actual, case.* They are technically not "authority" because not based on an actual trial, but in the petrified forest of the law they stand rigid and indestructible. Thus the question whether a convicted person is responsible or not, and whether he should accordingly live or die, is to this day decided on the opinion of fourteen Judges in 1843 why M'Naghten, who was reprieved, ought *not* to have been reprieved. As long as Common Law has existed, Judges have ruled by precedent; for the last century the fate of countless people has been decided by the anti-precedent of a fictional case, expressly constructed to reverse the precedent in a real case. Here is Wonderland logic in full, murderous bloom.

It is important to remember that the M'Naghten Rules were born in 1843—before the word "psychiatry" had been invented, before Darwin had published *The Origin of Species,* before it was realized that man has a biological past, has "animal" instincts and impulses which, though deplorable in the Victorian drawing-room, are his natural heritage, an explanation, and at least partial excuse, for his actions. Nor was it realized that childhood, education and social conditioning are largely responsible in forming character, including criminal character: 1843 was the year when a Royal Commission on mines first suggested that it might not be an altogether good thing to let women and children work fourteen hours a day in the pits. Yet even at that date the M'Naghten Rules were an anachronism, condemned by the majority of the medical, and the more enlightened of the legal, profession. In 1864, a meeting of the Medical Officers of Hospitals and Asylums for the Insane—and who was better qualified to talk about insanity than this body?—passed the following resolution:

That so much of the legal test of the mental condition of an alleged criminal lunatic as renders him a responsible agent, because he knows the difference between right and wrong, is inconsistent with the fact, well known to every member of this meeting, that the power of distinguishing between right and wrong exists very frequently among those who are un-doubtedly insane and is often associated with dangerous and uncontrolla-ble delusions.[2]

But the judges opposed any reform.

Ten years later, the greatest legal authority of the time, Stephen, tried to amend the M'Naghten Rules, but the judges opposed any amendment. It was on this occasion that Lord Bramwell (inventor of the "Limited Companies") made his famous remark, which I have already quoted, that the Rule "lays down such a definition of madness that nobody is hardly ever really mad enough to be within it, *yet it is a logical and good definition*".[3]

In 1922, a Committee was again set up under the chairmanship of Lord Justice Atkin to consider the matter. The Committee heard the views of the British Medical Association and of the Royal Medical Psychological Association and accepted their proposals for amending the Rules in such a way that a man should not be held criminally responsible if, owing to mental disease, he was acting under an irresistible impulse. The Government refused, as usual, to accept the recommendations of the Committee it had appointed, and referred the matter to the judges. Ten out of the twelve High Court Judges consulted, voted, as usual, against the reform, and the House of Lords, as usual, obliged by throwing the Bill out. Lord Chief Justice Lord Hewart referred in the debate to the proposed amendment as "the fantastic theory of uncontrollable impulse which, if it were to become part of our criminal law, would be merely subversive".[4]

Another quarter-century later, the Royal Commission of 1948 proposed that the M'Naghten Rules should be abrogated and the question of criminal responsibility be left to the decision of the jury; or, failing this, that the Rules should be extended to cover cases where the accused was "incapable of preventing himself from committing the act". It was substantially the same amendment which Stephen proposed eighty years ago, and the Atkin Committee twenty-five years ago. As usual, the judges opposed it. As usual, the Government refused to act on the proposals of the Committee which it had appointed.

An eminent psychiatrist said recently about some aspects of the Common Law of murder:

It would be difficult if one tried to pack into such small compass more vague, abstract nouns, ambiguous verbs, and untenable fictions. . . . The whole concept of "criminal responsibility" is itself fictional and logically untenable. . . . If it is true that justice is always done, it is not because of these rules but because of the common sense with which our courts *mis*-apply them. . . . If a man accused of murder seems a decent sort of bloke and has put up with much provocation from the victim—who might be said "to have got what was coming to her (or him)", and if at the same time the accused has some mental peculiarity not possessed by most of us, prosecuting counsel "pull their punches", judges err on the side of leniency in instructing the jury, and jurymen grasp at the slightest opportunity to avoid giving a verdict which would automatically be followed by the death sentence.[5]

In other words, we have reached the same situation with regard to murder, which prevailed in the nineteenth century with regard to petty thieving. When the jury had no choice but to find a wretch guilty of having stolen forty shillings' worth of goods, they fixed the value at thirty-nine shillings and cocked a snook at the outdated law; today, faced with a similar dilemma, they find him guilty but insane, though he isn't, because this is the only way out for them.

Sometimes they succeed in saving a soul, sometimes not. Much depends on their courage and determination in disregarding a severe judge's instructions; more on the humanity or inhumanity of the judge himself. When the judge is humane, he "stretches" the Rules. It is now fifty years since one of the greatest authorities on this question wrote that in such cases "the usual course is for the judge to adhere strictly to the terms of the answers, and then to stretch the plain meaning of the language of those answers, until the ordinary non-legal user of the English language is aghast at the distortions and deformations and tortures to which the unfortunate words are subjected, and wonders whether it is worth-while to have a language which can apparently be taken to mean anything the user pleases".[6]

But while some judges are humane, others adhere strictly to the Stone Age Law. Straffen was sentenced after the Judge had instructed the jury to disregard the fact that he was feeble-minded; Bentley, aged nineteen, illiterate, Grade 4 mentally defective, was hanged a year later; Lentchitsky, mentally defective, was hanged in the same year. In a number of opposite cases, convicted persons were sent to Broadmoor though sane, because the rigidity of the law prevented the reduction of the charge to manslaughter. The trial of a human life is the most solemn act of the law; when the law is reduced to absurdity, it becomes a game of roulette.

Yet even in this absurd and murderous game the table is loaded in favour of the black. The burden of "stretching" the rigid Rules lies mainly with the medical psychiatrists called by the defence. We have seen that the M'Naghten Rules came into being as an act of defiance of the Judges *versus* medical men. Ever since then, a more or less open warfare has been carried on in the courts of this country between the Judges favouring the Rules, and the psychiatrists who oppose them. Yet, as Dr. Hobson remarks,[7] "antagonizing a Judge may be hazarding a man's life". He goes on to give a typical example of a case in which "cross-examination by Counsel was easy to deal with", but where the judge in his summing up implied that the psychiatrist was incompetent and biased, and virtually instructed the jury to find the accused (a woman who had killed her baby) guilty of murder. The jury, ignoring the summing up, brought in a verdict of not guilty—but it was clearly a matter of luck, and a parody of justice.

The moral philosophy behind all this is summed up by the following exchanges between the Lord Chief Justice and the Royal Commissioners:

Q. Do you agree with the general view that it is wrong to hang those who are insane in the medical sense?—*A.* I think it very largely depends on what one means by "in the medical sense" . . . the test that ought to be applied in these cases is strictly a test of responsibility [i.e. the M'Naghten test] not merely whether a man may have been mentally abnormal in some respects.[8]

Q. Not even if he were certifiable?—*A.* It depends on what grounds he is certifiable . . .[9]

Lord Goddard was also asked whether he approved of the practice that, when a plea of insanity has been rejected by the jury, the Home Secretary frequently orders an inquiry to determine whether the convicted person was mentally fit to be hanged.

A. . . . if he has been found responsible, after due inquiry into his state of mind by a jury, and there is no change in that position after conviction, I cannot see that there is any ground for reprieve, and, as I say, I think it is a negation of trial by jury.[10]

This, of course, is plain nonsense. The reprieves granted in such borderline cases are not a "negation of trial by jury" but a negation of the M'Naghten Rules. The jury is bound by the Rules; the Home Secretary is not. It is this last escape-line from the stranglehold of the Rules which the Lord Chief Justice wanted cut off—as will appear from the next questions and answers:

Q. Do you mean that the same test of responsibility should be applied at both stages, both to determine whether he should be sentenced to death and also whether he should in fact be hanged?—*A.* Yes . . . if the jury finds . . . that he is responsible for the act he committed, within the definition of the M'Naghten Rules, I can see no reason why he should not be executed.[11]

Q. . . . In the evidence given by the Home Office there was some indication of the more common reasons for which the Home Secretary may recommend a reprieve? One of them is this: "When a murder is committed without premeditation as the result of some sudden access of frenzy and the prisoner has previously had no evil animus towards the victim, commutation is often recommended. In cases of this kind it is sometimes necessary to give weight to the consideration that the prisoner, though not insane, is weak-minded or emotionally unstable to an abnormal degree." I gather that that is the sort of thing to which you are now taking exception?—*A.* . . . I still think that it is an inroad on the conception of trial by jury, that the Home Secretary should take a different view after an inquiry conducted in private . . . It is most anomalous, especially considering the evidence which some people who call themselves psychiatrists have given in front of us.[12]

Pressed on the same point later on, the Lord Chief Justice added:

I do think that very often the opinion on which the Secretary of State acts is far too favourable to the convict. I have a note here of a recent case in which the Home Secretary reprieved a man, and I read very carefully the report of the three medical officers who went down to see him and recommended clemency, I confess I find it difficult to understand on what grounds.[13]

Q. May I act for a moment the role of advocate for the Home Secretary, and say to you: . . . What the jury have decided is whether this man knew the nature of what he was doing, and knew that what he was doing was wrong, under the M'Naghten Rules. What I have got to decide is something quite different, namely, whether this man is in a proper state to be hanged. What do you say to that?—*A.* I say that if the man is responsible within the M'Naghten Rules, and there has been no change, I cannot see any reason why the Home Secretary should take a different view.[14]

The Commissioners took him up on a specific case. It was the case of Ley (the so-called chalk-pit murder) which had been tried by Lord Goddard himself. He had referred to this case in his Memorandum to the Royal Commission, and had said that he "had no doubt that the prisoner was insane; his whole conduct showed a typical case of paranoia".[15] Ley was sentenced to death by Lord Goddard. The Home Secretary ordered a medical inquiry which found Ley insane; he was certified and sent to Broadmoor, where he died a few weeks later.

Q. Take the interesting case of Ley, whom you mentioned. You had no doubt that he was insane?—*A.* No; I thought he was insane from the way he gave his evidence. . . .[16]

Q. And he would hardly be covered by the M'Naghten Rules?—*A.* He was not covered by the M'Naghten Rules; at least, I thought he was not.[17]

Q. . . . I suppose you would not have wished that man to hang? You would not think it proper that he should hang?—*A.* I should have thought it very proper that he should have been hanged.[18]

We should be grateful to Lord Goddard. The strongest case for the abolition of capital punishment is made out by the arguments and mentality of its defenders.

V

THE CASE OF THE MACE-BEARER

I NOW PROPOSE to describe an individual murder story in some detail. It is a case that was tried in 1950 and given little publicity at the time or since. It was one of the cases in which the accused drew a red on the roulette: the jury returned a verdict of guilty but insane, though they knew perfectly well that he was not insane either according to Saint M'Naghten or in any accepted sense of insanity. It is a hum-drum story about ordinary people which demonstrates the absurdity of the murder law in a neater way than more dramatic cases.

Donald Martin * was at the time a respectable and respected citizen of the age of fifty. He was Town Hall Superintendent and Mace-bearer at the Borough of Notting Hill, and lived in a flat in the Town Hall called "caretaker's premises". On official occasions he walked behind the Mayor, carrying the mace in solemn procession. His wife Violet, also middle-aged, was working for the National Savings Association in the same Town Hall. They had one child, a pretty girl called Sally, aged seventeen.

On Wednesday, September 27th, 1950, Mr. and Mrs. Martin had lunch at a cafeteria in Baker Street and, returning to caretaker's premises, had an argument. Martin tried to persuade Violet to give up her job so that she could spend more time in looking after their flat, and also that she should consult the Marriage Advice Bureau. Violet refused, whereupon Donald hit her on the head— the first time in his life that he had hit her—then, leaving her lying on the floor, went to the kitchen, took his razor out of its case, replaced the case neatly at right angles to his brush and comb on the shelf, went back to Violet, cut her throat, and when satisfied that she was dead, telephoned the police. When the police arrived,

---

* The facts of the case are as stated; the names of the participants have been altered to avoid distress to their families. "Notting Hill Town Hall", which does not exist, stands for the existing Town Hall of a London borough.

he was sitting at the top of the staircase waiting for them, perfectly composed. He remained equally composed while waiting for his trial and never revealed any real remorse for what he had done.

Donald was the third in a family of eleven children, of whom ten survived. His father was a workman in the painting and decorating trade. His mother was a simple woman, who had led a very hard life. There was no hereditary mental disease in the family, and all of its members got on reasonably well in life. It is true that the father was said to have been a violent-tempered man who once broke the nose of one of his daughters with a blow, but such incidents, alas, are not very exceptional in a hard-up, working-class family of that size.

Donald was a normal child, average in school, got on well with his schoolmates and took an active part in all sports; he particularly excelled in boxing. According to his mother, he was always well behaved, never quarrelsome or violent; the only complaint about him was that he had been excessively "tidy and particular". Out of school hours he earned money for the family by polishing boots and selling newspapers. At fourteen, on leaving school, he held a job as a grocer's errand boy for twelve months, then another as a milkman for eighteen months. He subsequently worked in a rubber factory for a year, but did not like indoor work, and became a baker's roundsman.

At the age of nineteen, he enlisted in the Royal Tank Corps. He served altogether eighteen years in England, India and Egypt, reaching the rank of Sergeant and Acting Company Quartermaster-Sergeant. When he left the Army at the age of thirty-seven, his character was described as exemplary; he was awarded the long-service and good-conduct medal and granted a service pension. He then got employment at Notting Hill Town Hall, at first as a porter, and, during the next twelve years, gradually worked his way up to be Town Hall Superintendent and Mace-bearer.

A more decent and ordinary career could hardly be imagined. Yet Donald Martin bore a cross, part real, part imaginary, under whose weight he finally collapsed. He was, so to speak, a common-or-garden martyr of that commonplace Calvary: a marriage between incompatible partners.

He met Violet when he was twenty-two, while stationed with

his Company in Dorset. She was at that time a laundry-maid. A year later he became engaged to her; another two years later they were married; another fortnight later, during their honeymoon, she infected him with syphilis.

He did not realize this at the time. He only found out about it eight years later, when he was stationed in India, and a medical examination revealed a syphilitic infection of the central nervous system. The date of the infection was then traced back to the appearance of a small genital ulcer a fortnight after his marriage, which he had noticed at the time but ignored as harmless. He received treatment in military hospitals in England, India and Egypt, over a period of more than two years, and was then reported cured.

The medical examination which led to the discovery of the disease was caused by an incident at the Army Barracks in Poona. This happened in the eighth year of their marriage, and one year after Violet had given birth to their daughter Sally. They were living in married quarters. Donald suspected that Violet, who had been sexually cold towards him from the beginning of their marriage, was committing adultery with a Company Sergeant. There was a quarrel, after which he stole a revolver from the Armoury, intending to shoot Violet, the baby and himself. Before he could do so, however, an officer and N.C.O. came to arrest him for taking the revolver and ammunition without authority. He was court-martialled, but pleaded that he could not remember what he was doing. He was sent for observation into hospital; where, in the course of a medical examination, he was discovered to be suffering from syphilitic meningo-encephalitis.

Yet the idea of shooting Violet, the baby and himself had already occurred to Donald prior to this discovery. What had been going on during those first eight years of their married life to drive him to this point? We only have a few glimpses of the idyll between Donald and Violet. One of them is provided by Donald's repeated complaints about her sexual coldness towards him, and by his description "how she would merely lie on her side and go on reading a book whilst he had sexual intercourse with her". But in the law of murder this debasement of a sacrament to an obscenity, this mortal offence to the male's pride is not known as a provocation to a reasonable man.

Nothing could be more commonplace than the fact that during

twenty-four years of their married life Donald loved Violet desperately and Violet treated Donald like dirt. He was not a lovable man. He was narrow-minded, vain, pedantic and egocentric, obsessed with tidiness, and respectable appearances; a hypochondriac, constantly afraid of microbes and infections. Yet he forgave her the honeymoon present she had given him, and forgave her all that she did to him during the sixteen years that followed his first impulse to do away with her and himself and their child; in return, she kept adding provocation to provocation, of a kind not mentioned in the law books.

He kept himself under control. Only twice during all these years did he lose his temper: the first time when he was twenty-nine and had a fight with a soldier who taunted him; the second time, three years later, on the occasion when he got hold of the revolver. His Army record describes him as an excellent N.C.O., a good driver and mechanic, and a man who could confidently be recommended for any position of trust.

He was thirty-seven when he left the Army and started work at the Town Hall. The next ten years or so, the life of Donald and Violet was outwardly uneventful. He had an excellent work record. After being appointed Town Hall caretaker, he was responsible for porters and domestic staff and managed them well, though occasionally he was inclined to employ Army Sergeant methods. During the war he was superintendent of the local A.R.P. office, and an active member of the Civil Defence Club, to which Violet often accompanied him for dances and whist drives. He took great pride in his functions as a Mace-bearer. He did not betray the inner strain under which he lived and which he held in check by a rigid, meticulous, indeed fanatical, observance of his civic duties—as a man with a broken spine carries his head held stiffly up by a metal harness.

Perhaps the only odd thing about him was the exaggerated seriousness, verging on obsession, with which he took his duties. Having once been reprimanded for forgetting to hoist the flag for Princess Elizabeth's birthday, he wrote a letter to Buckingham Palace, asking for a complete list of royal birthdays. When the time came to ask for an increase in salary, he sent an inquiry to a number of other caretakers at town halls regarding their salaries; then wrote a letter of seven closely covered foolscap pages to the

Town Clerk, enumerating in detail all the important duties which he was called on to perform.

Since his main pride and obsession in life were order, discipline and tidiness, Violet, with the psychological insight that hatred provides, tormented him by being slatternly about their flat, never cooking a hot meal except once a week on Sunday, and turning caretaker's premises into a place of lewdness and abomination.

For by now the daughter, Sally, had become an attractive girl with an alarmingly developed temperament. At the age of seventeen, Sally had a "steady" named Horace, and besides him several sailor friends in the Merchant Navy. On one occasion, three of the sailors on different ships simultaneously applied for special leave to visit their fiancée, Sally Martin.

Horace, the civilian steady, was always hanging around caretaker's premises, and "carrying on" with Sally, with the consent and encouragement of Violet. This, of course, was a constant agony to Martin, the disciplinarian and prig; but he also had some additional reasons for loathing his daughter's young man. Horace had pimples on the back of his neck and Martin, who lived in horror of germs and infection, caught the pimples, so he thought, by washing out the sink after Horace had been there. On another occasion, he found a packet of contraceptives in Horace's pocket.

During the last year, the squalid cross became too heavy to bear. Donald believed that Violet and Sally were in alliance against him. At times they would "send him to Coventry" for several days on end. On one occasion they both left and were gone for a fortnight, leaving Donald to fend for himself in the flat. On several other occasions Violet left to stay with a sister, and threatened never to come back again. She knew that what he cherished most in life was his job at the Town Hall, and that if she left him he would lose it. She told him repeatedly that to sleep with him was repellent and distasteful to her, and encouraged him to have relations with other women. He tried this at the final stages, but it did not help.

Downstairs in the Town Hall he was still the strict and self-important Company Sergeant of Poona; upstairs at caretaker's premises he was virtually reduced to the state of an untouchable. In the Civil Defence Club he appeared, impeccably dressed, a paragon of respectability; in his sordid home he felt that he was drowning in dirt, pimples, contraceptives and fornications, real and imagined. He clutched at every straw. He implored Violet to give up her job because he thought that if she did so she would have more time to look after the flat, and all would be well. He sought advice from a doctor, who talked of sending him on to a psychiatrist, and then all would be well. He sought advice from the Marriage Advice Bureau, and implored Violet to go there, because they would talk to her sensibly and all would be well.

About six weeks before the end, Violet again left him. She went to stay with her sister in Dorchester, and said she would never come back. Whilst she was away, Donald cleaned, painted and decorated the flat. Then he followed her to Dorchester and persuaded Violet to come back and "give it another chance". Donald's old mother, aged seventy-four, was invited to an egg-and-bacon tea to welcome Violet on her return, and the old woman felt that a real reconciliation had taken place. Then Sally, who had also been away, came back too, and then Horace, and the contraceptives, and the pimples.

He became so miserable that he could hardly eat. Some time before the end he developed a duodenal ulcer. He was operated on and put on a gastric diet—which he could not keep because Violet refused to cook for him. He then became suspicious, and later convinced, that Violet was having sexual relations with their daughter's young man.

The incidents of the last three days are as drab, ordinary and commonplace as the rest.

On Monday, September 25th, Donald is reported to have asked Sally to help him with vacuuming the flat, which she refused. There were a few words.

On Tuesday, September 26th, Donald called on a Mrs. Tiplady, Sanitary Inspector at Notting Hill Town Hall, and asked her to inspect his flat in her official capacity, to confirm that his wife was neglecting it. Mrs. Tiplady obliged and wrote a report.

On Wednesday, September 27th, he again called to see Mrs. Tiplady, excitedly waving a *Daily Mail,* in which a sensational article on the neglect of the homes of married women who went out to work had appeared. Then he called at Violet's office, asking her to give up her job. Then they had lunch at the cafeteria in Baker Street, and they had an argument. Then they went on to the flat and he asked her again to give up her job and to consult the Marriage Advice Bureau. She refused, threatened to leave him again and spoke to him, as he described it, "in a manner she had never done before". Considering the time they had spent together, it must have been quite some manner to speak in. Then he hit her for the first time in his life; and then a quarter-century of repressed hatred burst to the surface, and he fetched his razor and cut her throat. She must have resisted, because there were cuts on her hands and arms.

While awaiting his trial, he slept well and ate well, and said he felt much happier now that he was in prison. In his statements he was frank and co-operative and unhesitatingly volunteered information which was prejudicial to him. He only made one misleading statement, at an early interview, when he denied having ever been unfaithful to Violet. His only complaint about conditions in prison was that he could not keep his clothes as tidy as he would like to and as he always had done. He did not seem to be aware that he had committed a crime and seemed to have no sense of guilt. He said to one of his visitors that a girl with whom he used to go out before he met Violet, and whom he had not seen for many years, had written to him on reading about the case: this had led to an amorous correspondence and her visiting him in prison. He hoped that if acquitted he could marry her.

When Donald Martin was tried for murder at the Old Bailey, the defence plea was guilty but insane. What else could Counsel plead? Not provocation, for Violet did not physically attack him, and her refusal to go to the Marriage Advice Bureau would hardly have caused a "reasonable man" to lose control of himself. Nor the absence of malice aforethought, since after knocking her down he went to the bathroom, extracted the razor, and put down the case with care and premeditation before he murdered her. There could also be no doubt that when he committed his act he knew what he was doing, and that what he was doing was wrong. There exists no paragraph in criminal law which Counsel could plead to reduce the charge from murder to manslaughter. There exists no paragraph in criminal law which would have enabled the judge and jury to spare the life of Donald Martin. Yet judge and jury, and even Counsel for the Crown, felt that it was not really necessary to hang Martin, either to avenge society or to protect society against other Mace-bearers who contract syphilis on their honeymoons. And because they all felt this strongly, charity and common sense prevailed; and the jury with a sigh of relief sent Mace-bearer Martin to be detained at the Queen's pleasure among the lunatics in Broadmoor, where he doesn't belong.

FREE WILL AND DETERMINISM

or The Philosophy of Hanging

1

Lᴇᴛ ᴜs ʀᴇᴛᴜʀɴ once more to the seemingly pointless question why we find the hanging of an animal so much more repellent than the hanging of a human being.

We saw that before the law as it stands, neither the horse which killed its master, nor the dog who stole the Sunday joint would have a chance of getting off, because they knew what they were doing and that what they were doing was wrong. Of course, the dog couldn't plead, except by wagging its tail and showing balefully the whites of its eyes; but some criminals behave as equally dumb creatures in the dock, and there is always counsel to plead for them. Yet, although we know that a well-trained dog knows its duty, and consequently knows right from wrong, and would be found "criminally responsible", we feel that man is nevertheless *more* responsible, or responsible in a different and higher sense, than an animal. We are ready to grant the dog or the chimpanzee the excuse that they were obeying an "irresistible impulse" and could not control themselves, whereas we assume more or less consciously that man *can* control himself, and that, when he commits a crime, he does it out of his own choice, independently from causative compulsion, out of his own free will.

We say: the dog couldn't help doing what he did, but the human criminal could have resisted the criminal impulse if he had "tried harder", "made a greater effort", "kept himself under better control". "Harder", "greater", "better"—than what? Than the effort or resistance which he actually did put up. Our belief that he *ought* and *could* have put up a greater effort than he actually did, implies the assumption that the same person faced with the same situation has the choice of reacting to it in two different ways. In other words, that *the same cause may lead to two or more different effects.* This assumption goes against the very foundations on which modern science is built. Yet it is this assumption which underlies the concept of "criminal responsibility", and which is implied in the whole body of the Law.

The issue of free will *versus* determinism is hardly mentioned at all in the century-old controversy on capital punishment. Yet it is really the heart of the matter. It is shunned because it is the oldest and most awe-inspiring problem of philosophy, and probably an insoluble one. Yet I will try to show that our inability to solve the problem is the strongest argument against capital punishment.

The dilemma is not one of abstract philosophy; it permeates all our actions in daily life. On the one hand I know that everything that happens is determined by the laws of nature, and, since I am part of the natural world, my conduct is *determined* by heredity and environment. But at the same time, contradicting this knowledge, I feel that I am *free* to choose whether at this moment I shall go on writing this text, or call it a day and have a drink at the pub. My scientific education tells me that the outcome is predetermined by my past, and that what I experience as my "free choice" is an illusion. It tells me, moreover, that the satisfaction that I shall feel tomorrow for having resisted temptation is equally illusory; if a man is compelled by the laws of nature to do what he does, we can no more praise or blame him for it than we can blame a watch for being fast or slow. From the scientific point of view a man's actions appear indeed as strictly determined by the genes which transmit his heredity, by the functions of his glands and liver, by his upbringing and past experiences which mould his habits and thoughts, his convictions and philosophy, as the functioning of a watch is determined by its springs, wheels and bearings, or as an "electronic brain" is determined by the circuits, amplifiers, resistances, rules of action and memory-stores which have been built or "fed" into the machine. If I feel a glow of satisfaction after a certain act, it is because I have been conditioned to experience just this type of emotion after this kind of act. If I feel guilt or remorse, it is because this type of reaction too has been hammered into me.

The function of education, then, according to the deterministic view, is to set up in the individual such habits and reaction-patterns that in a situation of conflict he will "automatically" tend towards the socially useful solution, because his expectation of outer reward or inner satisfaction will be one of the factors which determine his conduct; whereas the built-in expectation of punishment or remorse will act as an automatic deterrent. The function of the law from this strictly deterministic point of view is reduced to deterrence, plus reform through corrective reconditioning. Praise and blame, punishment as vengeance or retribution, have no logical place in a scientific world-view which treats man as part of the natural universe, and his character and actions as subject to its laws. He reacts in any given situation as he must, for *he could only act otherwise if either his character or the situation or both were different*. If Mace-bearer Martin had not killed Violet, he would not have been Martin and Violet would not have been Violet. To say that Donald ought not to have killed Violet means simply that Donald ought not to have been Donald.

In a consistently deterministic system of law, the definitions used in our courts would be regarded as pure nonsense. "Criminal responsibility" would be nonsense because "responsibility" implies a freely chosen course of action, whereas free choice is illusion and all action determined by the past. "I could not help it" would be a complete defence, for none of us can help being what we are and behaving as we do. Such a purely pragmatic concept of law has been advocated by various schools; it has a strong appeal to the scientifically minded and to all adherents of materialistic philosophy. It was, for instance, the basis of the Marxist theory of law up to and including the first years of the Russian Revolution. But developments in Russia are a vivid example of the difficulties which a strictly deterministic concept of the law must of necessity meet, for in no other country is the vindictive, retributive element of punishment more vehemently emphasized than under the Soviet régime. Its materialistic philosophy denies that man has a free choice in his actions, yet he is called a traitor, a "cannibal" or a "hyena" if he makes the wrong choice.

This paradox is not confined to the law; it has its roots in the common everyday experiences of every human being. For we all feel that, regardless of what we have learnt about causality and determinism, it nevertheless "depends on me" what I shall do within the next five minutes; or at least that it depends on me within certain limits. Henry Sidgwick [1] has formulated the dilemma in a very neat form:

Is my voluntary action at any moment completely determined by (1) my character as it has been partly inherited, partly formed by my past actions and feelings, and (2) my circumstances, and the external influences acting on me at the moment? Or not?

Detached reasoning will compel most of us to answer the question with a reluctant "yes". But our intimate, direct experience cries out a passionate "no". For, to quote William James, our "whole feeling of reality, the whole sting and excitement of our voluntary life depends on our sense that in it things are *really being decided* from one moment to another, and that it is not the dull rattling off of a chain that was forged innumerable ages ago".[2] This "sting and excitement" may of course be an illusion. But the point is, that even if it is an illusion, it is a useful and *necessary* illusion for the functioning of both the individual and society.

Let us assume that, by rational conviction, I adhere to a strictly determinist philosophy. I shall nevertheless feel satisfaction or remorse after a given choice of action, even though the choice was predetermined and the satisfaction or remorse are merely the results of my early training. Even on these premises, the experiences of satisfaction and remorse remain for me real mental events, and essential determinants of my future actions. Yet though the origin of these emotions is causally traceable, their message is a denial of causality, because the glow of my satisfaction and the sting of my remorse both derive from the implied conviction that I *could have acted in another manner* than I did. In other words, my conscience can only express itself in the emotional language of praise or blame, even if I know that logically there is nothing to praise or blame because I am not a free agent but a clock. In fact all education, whether guided by religious or purely pragmatic principles, always aims at setting up this kind of emotional orchestra in the mind which sounds its horns and trumpets in a permanent Judgment Day, *as if* the actions of the self were free. Thus the individual, though all his actions may be causally determined and though he may be intellectually convinced that this is so, cannot function without the emotionally implied belief in his own freedom.

Now let us take the opposite case: the person who rejects determinism and is convinced of the reality of free will. For him it is, of

course, much simpler to harmonize emotion and intellectual belief, conscience and conviction. His conviction may be erroneous,
and each time he believes that he is making a free choice he may
in fact be acting under compulsion. But in this case his disbelief
in determinism is one of the factors which determine his behaviour;
he can only execute the prearranged pattern by denying that it is
prearranged; destiny can only have its way by making him disbelieve in it. Thus in both cases: where a person intellectually believes in freedom and where he does not, the result is the same:
unconsciously and emotionally he acts on the assumption that he is
free.

The same paradox applies to society as a whole. The aim of the
historian, the psychologist, the social scientist, is to explain social
behavior by the interplay of cause and effect, by unravelling the
conscious and unconscious forces behind the act; and their approach must always be detached and ethically neutral. Their aim is
to trace and measure, not to judge. Nevertheless, moral judgments
seep into all our reactions and determine social behaviour; praise
and blame, approval and disapproval, whether scientifically justified
or not, are as essential to the functioning of society as they are to
the functioning of the individual. Man cannot live deprived of the
illusion that he is master of his fate; nor deprived of moral indignation when he sees a little brute blowing up a frog with a bicycle
pump, or a big brute gassing people by the million. Fatalism and
ethical neutrality may be the only correct philosophy, yet they are
denials of the brave and pathetic endeavour of the human species.

Here, then, is the dilemma. According to science, man is no more
free in the choice of his actions than a robot machine—an extremely
subtle and complex type of machine, yet a machine. But he cannot
help believing that he is free; moreover, he can only function by
believing this. Every human institution reflects this dilemma; and
the law, which is meant to regulate human behavior, reflects it in
the most concentrated manner, like a distorting mirror. Hence the
paradoxical nature of that part of the law which deals with the
supreme problem of the taking of life.

Its absurdity derives from the notion of "criminal responsibility". A man can only be held responsible for his act on the
assumption that he was not compelled to commit it, but chose
to do so of his own free will. The accused is considered innocent

until proved guilty, and the burden of proof rests on the prosecution. But he is considered responsible, i.e. having a free will, *unless proved insane* (according to M'Naghten); and the burden of proof rests in this case, and in this case alone, on the defence. It is not even necessary to labour the point that the archaic humbug of the Rules makes this proof impossible even in the case of the feeble-minded and persecution maniacs. If the Rules were amended and improved, the basic paradox would remain, that *the accused is considered to possess a free will unless the defence proves the contrary, namely, that he is subject to the universal laws of nature.*

This paradox is not confined to capital law. But in all other branches of the law there is a comfortable way out of it. The judge trying a burglar need not bother about the insoluble question whether burglars have a free will or not. He can bypass the problem, and judge each individual case on its merits, by the rule-of-thumb of his experience and common sense, because in all cases, *except capital offences,* the sentence is left to the discretion of the court. Consequently, it does not matter in non-capital cases that the notion of criminal responsibility is absurd, because this problem does not affect the outcome; hence the defence will hardly ever bother to raise the question of insanity. But in a murder trial the penalty is not left to the discretion of the court; in this case alone, in the whole criminal law, the penalty is rigidly fixed by statute. When a man is tried for his life, and in no other case, the abstract postulate of the freedom of the will assumes practical significance: it becomes the noose which breaks his neck.

2

However, we have seen before that the belief in freedom, even if illusory, has a necessary and useful function in society. Does it not follow, then, that the law is justified in adopting this useful belief and basing its notion of criminal responsibility on it? The answer is that free will may or may not exist; but the *kind* of free will which is implied in the law is self-contradictory and unacceptable to any scientist, philosopher or theologian with tuppenny worth of logic in his brain.

The word "freedom" can only be defined in the negative: it always means freedom *from* restraint of one kind or another. The physicist says that the molecules of a gas have more "degrees of freedom" than the molecules in a liquid, which again have more than those in a solid. Similar distinctions can be made between degrees of personal and political freedom, freedom from censorship, and so forth. Modern physics has come to grant to the components of certain types of atoms freedom in the sense that they are not restrained by the causal laws which govern the behavior of larger bodies. Whether a radioactive atom will or will not split at a certain time, is apparently not determined by any of the known forces which operate in our familiar, macroscopic world. But this freedom is not absolute. If the behaviour of radioactive atoms were subject to no law at all, the world would not be a cosmos but a chaos. In fact, though they enjoy freedom in the sense described, the total number of atoms which will split in a given quantity of a radioactive substance is rigidly determined at any given time. So much so, that the geologist measures the age of rocks and fossils, of meteors and of the earth itself, by the amount of radioactive decay that he finds in them. The breakdown of the classical type of causal determinism in modern physics merely leads to its replacement by a different type of statistical determinism.

Here again freedom means freedom from one kind of restraint—but not absolute freedom which would mean randomness and chaos. So when we talk of the "freedom of the will", we must at once ask "freedom from what?" *The freedom implied in criminal law means freedom from determination by heredity and environment;* it means, in Sidgwick's formulation, that the subject's voluntary action is *not* determined by his character and circumstances; "what free will requires is that our volition should be uncaused".[3] But a world in which every man at any moment performs uncaused and unaccountable acts, and yet is punished for some, glorified for others; a world in which free will reigns absolute, would be a logical absurdity, a tale told by an idiot. It is even more frightening than the determinists' robot man in a clockwork universe: that, at least, is a tale told by an engineer.

Once we deny that man's actions are determined by the physical order of events, we must either substitute a different kind of order or renounce reason. The denial of natural causation creates a void which can only be filled by the assumption of an extra-natural, or supernatural, kind of causation. To put it bluntly: *the concept of criminal responsibility implies the existence of a super-natural order; it is not a legal, but a theological, concept.*

Let me substantiate this somewhat abstract argument in a more concrete manner. When we say: "a man is guilty", this can always be translated as meaning: "there was insufficient effort". If only he had tried harder, made a greater effort, in action or restraint, he would not have become guilty.

A person can only become guilty in two ways: by inadequate positive effort or inadequate negative effort, i.e. restraint. Positive effort is required in all situations where the person drifts towards passivity through indolence, fatigue, lack of vital endowment. The student fails at an examination because he has not "concentrated hard enough"; a people becomes enslaved because it failed to "stand up" against tyranny; a man loses his job because he did not "pull his weight"; the mountaineer freezes to death because he did not make enough effort to stay awake. In every case the subject is found guilty, and moreover *feels* guilty on the assumption—unproved and unprovable—that he *could* have made a greater effort than he did, that there was *a reserve of psychic energy which he did not use.*

The more common type of guilt results from a failure of effort to *inhibit* a culpable impulse, the effort to resist provocation and temptation. It makes no difference whether the subject is prone to crime because his instinctual cravings are overdeveloped or perverted; or whether his restraining mechanisms are defective. Broadly speaking, the sadist and sexual delinquent belong to the former, the psychopath, the morally defective, the drug addict and the alcoholic to the latter type. But whether the offence was caused by too much steam or by defective brakes, the law assumes, and the repentant sinner also assumes, that there was in him an untapped reserve of effort, a hidden store of brake-lining, which he failed to find or to use.

Let me compare these assumptions regarding "effort of the will" with our assumptions regarding "efforts of the body". We know that an engine can only produce a limited number of horse-powers and that any person, even an athlete or weight-lifter, can only produce a limited and well-defined amount of energy. A man can hold his breath for so many seconds and not longer; he can cling with his fingers to a ledge over a precipice so long and not longer. And if the law of Ruritania decreed that a man is guilty unless he can carry a hundredweight on his back, we would call it a very foolish and barbaric law indeed.*

We have methods of measuring the physical resources of a man; if these are found to be below a certain standard, he will be unfit for Army service and certain manual jobs, but we do not blame or punish him for it. But we do blame, punish or hang a man because his psychic energy does not reach the required standard. We do not expect the colour-blind to "pull himself together" and achieve normal sight, but we do assume that a homosexual could turn to the opposite sex if he only tried a little harder.

The interrelation of mind and body is an exceedingly complex problem; it is even doubtful whether we are justified in making a distinction between the two. Yet we apply different and well-nigh opposite standards to efforts of the will and efforts of the body. We recognize that a person's physical powers are limited, but we assume that his will-power is not subject to quantitative limitation. We know that a man cannot lift a mountain, but we assume that he can "make", or manufacture, "moral" effort *ad lib.*, as if he were endowed with an unlimited quantity of spiritual adrenalin. Moreover, the question whether he will or will not draw on this additional source of moral energy, is not determined by the mould and pressure of the past—otherwise we would be back in the determinist clockwork universe. Hence, to say that the accused *ought* to have made a greater effort to restrain himself means to say that a man with a given self in a given set of circumstances is free to react in more ways than one; and that means that the decision which way he will react lies outside the circumstances and outside the self. It implies the existence of a factor "X", beyond time and causation, beyond the order of nature. It is, as I said before, a matter not for the lawyer but for the theologian.

When the Lord Chief Justice said about the maniac Ley that

---

* A person in danger of life will sometimes perform physical feats which in normal circumstances would be above his capacities, and may seem miraculous. But we know that this is caused by over-stimulation of his supra-renal glands under the effect of rage or fear, and that the adrenalin thus released into his bloodstream feeds additional energy in the form of glucose to his muscles. The same effect can be achieved by injecting the adrenalin, or some other drug, directly into his veins. It is a quite un-mysterious physiological process; and the additional effort thus induced has its strict limits.

since he passed the M'Naghten test "he could make his peace with God quite well" he was voicing the views of the law quite correctly. By assuming that man's actions are not determined by his heredity and upbringing, the law grants him a free will; and since this freedom cannot mean arbitrary, random choices, it is assumed that it somehow expresses the design of God. Why this design includes brutes who strangle little children is a headache for the theologian, not for the judge. Quite so. But to decide by the M'Naghten Rule, or by any other rule, that in one case the criminal obeyed the command of his endocrine glands and should therefore be spared, whilst in another case he used his metaphysical freedom to execute a higher design and must therefore be hanged, seems a rather arbitrary procedure.

The dilemma between freedom and predestination is the essence of the human predicament. The law rightly evades the horns of the dilemma by giving the court discretion regarding each individual sentence. The only exception which excludes the possibility of reasonable compromise is the capital sentence; which therefore is logically untenable and ethically wrong.*

* I have taken pains to state the case for both free will and determinism as objectively as possible. But once a writer ventures into this field it would be unfair for him to withhold his own personal beliefs. I shall state them as shortly as possible in this private footnote, for they are not meant to persuade, and do not affect the argument. I think that free will is a fantastic notion, but also that man is a fantastic creature. I believe in the unprovable existence of a factor x: an order of reality beyond physical causation, about whose nature only a negative statement is possible: namely, that in its domain the present is *not* determined by the past. If it were so determined, we would once more revert to the conception of the machine-universe. But a present *not* determined by the past is both a necessary and sufficient condition for the experience of relative freedom—not the freedom of anarchy and arbitrariness, but of an order based on the time-negating concept of the *creatio continua*. Continuous creation, a concept of theological origin, postulates that the world was not created once and for all by an act resembling the winding of a clock, but is continually being created—as, in the view of one school of modern physics, matter is constantly being created in interstellar space. If that be so, the experience of freedom, the possibility of making a choice which is influenced but not strictly determined, by heredity and environment would be the subjective reflection of an objective process negating time and injecting moral responsibility into the amoral edifice of nature.

LORD GODDARD
AND THE SERMON ON THE MOUNT

or *The Philosophy of Hanging Continued*

I

AFTER THIS metaphysical excursion, let us return to earth and the gallows. All punishment is supposed to serve three main purposes: retribution; protection of the society by deterrence; and reformation of the offender. Let us examine how the free-will controversy affects each of these three points.

We shall take deterrence first, for it is generally agreed that this is the main object of capital punishment. This in itself indicates that the modern trend is towards the determinist view: for the threat of the death-penalty is meant to act as a causative factor—which can only be effective on the assumption that environmental influences determine at least in part the criminal's actions. If the will were completely free, the threat would be pointless.

But this point is of merely academic interest in showing that unconscious determinist assumptions guide even the defenders of capital punishment. Apart from that, the question whether we side with the determinist's depressing robot-universe or his opponent's mystical world of freedom and moral responsibility, has no bearing whatsoever on the deterrence issue. The facts which prove that capital punishment is a more objectionable but not a more effective deterrent than its alternatives, are equally valid for the determinist and the mystic.

For the two remaining issues, however, retribution and reform, the free-will controversy is relevant. It will be simpler to treat the two issues together.

In our day, even among the upholders of capital punishment, the majority denies that they are guided by motives of vengeance against the criminal. In spite of these denials, retribution is a

...al unconscious motive which infiltrates and confuses the ...ner issues. The popular argument, "he deserves to be hanged", "you are only concerned with the murder not with the victim", etc. has a strong and lasting emotional appeal.

From the determinist point of view, vengeance against a human being is as absurd as punishing a machine. But even if I sometimes have the foolish desire to hit my old car on the bonnet for breaking down, it would be more logical to hit the garage mechanic, or the foreman, or the chairman of the firm who made it. If, guided by vengeance, we punish the criminal, then we ought also to punish the alcoholic father, the overindulgent mother who made him into what he is, and his parents' parents, and so forth, along the long chain of causation back to the snake in Paradise. For they all, including teachers, bosses and society at large, were accessories to the crime, aiding and abetting the act long before it was committed. Disapproval, punishment, vengeance, have no place in the determinist's vocabulary; the only legitimate target of his resentment must be the universe as a whole, and the laws of nature that govern it.

If, on the other hand, we accept freedom of the will with its inevitable religious consequences, then vengeance appears not as a sin against logic but a sin against the spirit. For if the murderer is not merely a robot with a faulty switch, but the executor of a mysterious design, then we move in a realm beyond the reach of human justice. If you believe that man is a recipient, for good or evil, of some influence beyond natural causation, then you have no right to break the vessel because you dislike the wine. If it is part of a higher design that children should be murdered or killed by epidemics, then the murderer can no more be the object of vengeance than the polio virus, for both are part of the same incomprehensible pattern. Every religion and every metaphysical system has to face the problem of evil: the fact that evil has been included in the design. No satisfactory answer has yet been found, or is likely ever to be found. The law assumes that man is free and responsible in his actions; it dumps the problem why God granted man the freedom to choose evil on the theologian, to the latter's embarrassment. During the Middle Ages, freedom of the will was one of the principal problems of theology, and every sect had a different answer to it. Some held that divine omnipotence amounted to "determinism by predestination", where the human automatons acted as foreseen and intended by God. Others taught that God allowed man sufficient rope to hang himself or climb on it to Paradise; this, however, was again held to contradict the notion of God's omnipresence. But if there is no final answer to the challenge, vengeance as an answer is the most futile, and a negation of the very essence of Christianity.

"Blood for blood, life for life" was the law of Israel during the Bronze Age, appropriate to the conditions of the time, and is still the law of the primitive nomads of the desert. It was repudiated in the Sermon on the Mount, and it was repudiated by Israel itself, which abolished capital punishment when it regained sovereign statehood. Orthodox talion justice survives in our time only in the vendetta codes of Sicilian bandits and organized gangsters.

In ancient Mosaic law, the death-penalty was statutory not only for murder, but for sabbath-breaking, slave-trading, blasphemy, the cursing of parents, adultery, and a number of other offences. But already the Babylonian Talmud reveals a completely changed attitude. "A Sanhedrin that effects an execution once in seven years, is branded a destructive tribunal; Rabbi Eliezer ben Azariah says: Once in seventy years. Rabbi Tarfon and Rabbi Akiba say: Were we members of a Sanhedrin, no person would ever be put to death." (Makkoth, 7a). Nor was the early Church's repudiation of the blood law accidental; it came from the core of the Christian teaching which makes punishment justifiable only in so far as its purpose is to reform the offender, and which states that no human being is evil beyond redemption. Yet the bloodthirsty shepherds were still going strong in the Lords' debate of 1948. Dickens knew them well when he wrote:

Though every other man who wields a pen should turn himself into a commentator on the Scriptures—not all their united efforts could persuade me that executions are a Christian law. . . . If any text appeared to justify the claim, I would reject that limited appeal, and rest upon the character of the Redeemer and the great scheme of His religion.[1]

So strongly did the early Church feel about abolition that the Emperor Julian had to disqualify Christians from holding certain administrative offices, because: "their law forbade them to use the sword against offenders worthy of capital punishment."

Perhaps the clearest formulation of the problem was given by St. Augustine, himself a reformed profligate and sinner, a saint with an endearing sense of humour—*vide* his famous "Give me chastity, but not yet". When some Donatists, a heretic African sect, had confessed to a heinous murder of Christians, Augustine pleaded with his friend Marcellinus not to inflict the death-penalty on the murderers:

We do not wish to have the sufferings of the servants of God avenged by the infliction of precisely similar injuries in the way of retaliation. Not, of course, that we object to the removal from these wicked men of the liberty to perpetrate further crimes, but our desire is rather that justice be satisfied without the taking of their lives or the maiming of their bodies in any particular; and that, by such coercive measures as may be in accordance with the laws, they be drawn away from their insane frenzy to the quietness of men in their sound judgment, or compelled to give up mischievous violence and betake themselves to some useful labour.[2]

The passage sounds curiously modern, almost as if it had been written by a member of the Howard League for Penal Reform. St. Augustine's opponents argued, as they argue today, that the times were too turbulent for such a daring experiment—he lived from A.D. 354 to 430, and in Africa to boot.

To sum up, vengeance as a motive for capital punishment is absurd from the determinist and indefensible from the free will point of view.

Yet though easy to dismiss in reasoned argument on both moral and logical grounds, the desire for vengeance has deep, unconscious roots and is roused when we feel strong indignation or revulsion—whether the reasoning mind approves or not. This psychological fact is largely ignored in abolitionist propaganda—yet it has to be accepted as a fact. The admission that even confirmed abolitionists are not proof against occasional vindictive impulses does not mean that such impulses should be legally sanctioned by society, any more than we sanction some other unpalatable instincts of our biological inheritance. Deep inside every civilized being there lurks a tiny Stone Age man, dangling a club to rob and rape, and screaming an eye for an eye. But we would rather not have that little fur-clad figure dictate the law of the land.

2

The problem of free will affects the criminal law in yet another, indirect but important, way. The gradual humanization of the penal system—juvenile courts, probation, parole, "open prisons", and so on—is due to our growing insight into the social roots of crime, into the influence of heredity and environment on the offender, into the causal determinants of human behaviour. Yet at the same time, the principle of criminal responsibility, which implies freedom of the will, cannot easily be dispensed with. The only possible course in this dilemma is, as we saw, to muddle along as best one can; and by and large the courts in this country muddle along quite well by tending to show leniency where there is reasonable hope of reform, by taking mitigating circumstances into account, and by trying "to make the punishment fit the crime". The only exception is the law concerning capital charges which, by its rigidity, makes compromise impossible, and prevents the court from taking circumstances into account which, in all other cases, would count as mitigating factors in assessing the sentence. Thus, it is up to the court to send a mentally defective person to an institution instead of passing sentence on him—in all except capital cases. If a mentally defective person "is charged with murder and the jury are satisfied that he committed the act, they have no option but to convict him of murder and the judge is obliged to pronounce the sentence of death".[3] The same applies to mercy killers and surviving partners in a suicide pact. They are, thank God, eventually reprieved; but before that is possible, the Judge must put on the black cap and pronounce the terrible words.

The Royal Commission's report stresses the inhumanity of the capital law over and again. It underlines the terrible anomaly that the *only* hope for a person who is proven to be epileptic, feeble-minded, suffering from delusions or otherwise mentally deranged, rests not with the law but with the person of the Home Secretary: "This is the natural consequence of a law which has the basic defect of prescribing a single fixed automatic sentence for a crime that varies widely in character and culpability. . . . The rigidity of a law that gives the court no discretion to select the appropriate sentence can be corrected only by the Executive [i.e. the Home Secretary]."[4] And again: "The outstanding defect of the law of murder is that it provides a single punishment for a crime widely varying in culpability." [5]

The Commissioners contemplated various reforms to make the capital law more elastic, and enable the court to exercise common sense and humanity, as when trying other offences. But they were well aware that minor reforms did not go to the core of the problem and that "a stage has been reached where there is little room for further limitation short of abolition".[6] They only made one really radical proposal, whose adoption would, however, not lead to a reform of the existing law but to its negation: the proposal to let the jury decide at their own discretion whether a man found guilty should suffer the penalty subscribed by the law, or not: "We have reached the conclusion that if capital punishment is to be retained and at the same time the defects of the existing law are to be eliminated, this is the only practicable way of achieving that object. . . .[7] We recognize that the disadvantage of a system of 'jury discretion' may be thought to outweigh its merits. If this view were to prevail, the conclusion would seem to be inescapable that in this country a stage has been reached where little more can be done effectively to limit the liability to suffer the death penalty, and that the real issue is now whether capital punishment should be retained or abolished." [8]

The reason why the law relating to capital punishment cannot be reformed is basically simple. It could only be reformed at the price of undermining the concept of criminal responsibility by such deterministic notions as "irresistible impulse" or "diminished responsibility"—that is, *by making determinism statutory,* as it were. This necessity does not arise in the case of other offences, because the sentence is elastic. Yet even by revolutionizing the basic concepts of Common Law for the sole purpose of making capital law a little less barbaric, its self-contradictions would remain. Since the frontiers between "responsible" and "irresponsible" are fluid, problematical and bedevilled by metaphysical problems, any drawing of the line by legal definition would be arbitrary. And since it is impossible to define when a man acted freely and ought to die, or when he acted under compulsion and ought to live, the only solution is to bring capital law into line with the remaining body of the Common Law by eliminating the unique, fixed, all-or-nothing penalty which admits of no gradations.

Yet it is precisely this rigidity which makes capital punishment so precious to the reactionary wing of the legal profession, and why they want to preserve it at all costs. For the death-penalty is the symbol and bulwark of an antiquated conception of justice; and if it falls the whole conception falls. This point was made abundantly clear in the arguments which the Lord Chief Justice used against the proposed relaxation of the murder law by introducing such notions as "diminished responsibility" or "irresistible impulse". They knew that these concepts would serve as a Trojan horse which, once admitted within the fortress of Common Law, would play havoc with it. Lord Goddard told the Royal Commissioners:

Once you begin to admit the doctrine of irresistible impulse, I do not know where it is going to end. I think that it is sometimes overlooked that if you once admit irresistible impulse as a defence, you are not going to admit it only with regard to murder, but you have got to admit it in every case. . . . Are you really going to say that this doctrine of irresistible impulse is to be readily admitted in the criminal law? There is the old case of the Judge who had the appeal made to him that the prisoner was suffering from the disease called kleptomania; he said: "This is just the disease that I am here to cure." [9]

He rejected on the same grounds the proposal that the gravity of a provocation should be assessed according to the character and temperament of the provoked person, in lieu of the test of the "reasonable man":

If you leave it to the question whether this particular man was provoked —well, any man is going to give evidence and is going to get his friends to come and give evidence that he is a peculiarly excitable person and you are letting in considerations there which do not apply to any other branch of the law.[10]

True; though in other branches of the Law people are not hanged, which after all is a consideration that should be "let in". But imagine the havoc if witnesses were called to testify that the individual in the dock *was* an irritable person, and *not* a reasonable man! The argument boils down to this: if we stop hanging murderers on the grounds that they acted under an inner compulsion, then judges would be encouraged to apply similar considerations to other offenders who acted under similar mental stress. If the hangman is no longer the correct cure for the mentally defective, then the "old judge" may no longer be the correct cure for the klepto-maniac. There exist, alas, modern judges, magistrates and juries who, disregarding Coke and M'Naghten, take social factors and emotional pressures into account when deciding the length of the sentence. But, fortunately, this danger does not exist in the case of a capital offender; the jury cannot alter the length of the drop, nor strangle him on parole, nor apply latitude in breaking his neck.

To sum up. The deficiencies of the capital law are irremediable because the death-penalty is based on a philosophical concept of criminal responsibility which does not admit the compromises with the determinist view practised in other courts. Regarding all other offences, the administration of the law is elastic; the death-penalty, by its nature, excludes gradings of culpability. This rigidity and finality, which is the very essence of the capital law, is at the same time the reason of its attractiveness and symbolic value for the anti-progressive forces in society.

DOOMED BY MISTAKE

or *What Is a Fair Trial?*

Innocent men have been hanged in the past and will be hanged in the future unless either the death-penalty is abolished or the fallibility of human judgment is abolished and judges become supermen. On this point both the defenders and enemies of capital punishment agree. They only differ on the consequences arising from this situation. There are three classes of opinion about it.

(*a*) Those who say hanging an innocent doesn't really matter;

(*b*) Those who say that the risk of hanging an innocent is so small that it must be accepted;

(*c*) Those who say that the danger of judicial error is inherent in the judicial system, and claims a larger number of victims than is generally assumed; and that this fact alone, in the absence of other arguments, would make the abolition of the death-penalty imperative.

Opinion (*a*) can be dealt with briefly, though it gives food for thought that it was not uncommon a century and more ago. It was put in its clearest form by that great oracle, Archdeacon Paley:

"He who falls by a mistaken sentence may be considered as falling for his country, whilst he suffers under the operation of those rules, by the general effect and tendency of which the welfare of the community is maintained and upheld." [1]

One wonders why the Archdeacon did not call for volunteers who would proudly take the drop for King and Country, and be awarded a posthumous medal. Nobody in our enlightened days would go on record with a similar statement; but who can assert that the callous indifference underlying it has really died out among the more sanguine partisans of hanging?

The second attitude is based on the assumption that the number of innocents who are hanged is very small. It was summed up in the evidence before the Select Committee by Dr. Maurice Hamblin Smith, a prison medical officer of long standing and humane views, who held that capital punishment should eventually be abolished but only after a great amount of prison reform has been carried out. He said: "I do not think the possibility of miscarriage of justice can be altogether excluded, but I think the possibility of a man being wrongly hanged is not of sufficient moment to weigh against Capital Punishment as desirable for other reasons. If you really thought it the best form of deterrent, then I would not allow the possibility of the occasional execution of an innocent man to stand in the way." [2]

The opposite view is expressed in a classic statement by Benjamin Franklin: "That it is better a hundred guilty persons should escape than that one innocent person should suffer, is a maxim that has been long and generally approved; never, that I know of, controverted"; [3] or in Lafayette's: "I shall ask for the abolition of the punishment of death, until I have the infallibility of human judgment demonstrated to me." [4]

I agree with the Franklin-Lafayette type of view, but this is a matter of personal philosophy which cannot be proved by logic. Hence, if (a) capital punishment were in itself a desirable thing, and if (b) the number of people innocently hanged were very small indeed, then the danger of an occasional miscarriage of justice would not represent a conclusive argument. The question, however, is not whether an occasional error is in itself an argument against hanging, but how often such errors occur, and whether they are *exceptional* phenomena or *inherent* in the system.

Let us go back to the last Royal Commission but one, the Commission appointed by Queen Victoria in 1864. The chief witness on the question of judicial error was Sir Fitzroy Kelly, the former Attorney-General and Solicitor-General, whose testimony was summed up in the Commission's report as follows:

After careful consideration and examination, he has come to the conclusion that it is not in any way reasonably to be doubted that in many instances innocent men have been capitally convicted, and in certain numbers of instances, few of course, but yet formidable numbers, have been actually executed . . . Well remembers that there were, between the years 1802 and 1840, 22 cases of capital convictions, seven of which resulted in the execution of convicts, and in the rest of which the sentence was mitigated, or a pardon granted. But in the whole of the 22 cases the innocence of these persons was established, or, at least, established satisfactorily to those who investigated the matter, and in most of the cases to the satisfaction of the advisers of the Crown.[5]

These were the cases where the innocence of the victims was virtually proven; but, Kelly continued, "There is presumptive ground for believing that [other] innocent persons have suffered death for want of having influential or wealthy friends to procure an investigation of their case, or to make such efforts as were successful in the instances of Kirwan, Dr. Smethurst, and others".[6] He added that the Sheriff of London, Mr. Wilde, "had given him the names and particulars of the cases of five persons who in a single year were erroneously convicted and sentenced to death".[7]

That, one may say, was a long time ago, and justice has improved since. But the annual number of executions has remained substantially the same since the beginning of Queen Victoria's reign (ten to fourteen executions per year), and the law and court procedure have also remained substantially the same.* It is not at all a reassurance to the public that in 1864 the possibility of judicial error was as pompously and categorically denied by the Law Lords and Home Secretaries as it is today. In 1864, before Kelly gave the evidence just quoted, Lord Wensleydale "was not aware of a capital case in which he thought the verdict illfounded"; in 1948, Sir Maxwell Fyfe stated with the same assurance that "there is no practical possibility" of justice miscarrying: "the Honourable and Learned Member is moving in a realm of fantasy when he makes that suggestion". A couple of years after Lord Wensleydale's statement, they hanged Mrs. Biggadyke for poisoning her husband—a crime to which a convict confessed on his deathbed. A couple of years after Sir Maxwell Fyfe's statement, we hanged Timothy Evans.

Every country and every age has its famous cases of men convicted by judicial error. In all cases, once a man has been found guilty, the proof of his innocence is an extremely arduous process, which demands the dogged efforts of lawyers and friends over a

* The only differences relevant to this chapter are that since 1896 the accused man has been allowed to give evidence from the witness box (which is often a doubtful blessing); and the establishment of the Court of Criminal Appeal.

great number of years. France had its Dreyfus case; in spite of the genius of Zola, it took twelve years to reverse the verdict. Austria had Hilsner, who was proved innocent after he had spent eighteen years in prison. In Hungary, Steven Tonka was hanged for the murder of his daughter in 1913 and proved innocent fourteen years later—when a farewell letter of the girl was found announcing her intention to commit suicide. In Holland, which has no capital punishment, Tuennisen and Klundert were convicted of murder in 1923 and found innocent six years later. But England, where the accused is supposed to have a fairer trial than anywhere else, again holds the record of famous cases.

Oscar Slater was sentenced to hang in May, 1909, but the sentence was commuted, forty-eight hours before his execution, to penal servitude for life. His trial was so grossly unfair that Sir Conan Doyle, after reading the verbatim report, decided that the man was innocent and started a campaign in his favour. In spite of Doyle's immense reputation, it took no less than nineteen years before the newly created Scottish Court of Criminal Appeal annulled the sentence. Had Slater been executed, who would have kept up an agitation for nineteen years to vindicate a man already dead?

This is the crux of the matter. Once a man is dead, the chances of proving that he was innocent are virtually nil. It is an axiom of the law that the burden of proof should lie with the prosecution; but when you try to vindicate a man, and a dead man to boot, it is up to the defence to establish positive proof of his innocence— and such proof is technically impossible, unless some extraordinary hazard intervenes. And since it needs a near-miracle for a judicial error to be detected, it is not unreasonable to assume that the number of undetected errors may be greater than we believe. If in a scrupulously clean hospital I find a fly in my soup, the inference is that there must be a host of them about.

To illustrate how exceptional the circumstances must be for proof of innocence to be possible, take the following example. In 1835, a man was found guilty of murder, sentenced to death and then transported for life to Australia. Nearly forty years later, he met the real murderer on that continent; even so, it took two Parliamentary debates and the eloquence of John Bright to obtain the Queen's pardon. The reader will say, "Ah, but such cases are rare and exceptional". He is making a common logical mistake. The exceptionality of the case does not mean that judicial errors are rare; it proves, on the contrary, that it needs exceptional luck to *detect* a judicial error. In spite of this, there is a long row of cases, stretching from Queen Victoria's days to ours, in which judicial error was either admitted, or all but technically proved. Biggadyke (1869) and Habron (1876) were proved innocent years after they were sentenced. Even the late Lord Birkenhead confessed to a lingering doubt about the justice of hanging Mrs. Thompson (1923); Marshall Hall was convinced of the innocence of several of his convicted clients; the cases of Podmore (1930), Rouse (1931), Thorne (1934), Hoolhouse (1938), Rowland (1946), Bentley (1952) belong to the same category; and in at least one case, Evans (1950), the Home Secretary who decided that "justice must take its course" admitted later on that Evans was hanged though not guilty as charged.

No doubt judge and jury always try, according to their lights, to give a man a fair trial. If judicial errors nevertheless continue to occur with monotonous regularity, this cannot be due to accident; *the probability of error is inherent in the judicial procedure.* I shall now briefly examine some of the main sources of error and uncertainty in murder trials. They fall under the following headings: (*a*) fallibility of witnesses; (*b*) fallibility of experts; (*c*) coincidence; (*d*) to (*h*) fallibility of juries, judges, appeal judges and Home Secretaries; (*i*) carelessness of solicitors and counsel; (*j*) unworkability of the M'Naghten Rules.

(a) Fallibility of Witnesses

Identification by witnesses is always more or less a gamble because no record is more notoriously unreliable than human memory. Sully, in *Mistaken Identity*, quotes a series of classic experiments, such as:

Fifteen students were subjects in a testimony experiment. Asked the date of a local flood, three gave the right year, but six gave a particular wrong year; asked the number of classrooms opening off a corridor, two gave the right number, but nine a particular wrong number; asked the colour of a particular book used in the school, five agreed in truth, but nine agreed in error.[8]

Every psychological textbook is full of examples of the illusions, suggestibility and tendency to self-deception of human memory, and a history of crime could be written as a comedy of errors by mistaken witnesses if the results were not so tragic.

In 1896, a certain Adolf Beck was sentenced to seven years for robberies from women. In 1904 he was again convicted of similar offences. He was identified on the first occasion by ten, on the second by five women. Nine years after his first conviction the real culprit, Smith, was found; all of the fifteen identification witnesses were proven wrong, Beck was discharged and paid five thousand pounds as compensation. If he had been convicted of a capital offence and executed, who would have bothered after nine years? Yet circumstantial evidence in murder cases depends on testimony of precisely this kind, as the following example will show.

The case of Walter Graham Rowland, hanged in 1947 for the alleged murder of a prostitute, is important for several reasons— among them the fact that Rowland is the only case in the present century of a reprieved murderer allegedly committing a second murder.*

On the night of October 19th, 1946, a prostitute named Olive Balchin was killed by hammer blows on the head, on a bombed site in Manchester. A week later, Walter Graham Rowland was arrested and charged with her murder.

Rowland was well known to the police. He had an uncontrollable temper. He had served a sentence on a charge of attempted murder, and a few years later was convicted of murdering a child, but the sentence was commuted on the grounds of his abnormal mentality. He was released during the war, having served only eight years, because men were needed for the Army. He seemed to have received no mental treatment in prison.

In the nine weeks which passed between Rowland's conviction and his execution, a man called David John Ware made three detailed voluntary confessions to the effect that it was he and not Rowland who killed Olive Balchin. Rowland's lawyers applied to the Court of Criminal Appeal, which rejected his application on

---

* In all passages referring to this case I am following Mr. Silverman's report[9] on the facts of the case, without necessarily subscribing to the inferences which he draws from the facts.

the incredible grounds that if they admitted Ware's confession as new evidence, they would prejudge Ware's case. The judgment will be discussed under heading (f), "fallibility of appeal courts". The Home Office instituted an inquiry which will be discussed under heading (g). The Home Secretary refused to recommend a reprieve and Rowland was hanged, protesting his innocence to the end. Four years later Ware walked into a police station in Bristol and said: "I have killed a woman. I don't know what is the matter with me. I keep on having an urge to hit women on the head." He was found guilty of the attempted murder of a prostitute under the same circumstances and by the same method (battering of head and face) as in the case of Olive Balchin. He was found insane and sent to Broadmoor.

The case against Rowland rested on so-called expert testimony, on motive and on identification by three witnesses. The expert testimony will be discussed under the next heading. As for motive, Rowland admitted that on previous occasions he had been sexually intimate with Olive Balchin, and had contracted venereal disease from her, which he strongly resented. But the main point was identification. The three witnesses who identified Rowland were Mr. Macdonald, who sold the hammer with which the victim was killed; Mrs. Copley, a waitress who had allegedly seen him in the victim's company before she was killed; and Mr. Mercer, who had allegedly seen them together on the bombed site.

Before being confronted with Rowland at identification parades, each of the witnesses had given a different description of the man they had seen, agreeing only on one point: that he had dark or black hair. Rowland's hair was fair. At a later stage it was suggested, to explain away the contradiction, that Rowland that evening had plastered down his hair with brilliantine; and from then on all three witnesses stuck unanimously to the brilliantine theory. E.g.:

Counsel for Defence: He has not got dark hair, has he?

Mrs. Copley: He had at the time, but he had greased it. Grease makes your hair look black.

Q. Grease does not make that kind of hair look black?—*A.* Yes, it did at the time, definitely.

Q. Did you say his hair looked black?—*A.* I did not say very black. I just said black.

Mr. Macdonald described a man "with thin features who was very pale". The waitress described a man of "fresh complexion"; Mr. Mercer, a man "with a full round face". They equally differed on the question of what colour shirt he wore, whether he had a mackintosh, and whether he carried a parcel or not.

Each of them was confronted with Rowland at separate identification parades. Mr. Macdonald was said to have picked out Rowland without hesitation, but on the next occasion, in the Magistrate's Court, when Rowland was not in the dock, "he looked carefully round the court and swore that he could not see the man to whom he had sold the hammer". He only identified Rowland when Rowland was asked to stand up: who asked Rowland to stand up was never established at the trial.

The second witness, the waitress, Mrs. Copley, took between five and ten minutes before she picked out Rowland in the identification parade, though she said she had seen him on three previous occasions in her teashop. She identified him with the words: "That looks like the man, but I am not sure." She first said in court that she had gone to the police on her own accord to tell them that Rowland, Olive Balchin and a third man had been to her café on the evening of the murder. But she denied having read about the murder in the newspaper, and thus had obviously had no reason to go to the police. She then admitted that it was the police who had come to the teashop to question her whether she had seen any "strangers" that evening in her café. She had then described a man "with a fresh complexion and black hair" who had come to the café in the company of an old woman and a "young girl" whom she identified in court from a photograph as Olive Balchin. Before she was shown the photograph she had referred to Olive six times as a "young girl"; and when asked whether her hair was going grey or not, she said "No. I noticed it was tinted. It was a bit sandy. She had it touched up auburn." The official description given at the *post mortem* examination of Olive Balchin, whom the waitress called a young girl with auburn hair, was as follows: "A woman of forty to fifty years of age, yellow hair turning grey, a few septic teeth in the lower jaw, none in the upper."

The third witness, Mr. Norman Mercer, a publican, saw a couple arguing on a street corner as he walked past them around midnight, taking his dog for a walk. He could see the woman full face, but the man only in profile. When shown a photograph of Olive Balchin in the Police Court, he said that "her features were similar to those of the woman I had seen the previous night". He saw Rowland on identification parade on November 4th—a full fortnight after his passing glimpse at the profile of a dark-haired man arguing with a woman at a street corner. He failed to pick out Rowland, but did so when the men were asked to turn half right.

At this point a word must be said about identification in general. A suspect may be "identified" by witnesses either in court or from police photographs or at a parade. If in court, the witness is solemnly asked: "Do you see that person in this room?" Whereupon the witness will turn towards the figure standing between two policemen in the dock and say cheerfully: "That's him. There he is." As for identification parades, the police are instructed that the suspect should be "placed among eight or more persons who are, as far as possible, of the same age, height, general appearance and position in life". When the parade is held in a prison, the participants in the parade are prisoners—who on this occasion are presumed to occupy the same "position in life" as the suspect, and are either dressed up in their civies taken out from the moth balls, or fitted out from the prison stores. If the parade is held in a police station, the participants are collected in a more imaginative manner. A half-hour or so before the appointed time, plain-clothed policemen scan the streets for passers-by similar in "age, height, appearance, position", etc., and ask them to volunteer for the parade.

In one case, the prisoner suddenly announced just before the parade that he usually wore spectacles, whereupon spectacles were obtained from the lost property room for all the persons paraded; but as none of the others were used to them, they all looked myopic and silly except, of course, the prisoner.[10]

From the psychological point of view, all identification parades are inconclusive to the point of being farcical. Most people have seen "thought-readers" performing in a music hall, who are able to find a needle hidden in the lapel of a gentleman in an audience of several hundred, by following unconscious hints, involuntary eye or muscle movements. A thought-reader, of course, is a trained man, but he has to find a needle in a haystack, whereas the witness only has to pick out a man, who *knows* that he is suspected, among half a dozen others who know that they are not. The gentleman with the

pin has a self-conscious look—and so has the suspect at the identification parade who knows that the officials at the parade *expect*
him to be picked out, and is under great nervous strain. It is an
amusing parlour game; as evidence to hang a man it is less amusing.

(b) Expert Testimony

It will be remembered that Adolf Beck (see the previous section,
p. 110), had been "identified" by altogether fifteen women as the
person who had robbed them, and that his innocence was only
proven nine years after his first conviction. Apart from these fifteen
witnesses, there was also a handwriting expert in the case, who
testified that certain letters produced by the prosecution were
written by Beck. They were not; they were written by the true
culprit, a man called Smith.

In 1931, a certain John Binney was convicted of writing blackmailing letters by the testimony of two handwriting experts. After
Binney was sent to Dartmoor, blackmailing letters in the same handwriting continued to arrive, and he was released.

In these cases, expert opinion was unanimous. But in murder
trials both sides call, as a rule, their own experts, and it is up to
the jury to decide which side to believe.

In 1925, Norman Thorne was hanged for the murder of a girl
friend. The defence claimed that the girl had committed suicide,
and that Thorne had buried her body in a panic. Medical witnesses
for the prosecution testified that there was no evidence of suicide
and that death had occurred in a certain manner. Three medical
witnesses for the defence testified that it was impossible for death to
have taken place in the manner stated by the prosecution, and that
in their view the girl had committed suicide. The jury of twelve
laymen decided to believe the prosecution experts and disbelieve the
defence experts, and Thorne was hanged.

The *Law Journal* commented that: "Thorne's execution would
leave a feeling of profound disquiet in the minds of many people."

In 1953 Mrs. Merrifield was convicted and hanged for the
poisoning of another woman by arsenic. The pathologist giving
evidence for the prosecution said the victim had been poisoned. The
pathologist for the defence said she had died a natural death. The
case is the more remarkable because the pathologist for the defence

whom the jury did not believe was Professor Webster, chief of the Forensic Laboratory in Birmingham for twenty years, who had been the *prosecution's* witness in every murder case of the Midlands Circuit for many years. We are left to infer that Professor Webster was a sufficiently reliable expert to secure a conviction, but not reliable enough to secure an acquittal even by "reasonable doubt". The summing up of the judge in that particular case will be described under (*e*).

We return to the case of Rowland (the case of the murdered prostitute, see pp. 110–113), in which expert testimony also played a part in the prosecution's case. The director of the Home Office laboratory at Preston testified that he had found grey hairs on Rowland's jacket "consistent with hair having come from the deceased, but I cannot put it any higher than that, no definite identity". He further found spots of blood on Rowland's handkerchief, a small bloodstain on his shoe, and debris of brick-dust in the turn-ups of his trousers which agreed with samples taken from the ground where the body was found. It is this kind of painstaking scientific detail which impresses the laymen on the jury. But the director of the Home Office laboratory admitted under cross-examination that the stuff in the trouser turn-ups could have come from any bombed site; the hair, if it was the victim's, could have got on Rowland's jacket on any of their previous meetings when they had been sexually intimate; and the blood on the handkerchief got there when a police officer shaved him in prison—as the police confirmed. Why was it put into the evidence at all? Lastly, the speck of blood on the heel of the shoe was too small to be analysed and could have got there either on the same occasion, or by stepping into any refuse or dirt.

But, as Mr. Silverman points out, to a forensic mind the expert evidence by its omissions speaks rather in Rowland's favour. Whoever gripped that hammer during the attack must have left fingerprints on it, but the prosecution was silent about fingerprints. And the physician who made the *post mortem* examination stated under cross-examination that Olive Balchin's injuries were such that blood must have spurted, in great quantities, because arteries had been broken. He also stated that he would have expected under the circumstances that blood would have spurted on to the clothes of the assailant. Yet the Home Office laboratory's evidence was that they couldn't find on Rowland's jacket, waistcoat or trousers one speck of blood. The lesson is that expert evidence, when properly presented, can make something out of nothing, and findings favourable to the accused appear unfavourable.

(c) Coincidence

In 1876, William Habron was convicted of shooting a policeman in Manchester. The policeman had been responsible for the previous arrest and conviction of Habron on a minor charge and Habron had publicly stated his intention to get his own back on him. Habron's boots were covered with mud of the same type as the soil where the murder was committed; his hobnails exactly fitted the footmarks in the vicinity of the crime. Who would believe that all this was due to coincidence? Because of his youth, Habron was granted a reprieve, and three years later the notorious Charles Peace, before being hanged, confessed to the murder for which Habron stood convicted.

There is no need to go on with examples; everybody remembers coincidences in his life which are so extraordinary that no court would believe in them. Yet coincidence plays a great part in murder trials—for a simple reason. A guilty man will always try to explain away the evidence against him as due to sheer coincidence; and this makes the law apt to disbelieve in real coincidence when it occurs.

(d) The Juror's Dilemma

I have said before that no doubt every jury, before whom a man stands on trial for his life, intends to give him a fair trial. But good intention is not enough to guarantee the result. How is a jury of laymen to decide which of the conflicting medical or psychiatric evidence to believe, which to reject?

An eminent lawyer, Mr. Pritt, Q.C., testifying on behalf of the Howard League before the Select Committee of 1930 had this to say on the subject:

I see every day, in civil cases, decisions arrived at, sometimes in favour of my clients and sometimes against my clients, and so far as I can exercise any judgment about them perhaps one-third of them are wrong. I have seen a certain number of criminal cases tried and I think some of those decisions have been wrong. . . . I regard it as impossible to believe that the only Court that never makes a mistake is the Court where a dozen men are placed together in a box, who may have never seen each other before, presided over by a Judge who may never have tried criminal cases before, sitting down there, and, to the best of their ability, trying to sort out the evidence on one side and the other, and trying to arrive at the truth of a very difficult story about which, *ex hypothesi,* someone is not telling the truth.[11]

Whatever Mr. Pritt's political opinions, he is an outstanding lawyer and he summed up the point neatly. Sometimes the jury must listen to controversial evidence and to counsels' speeches during three or more days. They are men and women of average—and sometimes, inevitably, of less than average—intelligence, without legal training. A clergyman recently wrote to the London *Times* that in conversation with jurors, "They have all emphasized the point that they found it well-nigh impossible to retain a clear impression of all that had been said to them in the course of the trial. They confess that, try hard as they did, they found it very hard to clear their minds of early prejudice and bias." [12]

In such cases much depends on the judge's summing up. This may last several hours. Yet when the jury retire, they have no written record of the summing up, nor of counsels' speeches, nor of the evidence. In recent letters to *The Times* several writers suggested that a written report, at least of the summing up, be given to the jury, or that the speeches, examinations and cross-examinations should be recorded on a tape recorder and played back to them at request. It seems fantastic that this minimum condition for a considered verdict should not exist. We live in an age where crooners and Light Programme skits are being recorded for posterity, but where a man's life is at stake, we leave it to the dubious memory of twelve tired householders to recall who said what and why.

In the February, 1955, debate in the House of Commons, the former Home Secretary, Mr. Chuter Ede, made a profoundly shocking statement on the subject. He said (my italics):

I wonder what goes on inside the jury room. I was once foreman of a coroner's jury. I have sat at quarter sessions and wondered by what processes jurors have, on occasion, managed to evade the specific hints which have been dropped to them by the chairman in his summing up. But I had a little enlightenment as to what happened, because, *on at least two, and, I think three occasions,* I had a letter from a juror after I had announced my decision about a recommendation.

The juror said, "You have let me down. I stood out for a long time against a verdict of guilty. Then the foreman said, 'We have been here a long time and you are the only person standing out. If we make a strong recommendation of mercy, will you then fall into line, and . . . you can rest assured that the Home Secretary will grant a reprieve.'" I did not grant a reprieve when, after consulting the trial judge and asking him the grounds on the evidence for making a strong recommendation for mercy, the judge said, "I really have not the remotest idea". That is what happened.[13]

So long as a Home Secretary is in office, he will always say that miscarriages of justice are a one-in-a-million chance. But when repentance makes him lift a corner of the veil of official secrecy, one shudders at the discovery how much of one's notion of a "fair trial" was built on illusion.

(e) *The Summing Up*

Sometimes jurors go against the judge's summing up—but by no means always in the interests of leniency. At the conclusion of the trial of Rouse (1931) for instance, the judge evidently thought that the evidence was not strong enough to convict, expected a verdict of not guilty and was deeply perturbed when the jury obliged him to put on his black cap. By and large, however, the learned judge's summing up is the only compass available to a jury adrift in the fog. And that compass is liable to very odd deviations indeed.

Take the case of Reginald Woolmington, who in 1935 was sentenced to death at Bristol for the murder of his young wife. I am quoting another ex-Home Secretary, Lord Templewood:

The jury at Somerset Assizes a few weeks previously had failed to agree, and a new trial had been ordered. The original failure to agree should have been a sufficiently clear indication that the case was not proved "beyond reasonable doubt". At the second trial, however, *the judge directed the jury to the effect that it was incumbent on the accused to prove his plea* that the death of his wife was the result of an accident. . . . Can there not have been other cases in which the wrong direction of a judge has led to an innocent man's death? [14]

The jury complied with the judge's direction and found Woolmington guilty. The case went to the Court of Criminal Appeal, which sustained the judge's decision and confirmed the verdict. However, the Attorney-General (Lord Caldecote, then Sir Thomas Inskip) granted permission for the case to go to the House of Lords, who ordered the release of Woolmington on the obvious grounds that the burden of proof must always remain with the prosecution. The *Law Journal* commented at the time: "It is interesting if unprofitable to speculate as to the number of murderers (to say nothing of innocent persons) lying mouldering in lime and ignomini . . . who would have been respectably alive and well if our Judges had known the law."

As a rule, however, the views of the judges are conveyed to the jury in subtler ways, and frequently in unreproachable terms. In the case of Mrs. Merrifield, who was hanged for poisoning another woman, in spite of the fact that the foremost Home Office pathologist in the Midlands testified that she had died a natural death, the jury's possible qualms of conscience were put at rest by being addressed as follows by Mr. Justice Glyn Jones in his summing up:

Counsel for the defence has said to you more than once that the prosecution must exclude every chance and every possibility that the inferences they ask you to draw are mistaken. . . . That is not the law. You need only deal with such possibilities of error as you may think to be reasonably likely. If juries are to be deterred from doing their duty because the ingenuity of counsel can propound some hypothesis, however unlikely, on which the evidence of crime can be explained in a manner consistent with innocence, then few persons charged with crime would ever be convicted.[15]

The operative words are "the ingenuity of counsel can propound some hypothesis, however unlikely". Just how unlikely is a hypothesis confirmed by a Home Office expert who is habitually relied upon by the prosecution? Does this sort of thing agree with the public's idea that the chance of error is so small as to be practically negligible? Does it agree with the statement by the ex-Home Secretary, Sir John Anderson, that "The risk, under the conditions as they exist in this country, of the capital penalty being executed on any one who was not in fact guilty of the crime of which he had been convicted is so small, indeed so infinitesimal, that that consideration can be dismissed"? [16]

In his summing up to the jury on the case of Craig, aged 16, and Bentley, 19, Lord Goddard not only left out any mitigating consideration of their mentality and background, but referred ironically to "the precious Bentley's skin" [17] where Bentley was being tried for his life.

In his work on *Courts and Judges in France, Germany and England*,[18] one of our outstanding writers on law, Sir R. C. K. Ensor, sums the matter up with refreshing frankness: "It is very easy for a bad judge, especially in a jury case, to defeat justice by the crassest stupidity or partisanship, without perpetrating any technical misdirection of the jury or explicit twist of the law, of which an Appeal Court could take cognizance." [19]

(f) The Court of Criminal Appeal

Sometimes, however, cases do go before the Criminal Appeal Court. Its existence is for the public mind an additional safeguard and reassurance that no mistakes can be made. Very few know even its composition. It is composed of the Lord Chief Justice and of two judges of the Queen's Bench Division—that is, the same judges who, when sitting singly, conduct the murder trials. Ensor comments: "It is scarcely plausible that an assembly of this same class of judges should be much wiser than the individuals composing it; and in fact the Court of Criminal Appeal has laid itself open to very considerable criticism." [20]

The Court of Criminal Appeal can neither re-try a case nor order a re-trial. Its view of its function is: "It is not sufficient to show merely that the case was a very weak one or that the members of the Court of Criminal Appeal feel some doubt as to the correctness of the verdict. If there was evidence to support the conviction, the appeal will be dismissed." [21] In the House of Commons Debate of February 10th, 1955, Mr. Scholefield Allen, Q.C., M.P., said: "The Court of Criminal Appeal had reversed a jury's decision on matters of law and misdirection, but [up to 1931] had never reversed the decision of a jury on evidence." [22]

I have already quoted the Court of Criminal Appeal's perplexing judgment in Rex *v.* Woolmington, which upheld the judge's direction that the accused must prove his innocence. I shall quote one more example of Appeal Court decisions: Rowland.

We have now examined the case of the unhappy Rowland from the angle of expert testimony, identification by witnesses, etc. He was found guilty and sentenced to death at Manchester Assizes on December 16th, 1946. When he was asked the usual question whether he had anything to say why the sentence of death should not be passed according to law, he answered:

Yes, I have, my Lord. I have never been a religious man, but as I have sat in this court during these last few hours the teachings of my boyhood have come back to me, and I say in all sincerity and before you and this court that when I stand in the Court of Courts before the Judge of Judges I shall be acquitted of this crime. *Somewhere there is a person who knows that I stand here today an innocent man.* The killing of this woman was a terrible crime, but there is a worse crime being committed now, my Lord, because someone with the knowledge of this crime is seeing me sentenced today for a crime which I did not commit. I have a firm belief that one day it will be proved in God's own time that I am totally innocent of this charge, and the day will come when this case will be quoted in the courts of this country to show what can happen to a man in a case of mistaken identity. I am going to face what lies before me with the fortitude and calm that only a clear conscience can give. That is all I have got to say, my Lord.

David John Ware came forward with his confession six days later. He was then serving a minor sentence at Liverpool prison, and confessed to the murder of Olive Balchin in a written statement to the prison governor. Two days later, he was interviewed by two police officers in charge of the Balchin case. He signed a second statement, agreeing that he had been cautioned, and then wrote out himself a third long statement in which he described in minute detail his movements on the day of the murder, and the murder itself. He was then interviewed by Rowland's advisers, and answered a number of further questions. No detail in his three statements was inconsistent with the circumstances of the death of Olive Balchin.

The Court of Criminal Appeal heard Rowland's appeal on January 27th, and adjourned to February 10th. Its members were Lord Goddard, Mr. Justice Humphreys and Mr. Justice Lewis. They rejected Rowland's appeal and set out the main reason for the rejection as follows:

If we had allowed Ware to give evidence before us, and he had persisted in his confession of guilt, the court would have been compelled to form some conclusion as to his guilt or innocence and to express that opinion in open court. In effect, therefore, the court would have been engaged in trying not only Rowland but also Ware and thereby usurping the function of a jury. It is true that we should not be empowered to pronounce finally upon the issue of guilt or innocence of Ware, who as the result of our judgment might have to stand his trial by jury on this charge of murder. In that event, the finding of this court could not fail to be prejudicial to his chance of an impartial trial. . . . Finally, we are not unmindful of the fact that there exists an authority in the person of the Home Secretary, who has far wider powers than those possessed by this court, who is not bound as we are by rules of evidence, and who has all the necessary machinery for conducting such an inquiry as is here asked for.

The Court also said that "upon the hearing of the appeal we were not referred to and we are not ourselves aware of any precedent for granting the present application". Yet a precedent did exist in which the Court of Criminal Appeal, on a plea of mistaken identity, had given an opposite ruling.

In 1932, Mr. Braddock, a city councillor in a provincial town, was convicted of incitement to riot. He appealed on the grounds that he had been confused with a Communist agitator named Man Boggin. The Court of Criminal Appeal allowed the appeal and quashed the conviction; in delivering the judgment of the Court, the then Lord Chief Justice, Lord Hewart, said:

The court has come to the conclusion that, if the witnesses whom they had heard, and who were not available at the trial, had been before the jury, the jury might have come to a different conclusion.

In other words, in allowing Rowland's appeal, the Court would not have prejudiced Ware's case; it would only have implied that whether Ware's confession be true or untrue, it would have introduced an element of doubt into the jury's mind; and that because of that doubt, the jury "might have come to a different conclusion". The rejection of Rowland's appeal was not only an offence to common sense; it also went against the sacred principle of basing law on precedent.

Mr. Silverman, in commenting on the rejection of Rowland's appeal, makes the sinister remark that since that day this decision has been followed *in at least one similar case.*

Let's get down to earth. If you were convicted for having murdered Mary Smith, and if afterwards Harry Brown confessed to the murder of Mary Smith, your appeal would be dismissed by the Appeal Court on the grounds that it is not their business to discuss Harry Brown.

But of course there is always the last hope: the Home Secretary. So Rowland's case went up to Sir David Maxwell Fyfe, whom we have quoted as saying that "there is no practical possibility of judicial error in a murder case".[23]

(g) Two Recent Home Office Inquiries [24]

We now come to the last but one station in our pilgrim's progress to the gallows. After a man has been sentenced to death and whether or not his case has been taken to the Court of Criminal Appeal, the Home Secretary has the power to order a further inquiry if he thinks that a miscarriage of justice may have occurred. Such inquiries are held in private and are not bound by the rules of evidence. Two such inquiries were held in recent times, on the Rowland case and on the case of Evans. In both cases, the investigator appointed by the Home Secretary reported that he was satisfied that no miscarriage of justice had taken place.

In the case of Rowland, the Home Secretary appointed a certain Mr. Jolly, Q.C., as investigator. Mr. Jolly started his investigation on February 21st, and four days later, on February 25th, he reported to the Home Secretary that he was "satisfied that there are no grounds for thinking that there has been any miscarriage of justice in the conviction of Rowland for murder". Another two days later, Walter Graham Rowland was hanged, having written in his last letter to his mother, "I die for another's crime. . . . Before my maker I swear that I am completely innocent of the death of that poor woman."

Another four years later, Ware attempted an exact repetition of the murder of Olive Balchin.

When Mr. Jolly started his four-day pressure-cooker investigation, six days before the scheduled date of the execution, he was faced with the situation of one man, Ware, having confessed to the murder of Olive Balchin and a second man, Rowland, denying it. Both men had a record which laid them open to suspicion. Ware had a criminal record of minor offences; he had confessed to the intended murder of a girl and had been discharged from the Army in 1943 on the grounds of manic-depressive psychosis. Rowland was mentally unstable and had an attempted murder and the murder of a child on his record. Both men had a motive. Rowland had, or thought he had, contracted venereal disease from Olive Balchin. Ware said in his confession that while standing "close together" on the bombed site, the woman had gone through his pockets and stolen a ten-shilling note: "I was aware of this but did not show her. I was ate up with hatred and felt immediately that I would like to kill her." Then follows the detailed description of the killing.

Mr. Jolly, like the Court of Criminal Appeal, was not called upon to decide whether Rowland or Ware killed Olive; only to decide whether if the jury had known of the existence and confession of Ware, they would still have found Rowland guilty "beyond reasonable doubt". Mr. Jolly, in his report, gives two reasons which appeared to him "conclusive" of Rowland's guilt, but he also added to these two reasons some "additional considerations". The quality of these additional considerations may be judged by two examples. Ware had said in his confession that the murder had caused bloodstains on his raincoat. Mr. Jolly states that there was no evidence of bloodstains on Ware's *trousers*. There is no mention of the raincoat, nor jacket nor shoes, but there is a mention that Ware's trouser turn-ups did not contain the debris which had been found in Rowland's turn-ups. But Rowland's turn-ups were examined a week after the murder, and Ware's three and a half months later. The other "additional considerations" can be found in Mr. Jolly's report, and in Mr. Silverman's discussion of the report (pp. 67-71).

The two *main* reasons were (a) that the three witnesses who had identified Rowland had failed to identify Ware and (b) that, interrogated by Mr. Jolly, Ware had withdrawn his confession.

On the identification question it is simplest to quote Mr. Silverman again:

With Ware's consent, an identification parade was arranged. Then Mr. Macdonald, Mrs. Copley and Mr. Mercer were each asked, separately, if they could pick him out. In each case Mr. Jolly began by reminding the witness that he or she had already given evidence identifying Rowland. He asked Macdonald whether he could see anyone on the parade who "in any way resembles Rowland *whom you have already identified as the man who bought your hammer*". . . . They all fail to pick him out. Then Mr. Jolly sends away the rest of the parade and confronts each witness with Ware and asks if he is the man. They all say no, with varying degrees of emphasis. . . . Here are three people who . . . have been swearing that Rowland is the man. Is it surprising that they refuse to change their minds?

Mr. Jolly must have been familiar with the minutes of the trial and with some elementary facts of human psychology. He must have known that all three had described Rowland as dark or black, had hesitated and contradicted each other and themselves. But once they had been led to make up their minds, they had remained unshaken. They were simple people who had been subjected to the awe-inspiring machinery of Magistrates Courts and identification parades; who had been bullied under cross-examination, and had testified under oath that their confused memories about a black-haired man and a young girl, and a dark man buying a hammer, and a couple standing on a bombed site, referred to Rowland and Olive Balchin. None of us likes to be made a fool: to testify solemnly in court to one thing, and then admit having been mistaken; particularly if this is rubbed in by a question like the italicized passage from Mr. Jolly. Four months had passed since that fateful day which subsequently was to cause those unhappy witnesses so much bother; by that time their originally fluid memories had hardened in their unconscious minds, and they had probably convinced themselves that they had never hesitated, and that the events were exactly as they had described them. For they were decent people, and without this certainty they were bound to doubt whether they had not helped to convict an innocent; and because such a doubt is intolerable, the mind in self-defence becomes rigid and dogmatic. Besides, they must have unconsciously felt that by pointing a finger at another man, the same torment must inevitably start again as when they had pointed at Rowland: more confrontations, cross-examinations, testifying under oath to the opposite of what they had testified before; and with another man's life at stake.

If the witnesses had changed their minds, the case against Rowland would have collapsed. The fact that they did not change their minds left it exactly where it had stood before. It did not prove any miscarriage of justice; it failed to lend support to Ware's confession; but it was no proof that that confession was false. One decisive question, and the only one, was whether Ware had told the truth when he confessed to the murder, or when he withdrew his confession. On this crucial point Mr. Jolly says:

I have considered this written statement [of Ware's withdrawal] in the light of the whole of my investigations and all the circumstances of the case and of my observation of Ware's manner, demeanour and mentality. I am satisfied that when Ware told me that he did not commit the murder he was then speaking the truth.

This statement refers only to the withdrawal, not to the various confessions. As regards the confessions, they are in all but two irrelevant details perfectly consistent with the manner in which the murder took place. Mr. Jolly dismisses this fact by suggesting that Ware based his confession on newspaper reports. This may be perfectly true. There is one detail which Ware could not have got from the newspapers, but his imagination may have supplied it. Ware's confession does not prove that he spoke the truth; but it is consistent with the truth; and so is the withdrawal.

There is only one consideration which casts serious doubt on the confession: the fact that he seems to have previously confessed to a murder or intended murder of a girl, apparently falsely; and that on retracting he explained his confession by saying: "I made the statement out of swank. . . . I thought I was putting myself in the position of a hero. . . . In the past I wanted to be hanged. . . . It was worth while being hanged as a hero. . . ." But as against this, his description of the murder, "I was ate up with hatred" and several other details, had an uncanny ring of truth about them. Mr. Jolly could not have known that four years later Ware was to attempt murder under the same circumstances, hammer blows on the face and neck of a prostitute. But once he based his conclusions on psychological considerations, he ought to have known that the morbid type, obsessed with the idea of murder, who confesses falsely in order to be hanged as a hero, is also capable of committing real murder, for precisely the same reason. Mr. Jolly says that Ware in his interviews showed "a morbid interest in the macabre" which "might well for exhibitional reasons" lead to a false confession. Mr. Jolly did not realize that the same morbid interest might lead to the real thing.

Ware is now in Broadmoor, having been found guilty of attempted murder, but insane. I do not know who killed Olive Balchin. Nobody knows. Mr. Jolly had no need to prove Rowland's innocence; he need not even believe Ware; all he had to decide was whether, if the jury had known the facts in his possession, they would still have been certain of Rowland's guilt. And to that question there is only one answer: no.

The other Home Office inquiry was concerned with the possibility of miscarriage of justice in the case of Timothy Evans. The report by Mr. Scott Henderson said there was not. The report was described in the House of Commons by Mr. Michael Foot as "not worth the paper it is printed on". It may be sufficient to say that though the inquiry was concerned with the vindication of Evans, the solicitors and counsel of Evans were excluded by Mr. Scott Henderson from the proceedings, and only admitted after the Law Society and other bodies had protested to the Home Secretary; but even so they were not permitted to put questions to Christie in vindication of their dead client. Evans's mother and sister had saved up to buy a copy of the shorthand transcript of his trial, but permission was refused to them. Few people know that, though trials are public, you need special Home Office permission to buy the transcript of a trial which, apparently, can be refused.

It is a relief that there is no need to go into the inquiry and reopen the sewers of the Christie-Evans case, since the Home Secretary who refused to grant Evans a reprieve has since admitted in the House of Commons [25] that Timothy Evans died as a consequence of a miscarriage of justice. After Mr. Chuter Ede's admission, the Scott Henderson report retains only academic interest. Mr. Reginald Paget, Q.C., in discussing the report, commented:

I have not been able to discover any case in which an inquiry of this sort has reported that justice did go wrong, and when I asked the Home Secretary whether historically a private inquiry had ever discovered a great miscarriage of justice, he, too, did not know of one.

The theory behind it all is, apparently, that any official admission of error would undermine the public's confidence in the fairness of British justice. It is not only an immoral but also a mistaken theory: if the full truth were known, it would not undermine faith in British justice, only faith in capital punishment. For the public have enough common sense to know it to be inevitable that judges and jurors should sometimes be mistaken. But if the full truth about a series of doubtful cases were known, public opinion would realize that the irrevocability of the death-penalty turns human error into inhuman error. We cannot avoid mistakes; but we can avoid the fatal consequences of mistakes.

(h) The Home Secretary

The Home Secretary is the last person who stands between the condemned man and God. He takes the decision whether a man should live or die, without being responsible either to the Cabinet or to Parliament. He is only responsible to God; but he has certain responsibilities towards the Police Force he represents; and to his political party; and to his future career. We have seen before what curious changes have occurred in several Home Secretaries' attitudes to capital punishment in general. As to particular cases, the effect of extraneous considerations became evident when mercy was refused to Derek Bentley in the teeth of public opinion, charity and precedent. Precedent demanded that Bentley should be reprieved on at least five grounds: the jury's recommendation; his youth; his mental deficiency; that he was said to be under arrest and cooperating with the police when the murder was committed; and that even had he been an accomplice to murder, accomplices are never executed unless the principal is executed too.

Norman Thorne, found guilty against the medical evidence for the defence that the victim committed suicide, was not reprieved. Mrs. Woolmington, found guilty against the Home Office pathologist's evidence, was not reprieved. Rowland, Evans, Bentley, were not reprieved. Yet the former Home Secretary, Sir John Anderson, stated in the 1948 debate: "Where there is a scintilla . . . of doubt—the Home Secretary has invariably advised commutation." Scintilla means "spark" or "atom". Some atom; some spark.

(i) The Handicap of Poverty

Money makes a great deal of difference in life; we assume that it makes no difference when a man is tried for his life. This is one more mistaken assumption.

The fees paid to the defence under the Poor Prisoners' Defence Act are shockingly small. In a recent letter to *The Times* a solicitor, Mr. N. M. Jordan, mentioned the fact that for defending a destitute person subsequently found guilty of murder, counsel for the defence received five guineas ($15), while the brief for the leading counsel for the prosecution was marked seventy-five guineas ($225)—both fees being paid out of public funds. The solicitors received for six appearances at the Magistrate's Court proceedings altogether three guineas ($9).[26] Where the plea is guilty but insane—and that is by the nature of things a most frequent plea for the defence—everything depends on obtaining the services of a highly qualified psychiatrist whose repute carries weight in court. Another solicitor, Mr. E. T. Williams, wrote on this subject to *The Times* as follows:

I was instructed to act in the defence of a man charged with murder in South Wales earlier this year, and after three to four months' hard work on the case counsel and I were duly rewarded with fees little higher than those received by Mr. Jordan.

Solicitors and counsel do know, however, that when they undertake work of this nature they can expect to be out of pocket at the end of it. But in the case in which I received instructions the defence was one based on insanity, and in these circumstances medical evidence had to be provided by a man well qualified in the highly specialized field of psychiatry. I wrote to the Clerk of the Assize some time prior to the trial setting out an estimate of the fees which the psychiatrist, who had been consulted in the case, proposed to charge, asking whether he considered them reasonable. I had a reply amounting to little more than an acknowledgment in which I was informed that the question of fees was one that would be decided by the Judge at the hearing.

The psychiatrist, a well-qualified man of the first rank, had eight interviews with the prisoner (in the main, at the prison), conducted several searching tests on him, attended three conferences with counsel and myself, prepared detailed reports for the benefit of the defence, and attended throughout the two days which the case lasted at the Assize Court. During this hearing he was subjected to examination and cross-examination in the witness-box for at least two hours, and was constantly being called upon by counsel for the defence to provide guidance on the medical evidence supplied by the prosecution. Had this psychiatrist been consulted in a civil case, he could have commanded a fee of between 70 and 80 guineas, but for all his labours in this matter he was allowed 12 guineas.

If the Court's attitude to highly qualified medical men in this type of case remains unaltered, solicitors may well expect to find themselves in some considerable embarrassment and difficulty in trying to find psychiatrists of the first rank to undertake such unrewarding work, and the question arises as to whether the public can feel satisfied that a poor person subject to a capital charge will always receive the best advice and assistance available.[27]

Let us look at the situation from the psychiatric expert's point of view. The psychiatrist I am quoting is Dr. J. A. Hobson, of the Middlesex Hospital, who gave evidence for Christie and in a number of other notable cases:

Recently there was a man awaiting trial for murder who, for two months between the proceedings in the lower court and the assizes, *was not seen by his solicitor.* Though the circumstances of his offence were such as to suggest the likelihood of mental abnormality, no effort was made for him to be examined by a psychiatrist. A leading counsel was called in at the last minute. He at once appreciated the omission in the preparation of the case, and on the evening before the trial asked me, apologetically, to examine the man. I did my best, but my examination was too brief to be complete. There was no time to make necessary outside investigations, which I should have done if I had been called earlier, and no time to write a report.

I found Counsel at his club and we had a short conference at 11 p.m. Next morning I gave evidence at the Central Criminal Court and was subjected to hostile examination by the Judge. His summing-up was against us, but the Jury brought in a verdict of "Guilty, but insane". I am sure that the verdict was the right one. . . . I am equally sure that if Counsel had not called in a psychiatrist at the eleventh hour, this man would have been found "Guilty" and might have been hanged.[28]

Dr. Hobson is a psychiatrist. Mr. Silverman is a lawyer and politician. He treats the consequences of the existing situation from a different angle:

Rowland . . . was quite penniless. . . . In such cases legal aid is invariably granted at an early stage. Such aid covers nominal fees to counsel and solicitor and the expenses of witnesses. No funds are made available for enquiries or investigations of any kind. There is no possibility of making available to the defence anything comparable to the complex, elaborate, nation-wide organization available to the prosecution for the preparation of their case: the detective force, the centres of forensic science and medicine, the expert witnesses.[29]

There is a stock answer to this, which may strike the reader as somewhat naïve and surprising. The answer is that the prosecution's business is not to secure a conviction or to "make a case", but to put before the court all the relevant facts both against and in favour of the accused. It is a beautiful theory but a somewhat abstract one.

According to theory the prosecution should put all relevant material unearthed by the police at the disposal of the defence, but this is not the practice. In the case of Rowland, the police took a great number of statements from a great number of people whom they did not call as witnesses. They gave a list of these persons to the defence, but they withheld the statements they had made. In a recent letter to *The Criminal Law Review,* Mr. A. E. Taylor reports:

In the course of the trial [R. *v.* Xinaris (1955)], leading counsel for the defence, having elicited from a witness for the prosecution that he had made a statement to the police, demanded that it should be produced for his inspection. Senior counsel refused.[30]

The judge, Mr. Justice Byrne, ruled that the defence was entitled to see the statement; and only at that point was a whole bundle of statements, which witnesses for the prosecution had made to the police, handed over to the defence. The fact that a specific ruling was required and that the ruling was found worthy to be reported in a technical journal, shows how completely abstract the notion is that the prosecution takes a paternal and objective interest in the man they are trying to convict. When Mr. Eddowes demanded in a letter to *The Times* that—

The names of all persons interviewed, and copies of all statements taken by the police, should be disclosed to the defence. At present it rests upon the shoulders of prosecuting counsel to decide which, if any, statements taken by the police and in his possession should be disclosed,—[31]

Miss Normanton, Q.C., answered that this was quite unnecessary and "would lead to an enormous increase to the clerical costs of trials".[32] All this gives the prosecution an immense and unfair advantage over the prisoner, and particularly so in cases where the defence has no funds for investigation of its own.

Everybody in trouble will try to get hold of the best physician, or the best lawyer, he can afford. It is a generally accepted state of affairs that one's prospects in the law court depend to no small extent on the convincingness and eloquence of one's lawyer. There are endless books about famous lawyers who saved their clients in seemingly hopeless situations. It is a terrifying thought that a poor man on trial for his life should have, other things being equal, a poorer chance than another.

There are two ways of looking at this. One is to say: short of living in Utopia, the advantages of a higher income exist in all walks of life; this may be deplorable, but it is part of a free, competitive society.

The second answer is: I accept the fact, whether I like it or not, that life in a competitive society is a kind of race with first come, first served, as its maxim; but in this case we must eliminate from the race-course that fatal ditch which the strong may clear in a jump but the weak and lame cannot. If there is even a slight risk that a man's financial means could influence his chances of suffering capital punishment, then a fair trial is only possible if we abolish either financial inequality, or abolish capital punishment. The impartiality of the immense machine behind the prosecution is abstract theory; the cases I have quoted are hard, everyday reality.

(j) The Laws of Probability

Miscarriage of justice can be understood in a narrower and a broader meaning. In its most limited sense we mean by it a man being found guilty of a murder which another committed: e.g., Evans and possibly Rowland; and cases where the victim may have died by natural death or suicide or accident (Thorne, Woolmington, Merrifield, etc.). I have already warned against the erroneous conclusion that because it requires an exceptional chance for such mistakes to come to light, therefore mistakes must be equally exceptional. There was, at the initial stages, nothing exceptional about the cases of Evans and Rowland. They were routine trials, based on identification by witnesses and circumstantial evidence which in both cases was fairly convincing. Both names would have been forgotten for ever but for the appearance of Christie and Ware on the scene.

When a man denies his guilt, he can only be convicted on evidence of this kind. Such evidence can never amount to certainty, only to near-certainty. The amount of doubt varies from case to case, but is never entirely absent, for it is inherent in the nature of evidence; we can reduce the amount of friction in a machine, but never completely eliminate it. In some cases, certainty amounts to nearly 100%; in others, where experts contradict each other and the memory of witnesses seems more erratic and vague than usual, the balance of probabilities degenerates considerably. If I am a juror in a trial where the accused denies the act, I can never expect 100% certainty; I can merely say to myself: "I shall vote 'not guilty' unless I am at least 95% certain that he did it."

Yet an average of 95% certainty means, according to the laws of probability, that every twentieth man convicted on circumstantial evidence is the victim of a miscarriage of justice.*

To measure certitude in percentages is of course an arbitrary procedure, yet any insurance company would base its policy as confidently on predictions of this type as they base their car insurance premium on the average number of accidents per annum. And if Lloyds were to insure every man on trial for his life against miscarriage due to "vagaries of memory, erroneous recognition, fallibility of experts and juries, faulty summing up, short-comings of legal aid, Appeal Court hazards, Home Secretaries' professional diseases, and other imperfections inherent and ingrained in the procedure commonly referred to as a 'fair trial' "—the premium would probably be much higher.

All this applies to errors of justice in the strictly limited meaning. But no hard-and-fast line can be drawn between miscarriages of this type and others due to the outdated and self-contradictory nature of the law, as exemplified by the M'Naghten test or the law of provocation. The fact that mental deficiency, epilepsy, paranoia, do not in themselves justify a plea of insanity makes the question

---

* Imagine a roulette table with nineteen white numbers and one black number. The nineteen white numbers represent the ninety-five per cent. certainty, the black number the five per cent. doubt. The chances then are that on an average one throw in twenty will draw a black.

whether a mentally deranged murderer will be found criminally responsible or not, quite literally into a toss-up; it replaces the symbolic scales of justice by a game of dice. And if we remember the answers given by the Lord Chief Justice to the Royal Commission's questions regarding the propriety of executing human beings thus afflicted, we realize that it is time to close this indecent game down.

The death-penalty is the only punishment inflicted by the law that is irrevocable. An irrevocable penalty, even if it could be morally and logically justified, presupposes an infallible tribunal and an omniscient law. Only if these conditions were fulfilled could a murder trial be justifiably called a fair trial. Without them a fair-minded judge, plus a fair-minded jury, do not add up to a fair trial. Once this is realized the "scintilla" of doubt will grow into an angry conflagration, and burn down the last, creaking Model T version of the Tyburn Tree.

Part III

THE END
OF
THE NIGHTMARE

THE ALTERNATIVE TO HANGING

1. The Nightmare

DOSTOIEVSKY SAYS somewhere that if in the last moment before being executed, a man, however brave, were given the alternative of spending the rest of his days on the top of a bare rock with only enough space to sit on it, he would choose it with relief. There is indeed a Kafkaesque horror attached to an execution, which goes beyond the mere fear of death or pain or indignity. It is connected not with the brutality but with the macabre, cold-blooded politeness of the ceremony, in which the person whose neck is going to be broken is supposed to collaborate in a nice, sensible manner, as if it were a matter of a minor surgical operation. It is symbolized in the ceremonial handshake with the executioner; it is present in the delinquent's knowledge that in the embarrassed stares of the officials he is already mirrored as a dead man with a blue face and ruptured vertebrae; and that what for him is the final, violent termination of life is for them merely an unpleasant duty, followed by a sigh of relief and a plate of bacon and eggs. The Romans deprived their victim of the dignity of death by throwing him to the beasts in the arena with a clown's mask attached to his face; we put a white cap over his head, and if the victim is a woman she is made to put on waterproof underwear on the morning of the execution.[1]

Officialdom wishes to make us believe that the operation itself is always quick and expeditious. This is not true. The truth is that some prisoners struggle both in the condemned cell and under the noose, that some have to be carried tied to a chair, others dragged to the trap, limp, bowels open, arms pinioned to the back, like animals; and that still other things happen which should only happen in nightmare dreams. In the Commons debate of 1948, the then Mr. Beverley Baxter mentioned one case which the Home Office did not succeed in hushing up, the case of a sick woman of twenty-eight whose insides fell out before she vanished through the trap. Everybody who took part in that scene suffered some damage to their nervous system. The executioner, Ellis, attempted suicide a few weeks later. The Governor of Holloway, Dr. Morton, was described a few days later by a visiting magistrate: "I think I have never seen a person look so changed in appearance by mental suffering as the Governor appeared to me to be." The prison Chaplain, the Rev. Glanville Murray, said of the scene of the execution: "When we were all gathered together there, it seemed utterly impossible to believe what we were there to do. . . . My God, the impulse to rush in and save her by force was almost too strong for me." When it was over, the Deputy Governor of Holloway, Miss Cronin, who was "not at all a sensitive or easily moved person", remarked of the hanged woman: "I think if she had been spared she could have become a very good woman." [2]

These nightmare scenes are not exceptional. When Pierrepoint, the hangman, was asked by the Royal Commission, "You must in so many executions have had things go wrong occasionally?" he had at first lied: "Never." Pressed further whether he had had any "awkward moments", he climbed down and said that he had had one awkward moment "with a foreign spy who had to be carried to the gallows strapped to a chair". Pressed even further, he said he had "probably three more" such cases "like a faint at the last minute or something like that, but it has not been anything to speak about".[3] It may not be much for Pierrepoint to speak about, but it should be enough for the nation to think about. For if it is proper that these things should be done in its name, then it is proper that it should hear about them.

The horror of the operation remains even if there is no struggle or dementedness in the condemned cell. The preparations on the previous day when executioner and assistant discreetly take the measure and weight of the victim to determine the length of the drop; the dress rehearsal of dropping a stuffed sack of the same weight to make sure that the estimated length of rope will neither strangle the victim too slowly nor tear his head off; the jolly domino game in the condemned cell while the preparations go on and the hour draws nearer; the stratagems to make him sit with his back to the door through which the executioner will enter; the brisk, businesslike opening of that door, the pinioning of the hands behind the back and the walking or dragging him in solemn procession to the execution shed and on to the white chalk mark on the trap; the tying of his legs while two officers stand at his sides on planks thrown across the trap, to hold him up; the fixing of the white cap and the noose with its sliding brass ring—in a few years' time, with God's help, all this will appear as unthinkable as drawing, quartering and pressing to death appear to us today.

The Royal Commissioners were much preoccupied with the question how long the penultimate act of the nightmare took, from the entering of the executioner to the drop. Mr. Pierrepoint, always an optimist, answered "the longest time" was twenty to twenty-five seconds. The Commissioners, no doubt acquainted with the secret Home Office instructions how to answer suchlike questions, were somewhat sceptical and insisted on witnessing a mock execution. The result apparently confirmed their scepticism:

Q. Did not today's execution take a little longer than usual?—*A.* That was not really an execution; the atmosphere was not there; and we had no assistant.

Q. What do you mean by saying that the atmosphere was not there?—*A.* You gentlemen there made the atmosphere different. We had no assistant executioner for another thing. You have not got the man there to perform on, you have to imagine a bit, and it all upsets your calculations a little bit. That this morning was very slow.

Q. As compared with the real thing?—*A.* Yes.

Q. Do you wear anything special in the way of clothing, like gloves?—*A.* No, just as we are.[4]

Q. . . . So it really means that you go into the cell, you tie up the man's hands, and you tie them up quicker than you did the officer this morning?—*A.* Yes.

Q. But he was much more willing to be tied?—*A.* He was not as willing, believe me.

Q. I should have thought he would have been more willing?—*A.* I should have thought so too, but he was not.

Q. So that took longer than usual, because he was unwilling?—*A.* Yes.[5]

As for the final surgical act itself, the Home Office states that "as now carried out, execution by hanging can be regarded as speedy and certain". The emphasis on "now" refers to the improved technique of a drop of variable length, and of the sliding ring which is supposed to hold the knot of the noose in its place under the left jaw. Before this innovation, the agony of slow suffocation without loss of consciousness could last up to twenty minutes, not to mention various forms of mutilation and lacerations, jaws torn off by hitting the edge of the trap, gashes torn in the neck, heads partly or entirely torn off, and people being hanged twice or even three times in succession. All that, we are told, are matters of the past; the new method is infallible; it causes instantaneous loss of consciousness by "a physical shock of extreme violence".[6] As a result of the improved method, the first, second and third cervical vertebrae are fractured or dislocated; the spinal cord is crushed or lacerated or torn from the brain stem, and if the initial shock is not fatal, the process is completed by strangulation. There is no chance, we are told, "of a later recovery of consciousness since breathing is no longer possible. The heart may continue to beat for up to 20 minutes, but this is a purely automatic function." [7]

Let us hope that this is true, or at least true in the majority of cases; though one is entitled to a certain scepticism regarding the infallibility of the improved method from the medical point of view, particularly where the extremely complex neurological problem of consciousness, and the loss thereof, are concerned. The *Encyclopaedia Britannica,* 1955 edition, which was published after the Royal Commission's investigations, expresses this scepticism in an indirect way:

It is said that the dislocation of the vertebrae causes immediate unconsciousness . . . the heart may continue to beat for up to 20 mins. but this is *thought to be* a purely automatic function.[8] (Italics mine.)

The fact is: we do not know for certain. A violent shock of this type is as a rule, but not always, followed by instantaneous unconsciousness. One classic example to the contrary is the so-called crowbar case, known to all neurologists and surgeons—a labourer whose brain was pierced from crown to jaw by a two-inch crowbar, and who walked, fully conscious, for medical help with the crowbar inside his brain.

A second reason for being sceptical about official assurances regarding the swift and painless character of the operation is that, like any other operation, the efficacy of breaking a neck depends entirely on the skill of the surgeon. On this point we can rely on the first-hand evidence of Pierrepoint. Questioned about the Scottish method of hanging which differs from the English, Pierrepoint said:

The Scottish [method] is very good, but I think it is very, very old, antediluvian. It is about time it was altered in Scotland.

Q. What is the difference?—A. The apparatus is very old . . .

Q. So it is much less exact?—A. It is not perfect. It is all right if you understand the job and you can work these things out, but a stranger can soon make a blunder of it.

Q. It is a question of getting new apparatus?—A. They want it badly in Scotland, badly, but their ideas are very good without that. . . .

Pierrepoint was then questioned on the English method:

Q. The knot, as you showed us this morning, must always be under the angle of the left jaw?—A. Yes.

Q. That is very important, is it?—A. Very important.

Q. Why is it very important?—A. If you had the same knot on the right-hand side it comes back behind the neck, and throws the neck forward, which would make a strangulation. If you put it on the left-hand side it finishes up in front and throws the chin back and breaks the spinal cord.

Q. It depends on where he is standing on the trap?—A. No, I do not think so. The knot is the secret of it, really. We have to put it on the left lower jaw and if we have it on that side, when he falls it finishes under the chin and throws the chin back; but if the knot is on the right-hand side, it would finish up behind his neck and throw his neck forward, which would be strangulation. He might live on the rope a quarter of an hour then.[9]

In one case, at least, we have direct evidence of a bungled execution, quite recently, after introduction of the improved technique: in case "L 1942" the report of the Coroner on a Pentonville Hanging contains the significant words "noose slipped on jaw".[10]

When the operation is over, the victim is buried within the prison walls. Unlike in America, the body is not handed over to the relatives, for a technical reason which sums up the obscene ignominy of the whole thing: in the words of the Royal Commission Report, "hanging . . . leaves the body with the neck elongated".[11]

Whereas in spite of all this evidence British belief in the "humaneness" of hanging remains unshaken, America takes a more realistic view. The Canadian Joint Committee recommended last year the substitution of electrocution for hanging, after the Canadian official executioner had explained in a statement that in "95% to 98% of cases" death was instantaneous, caused by the breaking of the spinal vertebrae, but in the remaining cases it was caused by strangling. Several American states switched to electro-cution or lethal gas precisely because of the haphazardness of hanging. Thus, for instance, the Attorney General of Oregon stated in his written answer to the British Royal Commission's question-naire:

In 1937, lethal gas became the means of executing the death-penalty. . . . In the use of the prior method . . . which was hanging, there were mishaps, two of which were horrible.[12]

If hanging is a modern form of the godly butchery, the alterna-tives of electrocution or the gas chamber are no better, and possibly worse, because of the long and ghastly preliminaries. Regarding electrocution, the following account of the procedure, practiced in the state of Washington, appears in the Royal Commission Report:

The execution takes place at 10 a.m. At midnight on the preceding night the condemned man is taken from the condemned cell block to a cell adjoining the electrocution chamber. About 5.30 a.m. the top of his head and the calf of one leg are shaved to afford direct contact with the elec-trodes. (The prisoner is usually handcuffed during this operation to pre-vent him from seizing the razor.) At 7.15 a.m. the death warrant is read to him and about 10 o'clock he is taken to the electrocution chamber. Five witnesses are present (including representatives of the Press) and two doctors—the prison medical officer and the city coroner. The witnesses watch the execution through a grille or dark glass and cannot be seen by the prisoner.* Three officers strap the condemned man to the chair, tying him around the waist, legs and wrists. A mask is placed over his face and the electrodes are attached to his head and legs. As soon as this operation is completed (about two minutes after he has left the cell) the signal is given and the switch is pulled by the electrician; the current is left on for two minutes, during which there is alternation of two or more different voltages. When it is switched off, the body slumps forward in the chair. The prisoner does not make any sound when the current is turned on, and unconsciousness is apparently instantaneous. He is not, however, pronounced dead for some minutes after the current is discon-nected. The leg is sometimes slightly burned, but the body is not other-wise marked or mutilated.[13]

* In some other States the number of witnesses is greater and in some places they are not separated from the prisoner by any form of screen.

The preparations for gassing are even more ghoulish. The following description in the Royal Commission Report of the procedure in North Carolina is typical:

A chamber or room, when the doors are closed, is hermetically sealed to prevent leakage of cyanide gas. This room contains two observation windows. One window is for observation by the required witnesses and the other for officials required to be present at the execution. . . . In this room is a wooden chair with leather straps for strapping the prisoner's arms, legs and across the abdomen to the chair. In the seat of this chair is a trap door electrically controlled which releases the cyanide pellets.

Prior to the execution all equipment is double checked and a pound of sodium cyanide pellets is placed in the trap in the seat of the chair. Twenty minutes before execution three pints of U.S.P. sulphuric acid and six pints of water are carefully mixed in a lead container. The container is covered with a lid of similar material and is placed under the chair in a position to receive the pellets when dropped.

There are two copper pipes adjacent to the chair which lead under the floor outside the physician's stand. At the end of the pipe in the chamber is a rubber hose which is to be connected to the head of a Bowles stethoscope strapped to the prisoner's chest. Attached to the other end of the copper pipes at the physician's stand are the earpieces of a stethoscope for determining the time of the prisoner's death.

The prisoner has been previously prepared in his cell in this manner: clothing removed, with the exception of shorts; the head of a Bowles stethoscope strapped over the apex of the heart with broad strips of adhesive.

After the above preparations the prisoner walks to the execution chamber preceded by the Chaplain and followed by the Warden or one of his Deputies. He is then strapped in the chair under the supervision of the Warden or Deputy; a leather mask applied to the face; the stethoscope head connected with aforementioned tube; the Chaplain's prayers completed and all officials leave the chamber. The last person leaving the chamber quickly removes the cover from the acid container. The doors to the chamber and ante-room are quickly closed and the pellets dropped in the acid by the electrically controlled switch. . . .

When this method was first employed, medical opinion was not unanimous about it; there were some who thought that the gas had a suffocating effect which would cause acute distress, if not actual pain, before the prisoner became unconscious. It seems to be now generally agreed that unconsciousness ensues very rapidly.[14]

The report adds: "No sedatives, narcotics or any other drugs are administered to the prisoner before execution."

The alternative to capital punishment is imprisonment "for life". This really means imprisonment for a length of period determined by the demands of public safety and the rehabilitation of the prisoner.

The arguments most often heard against this alternative can be classified as follows:

(a) It is *unsafe*. The murderer serving a life sentence is usually let out after a number of years and may commit another murder.

(b) To keep a murderer, who cannot be reformed, in prison to the end of his life is *more cruel* than a quick death.

(c) Imprisonment is *not cruel enough;* modern prisons pamper the criminal instead of punishing him—plus the subsidiary arguments about the burden to the taxpayer, the strain on prison warders, the danger of escape.

2. *Murderers as a Class*

That it would be *unsafe* to let murderers live is an argument in which many well-meaning people believe, though they loathe the idea of hanging and would rather do away with it. But the public's idea of the murderer is modelled on exceptional and untypical cases (Heath, Haig, Crippen, Christie), which receive the widest publicity and are part of the national folklore. The murderer is either thought of as a homicidal maniac, or a hardened criminal, or a monster planning the "perfect murder". But these popular figures who impress themselves on the public imagination are no more typical of murderers as a class, than Lawrence of Arabia was of British subalterns as a class.

The figures quoted in Chapter II show that during the fifty years 1900–49 only in one out of twelve cases was the murderer found so dangerous for public safety or his crime so "unpardonable" that he was executed—that means only 8% of the total. In Scotland, the proportion was even lower: 4%. Every analysis of the motive and circumstances under which the crime was committed, shows the extreme rarity of the cold-blooded type of murder. Half a century ago, Sir John Macdonell, Master of the Supreme Court, analysed the criminal statistics from 1886 to 1905 and found the following result: 90% of the murders were committed by men, and nearly two-thirds of their victims were their wives, mistresses or sweethearts. The peak day for murder is Saturday, and the peak hours 8 p.m. to 2 a.m. Approximately 30% of the murders were caused by drink, quarrels and violent rage, another 40% by jealousy, intrigues and sexual motives, and only 10% by financial motives. Sir John Macdonell concludes his survey in the following words (my italics):

I hesitate to draw any conclusions from imperfect data as to matters of great complexity, but I am inclined to think that this crime is *not generally the crime of the so-called criminal classes* but is in most cases rather an *incident in miserable lives in which disputes, quarrels, angry words and blows are common.* The short history of the large number of cases which have been examined might be summed up thus: Domestic quarrels and brawls; much previous ill-treatment; drinking, fighting, blows; a long course of brutality and continued absence of self-restraint. This crime is generally the last of a series of acts of violence.[15]

Half a century later, the Royal Commission examined the statistics of the years 1900–49 and came to the conclusion that they "confirm Sir John Macdonell's statement that murder is not in general a crime of the so-called criminal classes".[16]

3. The Behaviour of Murderers in Prison

Next, let us examine, from the point of view of public safety, the conduct of murderers who have been convicted and reprieved. The people best qualified to decide this question are evidently the prison governors, warders, prison chaplains and Home Office experts. These were heard both by the Select Committee and by the Royal Commission. Their opinions are quoted below; they were unanimous and without dissent. Since this point is of great importance in correcting popular misbeliefs about murderers as a class, I am quoting in full the relevant passages from both reports. First, the Select Committee of 1930:

High tribute was paid to the general conduct in prison, and on release, of reprieved murderers. . . . The testimony of the Home Office witnesses was as follows:

"A very large number of murderers are, in other respects, perfectly decent people, and a very large proportion of them, if they were let out, would be very unlikely to commit any other murder or any other crime. They are really a class by themselves; they are quite different from the ordinary criminal as a rule. . . . It is certainly not common experience that a murderer who has been released after serving part of a life sentence returns to prison . . . as to . . . committing further murders on release, that might be entirely ruled out."

Lord Brentford [Home Secretary, 1924–29] said of the reprieved murderer that he was a man who had committed one crime and, not being of a criminal type or of a criminal mind, he made a very good prisoner. He did not think he had come across a single case of a reprieved murderer committing another murder.

Colonel Hales, Governor of Parkhurst Prison, could not recall one who, from the moment he was discharged, had not made good. The same testimony was given by Revd. William Lewis Cottrell, M.A., Chaplain at Wormwood Scrubs, by Mr. Walter Middleton, Chief Officer of Pentonville Prison, and by Captain Clayton, Governor of Dartmoor.[17]

None of the prison governors or officials dissented from this opinion, although the majority were probably anti-abolitionist. Twenty years later the Royal Commission came to the same conclusion:

There is a popular belief that prisoners serving a life sentence after conviction of murder form a specially troublesome and dangerous class. That is not so. Most find themselves in prison because they have yielded to temptation under the pressure of a combination of circumstances unlikely to recur. "Taking murderers as a class", said one witness [Major Benke, Governor of Wandsworth Prison and Chairman of the Panel of Prison Governors] "there are a considerable number who are first offenders and who are not people of criminal tendencies. The murder is in many cases their first offence against the law. Previous to that they were law-abiding citizens and their general tenor of life is still to be law-abiding. . . ."[18]

In August, 1952, there was a total of 91 reprieved murderers among the prison population of England and Wales, out of which 82, that is, more than 90%, belonged to the star class.[19] Thus the large majority of reprieved murderers are unusually well-behaved model prisoners. What happens when they are let loose on society after serving their sentence? Do the reformed lambs turn into wolves again?

4. Murderers Turned Loose

The answer is given in the statistics of the Home Office, of Scotland Yard and the Central After Care Association. During the twenty-year period 1928–48, 174 people were sentenced to life, and of these 112 had been released at the end of the period in question.[20] Of these 112, only one was alleged to have committed a second murder: Walter Graham Rowland; and he was, as we saw, one of the most probable victims of mistaken identity. Yet Rowland is, as far as one can gather from existing reports, the only case of a "sane" reprieved murderer being convicted of a second murder in the United Kingdom in the course of the twentieth century.* None of the other released "lifers" during the twenty-year period ending in 1948 committed crimes of violence against the person; and only five committed offences against property. In Scotland, eleven reprieved murderers were released during the same period: only two of these were re-convicted, one for theft and one for "lewd practices".[21]

The evidence before the Royal Commission from the Commonwealth countries and the U.S.A. was as follows:

New South Wales: In general such prisoners after release behave well. Very occasionally . . . the murderer with a previous record of criminality . . . will again come into conflict with the law, but seldom for a serious offence.

Queensland (capital punishment abolished): In the fifty years 1900–50, four released murderers committed subsequent offences: one attempt to kill, one indecent assault, one infliction of bodily harm, one cattle stealing.

South Australia: No prisoner released after life sentence has been returned for breach of conditions.

Canada: The average of failures is estimated to have fluctuated around 3%:

Ceylon: No accurate information available, but cases where murderers returned to prison are exceptional.

New Zealand: So far as memory goes, no prisoner released after a conviction of murder has broken any of the conditions of his release or committed any offence or been returned to prison.

South Africa: Recommittals of this class of prisoner are extremely rare occurrences.

* Straffen was not released; he escaped from Broadmoor.

U.S.A.: Generally speaking, I doubt if there are any facts which would indicate that persons originally convicted and later commuted and released under parole have any higher degree of failure on parole than any other group. There have been a few notorious cases where persons have lapsed into delinquency again, but it is usually a comparatively minor sort of crime as compared to the one which originally got them into trouble. Cases of murder committed by persons pardoned from the death-penalty are rare if not almost unknown.[22]

It may be objected that this unanimous body of evidence refers only to the more harmless type of murderers who were reprieved precisely because they were considered harmless. But the experience of countries which have abolished capital punishment and where, therefore, every murderer is automatically reprieved, whether considered "harmless" or not, is exactly the same as in countries where murderers are still being executed.

Regarding the Dominions, we have already seen that in Queensland and New Zealand, both abolitionist during the period in question, only one case is known of a reprieved man attempting murder in the last fifty years. In Europe, the Royal Commission's inquiry embraced six countries: Belgium, Denmark, the Netherlands, Norway, Sweden and Switzerland. *In these six countries altogether six convicted murderers have committed crimes of violence after their release in the course of the last thirty years.** The Royal Commission concludes:

"Even in countries which have abolished capital punishment the protection of society is rarely thought to require that murderers who are mentally normal should be detained in prison for the remainder of their life or even for very long periods. . . . The evidence that we ourselves received in these countries was also to the effect that released murderers who commit further crimes of violence are rare, and those who become useful citizens are common".[23]

These facts are so amazing and contrary to public belief that they call for some explanation. It is partly contained in the statements of the prison governors and Home Office experts which I have quoted: namely, that with rare exceptions, murder is not a crime of the criminal classes, and that the average murderer is *not* an "enemy of

* Two in Belgium and four in Denmark.

society" in the broad sense. This general statement was borne out by the statistics on the motives and circumstances of murder. It was confirmed by the experience of abolitionist countries which show that released murderers are less apt to relapse into crime than other offenders. Broadly speaking, it boils down to this: that the vast majority of murderers are either "crazy" in the elastic, non-legal sense of the word, or momentarily "crazed" ("mad" in American parlance); because a normal person in a normal state of mind just doesn't commit murder. Hence murderers are, by and large, either mentally abnormal, or acting under abnormal circumstances. The former belong not to prison but to an institution; the latter are easier to reform than any other type of criminal.

There remain the rare exceptions—the Christies and Haigs—who, in all likelihood, cannot be reformed and would have to be kept safely locked away to the end of their natural lives. But these "monsters" who so much agitate public imagination, form such a small percentage as to be almost negligible as a social problem. Moreover, they do not affect the question we are discussing—life imprisonment as an alternative to the death-penalty—because they do not belong to prison but to an institution. The Royal Commission says about them: "We agree with the Home Office that any convicted murderers whom it would be unsafe ever to release are likely to be in the category of the mentally abnormal." [24] They belong to a category apart, since the protection of society against them becomes the responsibility not of the legal but of the medical profession.

The practical consequences of abolition would in fact hardly be felt or noticed by the country. The cessation of the death-penalty would simply mean that on an average thirteen persons per year would be added to the British prison population. Even the Home Office, traditionally opposed to abolition, agrees that these people "would not be likely to give any exceptional trouble to prison officers".[25] And furthermore, that those who could not be safely released in due time would form a very small proportion of the whole, and would be found in the category of the mentally abnormal and in that category alone.[26]

For the thirteen men and women who are annually hanged with the nation's tacit consent are by no means "monsters" and "irretrievables". We saw how the rigidity of the law and the anachronism of the M'Naghten Rules transform justice into an unholy roulette game. Mrs. Ellis, Mrs. Thompson, the boy Bentley, all of whom were hanged, were no more "irretrievable" than Mace-bearer Martin, who was spared. The late Sir Alexander Paterson, Director of Convict Prisons, had this to say about the thirteen whom we annually hang: "If the estimate of [the condemned person's] character, formed by those who have to look after him for several weeks while awaiting sentence, could be taken into account by those who have to advise the Secretary of State, a considerable number might be respited." [27] And the Chaplain at Wormwood Scrubs Prison, the Rev. W. L. Cottrell, summed up his experience as follows:

Of the 15 men whom I have seen executed I have felt very much indeed that a proportion of those men, perhaps half of them or even more, might really have been allowed to live, and had they been allowed to live I have felt that they would really turn into decent honest citizens. That is not emotional sentiment that has carried me away, but it is the real hard facts of the men whom I have known, because a chaplain gets very intimate with these men before they die, and I have felt that many of them, like so many reprieved murderers have done of whom I know today, would really have been quite decent honest citizens and could have taken their place in the world and in Society.[28]

The precautions taken by the Home Office before a man sentenced to life is released, will be discussed later. But the evidence of the extreme rarity of the cases where a murderer found fit for release committed a second crime, is in itself sufficient to show that the risk run by the community through the substitution of life for death sentences, is almost entirely an imaginary one. It is certainly smaller than the joint risks of executing innocent people and of letting guilty people off because the jury is not certain enough to hang the man, but would send him to prison in the knowledge that the case can be reopened. We have seen that these are the inevitable consequences of an outdated law, and the chances are that there are more murderers at large for this reason in England than in countries where capital punishment was abolished.

5. The Length of a Life Sentence

We now come to the argument that a quick death is less cruel than a long prison sentence. It comes from two categories of people:

those who rationalize their sadistic tendencies by a pious "break his neck for his own good", and from genuine humanitarians who, ignorant of conditions in modern prisons, base their apprehensions on vague notions of gaol-life in Dickensian days.

The person best qualified to judge whether prison is preferable to execution is evidently the prisoner himself. Sir Basil Thomson, an outstanding authority, wrote that "no Governor has ever yet met a condemned prisoner who would refuse a reprieve or who did not ardently long for one".* Calvert quotes another ex-prison official as stating "that of the thirty reprieved murderers whom, in the course of his duties, he had come to know intimately, there was not one but had testified, after years of imprisonment, to his thankfulness for the respite".[29] Yet at that time prison routine was much grimmer and more depressing than nowadays.

The actual length of a "life" sentence is determined by the Home Office. It is not decided in advance, but according to the reports received on the prisoner's character and conduct. Each case is reviewed at least every four years. In exceptional cases the reprieved prisoner may be released almost instantaneously. Home Office statistics [30] show that during the decade 1940–49, 93 people were released from serving commuted life sentences. Of these, 6 had served less than a year—among them a woman who had gassed her son, a hopeless imbecile of thirty who had to be nursed like a baby; and a Jewish refugee woman from Nazi Germany who, together with her mother, tried to poison herself during the war for fear of a German invasion. The mother died, the daughter survived and was convicted of murder as a survivor of a suicide pact.

Of the others, on an average 5 persons were released each year between their second and sixth year in prison. This makes a total of 32 persons out of 93, released after serving less than seven years. All of these were obviously pathetic cases, who could not be of the remotest danger to society. The peak years of release were between the seventh and eighth years after conviction—36 cases, amounting to 40% of the total. Of the remainder, 10 persons were made to serve nine years, 8 persons ten years, 2 eleven years, 3 twelve years, 1 thirteen years and 1 fourteen years. Nobody was released who had

* While awaiting trial, many prisoners are indifferent to their fate. But after sentence of death has been passed on them, the instinct of survival seems to reassert itself with a vengeance.

served more than fourteen years. The table does not say how many prisoners there were who had served more than fourteen years and were *not* released; but the Home Office states that "only most exceptionally would anybody serve more than fifteen years under the present practice; the normal is much less than that".[31] From this we must conclude, that most of the "over-fifteen-years", i.e. the irretrievables, are in Broadmoor. Yet, as we saw, there was only one case in England, Wales or Scotland, during the last fifty years, of a released "lifer" committing an act of violence—and that was the enigmatic case of Rowland.

6. How a Life Sentence Is Spent

So much for the length of time spent in prison by reprieved murderers before they are considered to have expiated their crime, and safe to be released. How is that time spent?

Long-term prisoners in England are divided into two classes: "star" and "ordinary". The star class comprises all first offenders unless they are considered a bad influence, but also prisoners with previous convictions if they are supposed to become a good influence; there is no rigid rule.

In August, 1952, the prison population included, as previously mentioned, 91 reprieved murderers, 82 of whom were in the star class. The men of the star class were serving their term partly at Wakefield, partly at the new "open prison" at Leyhill; the women, either at Aylesbury or at the "open prison" at Askham Grange. Others were undergoing hospital treatment, or waiting for their transfer from local prisons.[32]

The "open prisons" are a recent experiment, dating back to 1946. There are no walls around the prison, no bars on the windows, no locks on the doors, and no guards are posted. Leyhill houses on the average 250 to 300 prisoners, of whom, in 1952, 20 were reprieved murderers. Escape is, of course, child's play—but it is not in the interests of the type of prisoner sent to an "open prison". In 1947, the first year after the experiment was started, fourteen escaped; in 1948, eight; in 1949, five; in 1950, one; in 1951, one; in 1952, nil.[33]

Yet the great majority of reprieved murderers serve part of their sentences—often a large part—in "open prisons".

The major part of the day—seven to eight hours—is spent by the prison population much in the same manner as by the ordinary free population: on work. "Work" for the prisoner under the old régime meant "the treadmill, the shot drill and the crank, of which the deliberate intention was to be irksome, fatiguing and—because totally unproductive—degrading".[34] Today "work" means nearly anything in the prisoner's own trade or a trade learnt in prison: from farming and market gardening to printing and bookbinding. At Wakefield, prisoners are engaged in: weaving, tailoring, precision engineering, bricklaying, foundry work, painting and decorating. At Leyhill: in carpentry, shoemaking, printing and binding. Some Leyhill prisoners work on local farms, or at road-mending, or as bricklayers and builders. They bicycle to their places of employment without any escort, and work without prison supervision. Other prisons send out parties of up to twenty prisoners with a single officer accompanying them, to do agricultural or forestry work. In women's prisons, the main trades are needlework, dressmaking, knitting, cleaning, painting, gardening and laundering. Some prisoners manufacture fishermen's nets, others footballs, others gloves and pullovers. The customers of their produce are the prison administration itself, other Government departments, public and local bodies and, to a small extent, private firms.

All prisons in which long sentences are served have vocational courses for those prisoners who had no skill or trade, or who wish to acquire a new one. They take the form of a six-months course of both practical and theoretical instruction based on a Ministry of Labour syllabus. They include, for men: precision engineering, carpentry, fitting, bricklaying, painting and decorating, foundry work, weaving, printing, bookbinding. For women, there are courses in cookery and general housewifery, tailoring, and so forth.

The pay is very small. It normally does not exceed four shillings a week. The idea behind this seems to be that the surplus value of the prisoner's work should pay for his upkeep. On the Continent the rates of pay are generally much higher: in Belgium, prisoners earn up to thirty shillings, in Denmark up to two pounds a week, half of which can be spent in prison, the other half kept until release. However that may be, the system answers the old idiotic argument that abolition of the death-penalty would increase the taxpayer's burden. The average of thirteen broken necks per annum costs the taxpayer ten pounds per neck to Mr. Pierrepoint, plus the fee to his assistant, to which have to be added travelling expenses for both; not to mention the outlay for warders going sick after each operation; maintenance of the apparatus, wear and tear of the rope, and so forth. The reprieved convict, on the other hand, earns his keep, plus a surplus for the prison administration. The costly prisoners are those who serve short sentences in local prisons, such as vagabonds and petty thieves. From the anxious taxpayer's point of view, it would be more logical to hang these.

Outside working hours there is a large and growing programme for various activities in both the field of education and entertainment. There are lectures, theatre performances, film shows and concerts. In some prisons the prisoners have their own orchestras and dramatic societies. All have libraries, but prisoners may also receive books and periodicals from outside and subscribe to correspondence courses for any trade or hobby. Games are played at weekends, and physical training is given to younger prisoners. At Wakefield there are five courts; at Leyhill, the cricket and football teams play against the local clubs; the inmates can have their own gardens, competing in the annual flower show; they have a putting course, a deck-tennis court, a swimming pool, ping-pong, billiards and a wireless room.

It can hardly be said that detention under these conditions is "a doom far worse than death", as the Lord Chancellor of the day, Lord Jowitt, and the previous Lord Chancellor, Viscount Simon, said in the House of Lords debate in 1948. These worthies, whom I had occasion to quote before, were referring to some long bygone horrors of the Belgian and Italian prison systems as the only conceivable alternative to hanging. It is worth a digression to listen to the Lord Chancellor:

In Belgium the position is that a murderer who is sentenced nominally to imprisonment for life is usually allowed out after some twenty-five years, but he serves the first ten of the twenty-five in solitary confinement. . . . Speaking for myself, I do not for a moment doubt that these are fates worse than death, and I am quite certain that nobody in this House or in another place would for one moment tolerate the conception of any such penalty as that.[35]

The facts are that even in Belgium, which has a harsher prison régime than any other European country, solitary confinement "has been gradually abandoned since 1920. . . . It must be emphatically stated that solitary confinement in Belgium . . . no longer exists." [36]

But even if the Lord Chancellor's information had been correct, and not outdated by twenty years, why on earth would England have to imitate just that one example? Lord Jowitt had thought of this objection, and had the following answer to it:

Logically, one is perfectly entitled to say, "Look at what has happened in Belgium." One can say, "Well, you see, the abolition of the death-penalty had no ill-effects; there are no more murderers." On the other hand, if one says that, then, logically [sic], one must be prepared to say, "I will accept the Belgian remedy." Yet none of us would accept that. Therefore, I come to the conclusion that, logically, it is fallacious to rely on the experience of foreign countries, unless one is to accept the remedy which they propound.[37]

I have said before that the strongest case for the abolition of the death-penalty is to be found in the arguments of its upholders.

7. Pampering the Murderer

The majority in the House of Lords which in 1948 defeated abolition for a trial period was based on a holy alliance between those who proclaimed with the Lord Chancellor that a life sentence was a cruelty "worse than death", and those who thought with Lord Sandhurst that it was not cruel enough.

Unless we look out (that noble Lord warned the House), prison will become a home from home, and the next thing will be that they will be giving the beggars weekend leave. . . . We have to remember that quite a large proportion of the criminal population come from, and are the result of, bad housing and bad homes. The effect would be to make prison more comfortable than home, and even now such people know that when they go to prison—and the magistrates' courts produce evidence of this—at least they will be warm throughout the winter. . . . The general view of the police is dead against this suggestion [suspension of the death-penalty]. I think it was well summed up by the Commissioner when he said that it is safer to commit murder than to cross the road. At the present moment, that is perfectly true. If you commit murder, you know that you will be out of danger of everything except of a natural death for the next ten or fifteen years. Not one of us in this House can say that. So long as we are free to roam about the streets freely, as some people do, we are liable to come to a sudden and abrupt end at any moment.[38]

Which proves that Hansard can be funnier than P. G. Wodehouse. For if there are people in this nation living under such wretched conditions that even prison is preferable to them, then decency demands that housing conditions should be improved and not that prison conditions should be made more wretched. Fortunately, people attracted to prison on these grounds exist mainly in the noble Lord's imagination, and among picturesque characters in Dickens's and Joyce Cary's novels.

But this kind of nonsense apart, it may still be thought that the swimming pool and dramatic society of Leyhill mean going too far towards coddling the criminal. The answer is that conditions even in the most modern prison seem more idyllic when one reads about them than if one has to live in them. A quarter-century ago, before the great prison reform got under way, Sir Alexander Paterson told the Select Committee:

Whatever means of education, stimulation and recreation may be employed, however you may seek to ring the changes on handicrafts and literature, skittles or chess or ping-pong, despite the invaluable labours of most devoted voluntary workers, it requires a superman to survive 20 years of imprisonment with character and soul intact.[39]

Since this was said, prison conditions have been radically changed, and terms of detention shortened. Yet even so, detention for six, eight or ten years is a very dreadful thing. It is a modern purgatory with welfare services, skittles and ping-pong, yet a purgatory nevertheless which those who never lay in gaol cannot really visualize even if endowed with sympathy and imagination.* In its matter-of-fact language, the Royal Commission says that:

The deterrent effect of imprisonment on the individual offender lies primarily in the shame of being sent to prison and the fact of being in prison, with all that that fact in itself implies—complete loss of personal liberty; separation from home, family and friends; subjection to disciplinary control and forced labour; and deprivation of most of the ordinary amenities and intercourse of everyday life. An offender is sent to prison *as* a punishment and not *for* punishment.[40]

However terrible the act that landed him in limbo was: the cracking of a human skull or the stopping of a human breath, the

---

* This writer has only spent a little more than a year in prisons in various countries (as described elsewhere), yet this short taste of limbo was sufficient to alter his whole outlook on life.

delinquent is chewing the cud of his deed and vomiting it out and swallowing it again at least once a day, multiplied by 365, multiplied by 5, 6, 7, 8, 9, 10, repeating to him or herself "if only at that moment I hadn't. . . ." Atonement consists in the knowledge, or the illusion, that one could have acted otherwise than one did; purgatory is the internal combustion of the missed chance. It is not a continuous process. It may stop after a while, or diminish and then start again in a furious crescendo: "if only . . . then I wouldn't be here." Until gradually, with ups and downs, periods of depression and periods of excitement, which are all in a day's, week's, year's work, gradually the past is burnt out and the future becomes real again; and the "I wouldn't be here" is replaced by "when I get out". At its worst, prison is limbo; at its best, it is a forced residence for adult, full-blooded and mostly temperamental people in a kind of boarding-school-cum-Y.M.C.A.-cum-Salvation-Army-dosshouse, mitigated by lectures, skittles and games on Sunday.

The worst of it is not the absence of sex, or drink, or even of the family. The first two lose their sting after a while, and at times surprisingly quickly; and the intense friendships and tensions of a convict community substitute for the third. The worst is the loss of one's adult manhood or womanhood—in the non-sexual, purely human sense. A prisoner feels as if he were castrated—not because he can't sleep with women, but because he has been deprived of the dignity of his manhood and reduced to a schoolboy or ward, to an infantile and helpless state, no longer the master of his destiny but its victim, deprived of responsibility, under constant observation: a marionette in a fair and enlightened puppet-player's hands, yet still a marionette. Even when working without supervision or playing soccer, convict team against village team, he feels that he is not quite human—a man not exactly despised, yet not exactly trusted, crippled in his rights, diminished in his self-esteem—a star prisoner, treated with benevolence, in a word a creature *almost* human.

Whatever reforms are introduced, even if the bars vanish and the prison is an open one, this basic defect cannot be remedied because it is the essence of the prisoner's condition, the irreducible core of his punishment. That is why that very wise White Paper says: "An offender is sent to prison *as* a punishment and not *for* punishment."

That is also the reason why "lifers" are so reasonable and well behaved, and give less trouble than the small fry. The primary motive is not the hope for privileges and remissions—though, of course, the earning of privilege and remission is for the prisoner the equivalent of the freeman's pursuit of career and material gains. The true reason is that the only way open to the prisoner to save the remainder of his human dignity, and to avoid further humiliation, is to be a model prisoner. That means not only outwardly obeying the rules, but inwardly accepting them as a condition of existence; or, which amounts to the same thing, to treat the rules as if they were non-existent by conforming to them, thus avoiding that they be enforced. Moreover, well-behavedness among long-termers is not regarded as "sissy", nor is unruliness and showing off regarded with approval, for it makes life more difficult for everybody, and because every disciplinary action makes a prison more grim and prison-like. On the other hand, correct and disciplined behaviour will, apart from its practical benefits, gradually earn the prisoner the respect of the warders. This, in turn, will raise his self-respect and diminish the span between the almost-human and the human condition—which he will only re-attain when he is set free.

To quote the saying about the repentant sinner who causes more rejoicing, and so forth, would be sentimental and out of place. But it is no exaggeration to say of a man who has been condemned to die and has worked himself through purgatory and finally regained his freedom, that he has earned every moment of it at a much higher price than ordinary mortals, born under kinder stars.

8. The Return to Freedom

When the prisoner has served his six, or eight, or twelve years, according to the case, he is not simply turned loose with a "go and sin no more". Steps for his reintegration into society start in fact as soon as he arrives in prison. At that stage he is interviewed by a representative of the Central After Care Association (a voluntary body under a Council appointed by the Home Secretary), who discusses his future plans with him and henceforth visits him regularly to help and advise. His progress is reviewed periodically by the Governor, medical officer and prison chaplain. Where the need arises, the co-operation of the local authorities and of the Ministry of Education or Labour is obtained. As the end of his term of imprisonment approaches, he may be granted permission to go home on leave for periods of five days, not earlier than four months and not later than two months before the date of discharge. The object of this innovation (which dates from 1951 and follows the practice of other countries) is "to contribute to the restoration of the prisoner's self-confidence by placing trust in him under conditions of complete freedom, and to give the prisoner an opportunity before his final release from prison to make contact with prospective employers, to deal with domestic problems and to renew his home ties, in order to facilitate as far as possible his absorption into society".[41]

According to the Central After Care Association's report to the Royal Commission, during the fifteen years 1934–48, the number of male prisoners convicted of murder and discharged after serving their sentence, in England and Wales, was 129. Out of these, 112 "settled down immediately". The corresponding number of females was 27, out of which 19 settled down "immediately", and 4 "fairly well".[42] Some prisoners are released on a licence which binds them to report any changes of address to the After Care Association, and to comply with certain other conditions, but they are the exception, not the rule. The general tendency is that once an ex-murderer is considered worthy and safe to be released, he should be allowed to resume a normal life without ties and reminders of the past.

It is reassuring to note that the police who, as a body, are the stoutest supporters of the death-penalty, are most co-operative in helping a man who has escaped that fate, to find his feet again. The directors of the Central After Care Association were unanimous in testifying that they have found the police in all cases most helpful, and that sometimes they go out of their way to be so. The same paradox applies to the Home Office, which stubbornly defends capital punishment and yet engages in bold, humane experiments, like "open prisons" to ease the life of those who have been spared.

9. The Answer to Straffen and Christie

A special problem is the category of murderers who are mentally abnormal, but not technically insane. As we saw before, the Home Office and the Royal Commission agree that in this class "and in it alone, are likely to be found any prisoners whom it would be unsafe ever to release".[43]

But the Christies and Straffens are not the only type who belong to this borderline category. "These prisoners do not form a homogeneous group. Some are suffering from minor forms of mental disease or mental defect, from neurosis or some kind of epileptic condition; others are psychopaths. It is this latter group with whom we are particularly concerned, since . . . there is no recognized and accepted method of treatment that can be applied to psychopaths, and many doctors believe that no treatment is effective. In the first group there are types of disorder which may respond to psychiatric treatment; of those in the second some improve as they grow older, but some never improve and are always a danger. They constitute a more solidly intractable problem than the first group, and are a persistently disturbing element in prison society." [44]

The only possible solution for this group is confinement in a special institution, half-way between ordinary prison and mental hospital, where they are treated and kept during an indeterminate period—which in some cases means to the end of their lives. A special institution of this kind is now in the process of being created in this country. On the Continent, there are several of them—the best known at Herstedvester, in Denmark. Sex offenders form the largest group; in Denmark and Holland they may be castrated on their own wish, and as a rule this leads to the extinction of the criminal impulse. But otherwise the chances of cure and release for sex offenders and psychopaths are small; whereas in other categories they are better. At the worst, a part of the mentally sick must be regarded as the drones of society, as we regard their brothers and sisters in misery, the certified insane. The distinction between the two is a matter of technical definitions, and since we regard it as a barbarity to kill the insane, it is equally barbarous to kill those whose sickness our courts deny on the strength of a diagnostical rule, established by lawyers in 1843.

The matter is simple enough. But not so to the Ellenborough-Goddard axis. . . . Let us return, for the last time, to the Lords' debate in 1948, when Lord Goddard had, among other things already quoted, this to say on the subject:

If the criminal law of this country is to be respected, it must be in accordance with public opinion, and public opinion must support it. . . . In my humble opinion, I believe that there are many, many cases where the murderer should be destroyed. . . . Let me give your Lordships two instances to justify my view that some of these bestial murderers should be destroyed. Last November, I tried a case at Bristol. The prisoner, thank God, was not a British subject. He was a Pole, but he had been here for quite a long time. On his own confession, having finished his supper, during which he had only a moderate quantity to drink, he said that he had an overwhelming desire for sexual intercourse. He went out and, finding no young girl near his camp, went to a little village alehouse on the outskirts of the village, kept by an old woman of seventy-six. He entered that woman's house at dead of night, he went into her room, he raped her, he committed another nameless offence on that poor creature's body, and he killed her. At the end of last sittings, another case came before me in the Court of Criminal Appeal. I regret to say that this time the prisoner was a British subject. In a mining village in South Wales, a young man of about twenty-two years of age who had had a little to drink —not much, for no one suggested he was drunk—while pushing his way down an alley knocked against an old woman who reproached him—reviled him, if you like, for I expect she used strong language at him. He struck at her so that she fell on the sidewalk and fractured her skull. Then he kicked her to death and raped her as she was dying on the pavement. . . .[45]

It is somewhat odd that both cases which the Lord Chief Justice selected to regale their Lordships with were sexual murders committed on old women. It would be even odder if he did not realize that a lad of twenty-two who raped an old woman *on the pavement* and kicked her to death, and the other man who raped a woman of seventy-six and committed "another nameless offence" on her, were both pathological, mentally sick cases. He did not deny that they were insane; he merely concluded that some cases were so awful that the prisoner should be destroyed. And he made his meaning unmistakably clear in his evidence before the Royal Commission when he stated that though he knew that Ley was insane, he "thought it very proper that he should have hanged".[46]

Both the law of the land and the law of humanity take the opposite view: that disease of body or mind is not a reason to destroy a man. The Royal Commission went out of its way to reject the philosophy of the highest judge of the country:

We make one fundamental assumption, which we should hardly have thought it necessary to state explicitly if it had not lately been questioned in some quarters. It has for centuries been recognized that, if a person was, at the time of his unlawful act, mentally so disordered that it would be unreasonable to impute guilt to him, he ought not to be held liable to conviction and punishment under the criminal law. Views have changed and opinions have differed . . . but that principle has been accepted without question. Recently, however, the suggestion has sometimes been made that the insane murderer should be punished equally with the sane, or that, although he ought not to be executed as a punishment, he should be painlessly exterminated as a measure of social hygiene. . . . Such doctrines have been preached and practised in National-Socialist Germany, but they are repugnant to the moral traditions of Western civilization and we are confident that they would be unhesitatingly rejected by the great majority of the population of this country.[47]

X

THE MONTHLY SACRIFICE

We shall look upon crime as a disease. Evil will be treated in charity instead of anger. The change will be simple and sublime. The cross shall displace the scaffold. Reason is on our side, feeling is on our side, and experience is on our side.

VICTOR HUGO

In 1938, a Gallup poll on the question whether the death-penalty should be maintained or not, showed 50% "ayes" in favour of hanging, and 50% "nays" and "don't knows". Nine years later, in a similar poll, the "ayes" in favour of hanging had increased to 68%. Another eight years later, in July, 1955, the *Daily Mirror* arranged a new poll which revealed a complete reversal of public opinion: 65% voted against the death-penalty—about the same proportion which previously had voted for it.

Such wild fluctuations of public opinion are unusual in a country where the floating vote amounts only to a small fraction of the total, and General Elections are decided by narrow margins. There is, no doubt, a steady, gradual increase in the number of people who favour a more humane administration of the law; but this slowly mounting tide does not account for the violent gales which blow now in one direction, now in the other. When the vision of the gibbet appears on the nation's horizon, opinion swings and twists like the body suspended from it; eyes bulge and reason is strangled. If the last victim happens to arouse pity—a feeble-minded boy for instance, unhinged by the movies, or a mother of two children, half-crazed by gin and jealousy—up go the "nays" of mercy like a flight of doves; if he is a cool customer like Christie, up go the "ayes" like a swarm of vultures. Let us agree that this is not a dignified or desirable state of affairs.

The manner in which governments and politicians handle the problem of the death-penalty is no more dignified, though less excusable. Public opinion swings, moved by passion and pity, but

Home Secretaries, as we saw, obey a peculiar swing-rule of their own. In recent Parliamentary debates, Home Secretary, Major Lloyd George, who, in 1948, had voted for the abolition of hanging, defended it on the familiar grounds: its unique value as a deterrent, the difficulty of finding a satisfactory alternative punishment and, lastly, that public opinion is opposed to abolition. All this is as old as Methuselah and no more need be said on the first two points; but the third, alas, cannot be dismissed. It is true, of course, that governments only use public opinion as a shield when it is convenient to them. When public opinion demanded that Bentley be reprieved, the Government disregarded it. On a previous similar occasion, the then Home Secretary, Lord Brentford, explained that "no Secretary of State worthy of his name could permit himself to be influenced in a matter of that kind by public clamour". Mob mercy, he continued, was as bad as mob execution. There was no difference between a lynching mob and a mob trying "to usurp the office of the Minister" by petitioning for a Royal reprieve.[1] Thus the argument proved to be beautifully reversible: Heads I win, tails you swing.

An example of this double-think was given by the Home Secretary in a recent debate. A few minutes after he had refused to consider abolition because the public was in favour of hanging, he was asked the following question:

Mr. Price (*Lab. Westhoughton*): Does he realize that British public opinion was shocked and scandalized by the gross commercialism of certain showmen in Blackpool who put on exhibition an effigy of Ruth Ellis, one day after she was hanged at Holloway Gaol?

Major Lloyd George: . . . It would hardly be practicable or indeed desirable if every departure from public opinion . . . in this country was made the subject of legislation.[2]

Thus hanging cannot be stopped, because we must listen to public opinion; and the desecration of a dead woman cannot be stopped because we must not listen to public opinion.

Nevertheless, public opinion is still the strongest passive support of the hang-hards. The main reasons for this are ignorance, traditional prejudice and repressed cruelty.

The public's ignorance of the facts and arguments of the issue is of course artificially fostered by official spokesmen and other oracles. The bogies conjured up by Ellenborough have not lost their

effect even after a century and a half. The public is made to believe
that only the hangman can protect them against "the hardened robber"; that it is quite impossible for an innocent to be hanged; that
no mentally sick person is hanged; that all the burglars of the realm
are impatiently waiting for Abolition D-Day to arm themselves with
guns, and that the day of the hanging judges is past. They are also
being given the impression that hanging is a normal thing outside
England in the contemporary world, that only some small freak
nations, like Switzerland or Norway, have engaged in freak experiments of penal reform, that all murderers are Haigh-type monsters,
that sex-maniacs must either be hanged or turned loose, that thirteen
reprieves per year would cost the taxpayer millions and that the dislocation of the cerebral vertebrae and rupture of the jugular vein
is a humane and instantaneous procedure which is always carried
out swiftly and without a hitch.

The effect of this official smoke-screen is that the stark reality of
the gallows is hidden in the background, and, at the same time, the
public is led to believe that the whole subject is a highly controversial one in which the arguments of both sides are evenly bal-
anced and can only be judged by experts. Once the smoke-screen
is dispelled, people will realize that hanging is simply a stupid and
cruel relic of the past, much more stupid and cruel than they ever
imagined. About half a dozen books were written in the last few
years crammed with facts in favour of the abolition of hanging. Why
has nobody written a book in defence of it? I believe the reason is,
as I have tried to show, that the strongest case against capital punishment is to be found in the arguments of its defenders. I challenge
them to produce quotations from abolitionists as silly or ignorant
or dishonest as the collection of pro-hanging quotations in this
book.

Ignorance can be cured, but not callousness. Those who feel
strongly that this nation should continue to break people's necks
or strangle them to glory, display a curious mixture of insensitivity
and sentimental traditionalism which makes them impervious to
reasoned argument. They believe that legal murder prevents illegal
murder, as the Persians believed that whipping the sea will calm
the storm. They will say that England cannot do without hanging,
and when you point to the example of other countries which get
along perfectly without it, they will say that foreigners are differ-

ent. They will say that English justice makes hanging by legal error impossible, and when you quote names of people who were hanged in error, they will answer that you cannot expect any system to be perfect. They will say that hanging is the most humane method of execution, and if you quote cases of a man having to be carried to the drop "strapped sitting in a chair" or women dragged to it in a free-for-all fight, they will answer that mentioning such matters is in bad taste. As a former Home Secretary said: "The less said at the inquest, the better; it is preferable to draw a veil over these cases." [3] What matters is that the victim is dead, not the manner in which he was made to die, and the nation is busy washing their hands.

Those who are determined that this barbarity should continue are to be found in all classes and professions, from retired Colonels to bus drivers; the boundary is not defined by income or education. George Bernard Shaw wrote that the treatment of the "human vermin in the Commonwealth", including idiots and morons, ought to be "kill, kill, kill, kill, kill them". His arguments were essentially the same as the charwoman's "What I always say is let 'em swing; that's what I always says"; which again are essentially the same as certain speeches I have quoted from the House of Lords. The division is not between rich and poor, highbrow and lowbrow, Christians and atheists: it is between those who have charity and those who have not. The Bishops who in 1810 voted death for a five-shilling theft had no more charity than the atheist Shaw.

In this age of mass production, charity has come to mean dropping sixpence into a box and having a paper-flower pinned on one's lapel. But originally it had a different and revolutionary meaning: "Though I speak with the tongues of men and of angels, and have not charity, I am become as sounding brass, or a tinkling cymbal. And though . . . I have all faith, so that I could remove mountains, and have not charity, I am nothing. And though I bestow all my goods to feed the poor, and have not charity, it profiteth me nothing." Charity in this ancient meaning of the word is about the most difficult virtue to acquire: much more difficult than equity, mere kindness, or even self-sacrifice. For true charity presupposes a rare combination of gifts: humility-plus-imagination. Humility without imagination makes the pious bore; imagination without humility makes the brilliant cynic. But where the two appear together, they are an active healing force for the ailments of man and the wounds of society—and a burden on him who is blessed and cursed by possessing it. For his motto must then be: *homo sum: humani nihil a me alienum puto*—I am human and nothing human is alien to me. And one must be very humble indeed, and very imaginative indeed, to accept this; for it means that neither Hitler nor Christie, neither young Bentley nor old Mr. Pierrepoint, can be excluded from the demands of charity—since what we dislike in them is merely an extreme development of some of the less palatable aspects of ourselves, of some human quality in which we all share. The test of one's humanity is whether one is able to accept this fact— not as lip service, but with the shuddering recognition of a kinship: here but for the grace of God, drop I.

This guilty recognition of an inner kinship may, however, be repressed from consciousness and turn with a vengeance into the opposite of charity. When Ruth Ellis had shot her lover in a frenzy of jealousy and resentment, women were in general less inclined to demand a reprieve than men. Many of them, involved in similarly unhappy circumstances, may have felt some unconscious envy at the thought that if they were denying themselves the luxury of murdering a faithless lover or husband, then those who indulge in it ought to pay the price. Their apparent moral indignation was a mixture of envy and vindictiveness. Sexually frustrated women will persecute their luckier sisters under the same cloak of moral righteousness.

There also exists a kind of pseudo-charity, expressed in sayings like "you ask for sympathy for the murderer, but what about the poor victim?" The answer is that we sympathize with the victim but we do not wish to add a second crime to the first. We sympathize with the victim's family, but do not wish to cause additional suffering to the murderer's family. We did not abolish drawing and quartering for lack of sympathy with the victim, but because cruelty is incompatible with the notion of charity.

There is a spoonful of sadism at the bottom of every human heart. Nearly a century ago, Charles Dickens wrote that "around Capital Punishment there lingers a fascination, urging weak and bad people towards it and imparting an interest to details connected with it, and with malefactors awaiting it or suffering it, which even good and well-disposed people cannot withstand". His contemporary,

John Bright, knew that "capital punishment, whilst pretending to support reverence for human life, does in fact, tend to destroy it". And even earlier, Samuel Romilly said that cruel punishments have an inevitable tendency to produce cruelty in people. The image of the gallows appeals to their latent sadism as pornography appeals to their latent sexual appetites.

There is a famous saying by a Press tycoon that what the newspaper reading public wants is blood, sex (he used a more anatomical expression) and the national flag. It was the *Daily Mail* version of Freud's discovery that the sexual instinct and the instinct of aggression are, beside tribal loyalty, the most powerful biological drives. Civilization obliges us to keep the little Stone Age man inside us under strict control; but while the sexual appetites find a reasonable amount of authorized or tolerated outlets, aggression has almost none. Competitive sports are supposed to provide such an outlet, but it does not amount to much: cricket and soccer do not allow scratching, biting and strangling. So, on peaceful Sunday mornings, before setting out for Church, we avidly gulp down the *Dirt in the World*. True to Northcliffe and Freud, the largest space in the popular Press is given to divorce and murder cases, catering to the two basic instincts. Some fifty million readers of the popular Press express their unctious disgust about this state of affairs, yet they lap up the contents of the slop-basin to the last drop, for *homo sum* and such is human nature.

The point is not to deny the existence of the fur-clad little man in us, but to accept him as part of the human condition, and to keep him under control. Newspaper editors who have to earn money for the proprietors cannot be expected to stop making the most of hanging, so long as hanging exists. In countries from which the death-penalty has vanished, this dirty sensationalism has vanished too, and murder trials do not get more publicity in the Press than cases of burglary or fraud now get in this country. For the fascination of the murder trial, and its appeal to unconscious cruelty, lies in the fact that a man is fighting for his life like a gladiator in the arena, and in the thrilling uncertainty whether the outcome will be thumbs up or thumbs down. One only wonders why the bookmakers and tote do not come in.

A short time ago, there was a national outcry against horror comics, particularly from the judges who defend the real horror of hanging.

Yet a horror comic is always less exciting, because it deals with fictitious events, than the matter-of-fact statement that a real person,
whose photographs we have seen, whose words we have read, has
been officially strangled. The drawings of monsters and mad sextons
enamoured of drowned blondes are less pernicious, because of their
science-fiction remoteness, than the studiedly sober report about the
traces of brandy found in the executed woman's stomach. Moral deterrent, public example, reverence for human life—what bloody
hypocrisy! So long as there are bull fights there will be *aficionados*,
and so long as there are gladiators there will be a circus audience.
There is a poisoned spray coming from the Old Bailey which cor-
rupts and depraves; it can only be stopped by abolishing its cause,
the death-penalty itself. Two centuries ago, visitors to this country
were puzzled to find the road to London dotted with grizzly gibbets.
They are still puzzled by the same contradiction between the Englishman's belief in the necessity of hanging and his proverbial virtues
of tolerance to man, kindness to animals, fussing over plants and
birds. They fail to understand the power of tradition, his reluctance
to abandon any of his cherished prejudices. Tradition has a hypnotic
effect which commands blind belief, an instinctive recoil from any
new departure as a "dangerous experiment", and unwillingness to
listen to reasoned argument. This is why the principal defenders of
hanging have always been the most tradition-bound bodies of the
nation: the House of Lords, the Bishops' Bench, the upper ranks of
the gowned and wigged profession. Yet in spite of their power and
influence over the public mind, chunk after chunk of sacred tradition has been wrenched from their hands: the pillory and the duck-
ing chair, the stake and the gibbet, the cat-o'-nine-tails; and within
the next few years the strangling cord will be wrested from them too.

For despite the inertia of man's imagination and its resistance to
reason and fact, public opinion is at long last beginning to realize
that it does not need the hangman's protection; that the deliberate
taking of life by the State is unjustifiable on religious or philosophic
or scientific grounds; that hanging by mistake will go on as long
as capital punishment will go on, because the risk is inherent in its
nature; that the vast majority of murderers are either mentally sick
and belong to the mental sick ward, or victims of circumstance, who
can be reclaimed for human society; and that the substitution of the
life sentence for the death-penalty exposes the peaceful citizen to

no greater risk than that of being killed by lightning in a bus queue, and considerably less than the risk of being a passive accomplice in the execution of an innocent or a mentally deranged person, which the citizens of this country run on the average thirteen times a year.

It is not only a question of the thirteen individual lives which we offer annually as a sacrifice to the stupid moloch of prejudice. The gallows is not only a machine of death, but a symbol. It is the symbol of terror, cruelty and irreverence for life; the common denominator of primitive savagery, mediaeval fanaticism and modern totalitarianism. It stands for everything that mankind must reject, if mankind is to survive its present crisis.

APPENDIX I

The Experience of Foreign Countries

THE FOLLOWING summaries of the consequences to which the abolishment of the death-penalty led in various countries are based on the 1929–30 Select Committee's and the 1948–53 Royal Commission's Reports and Minutes of Evidence and on B. Duesing's *Die Geschichte der Abschaffung der Todesstrafe,* Offenbach/Main, 1952. I am referring only to capital punishment for civil offences in peacetime.

Austria. Capital punishment abolished in 1950. No recent statistics available.

Belgium. Capital punishment in abeyance since 1863.

Conclusion of the report submitted by the Belgian Ministry of Justice to the Select Committee in 1930:

The lesson has been learnt that the best means of inculcating respect for human life is to refrain from taking life in the name of the law.[1]

Conclusion of the Belgian Government's Report in answer to the Royal Commission's questionnaire:

Since the practice of commuting all death sentences for civil offences was introduced, no increasing crimes or offences have been observed which could be attributed to the failure to carry out the death-penalty.[2]

Denmark. Capital punishment in abeyance since 1892; abolished in 1933. Mr. Eric Kampmann, Director General of Danish Prisons, testifying before the Select Committee, stated that crime has decreased since the death-penalty was allowed to fall into abeyance.[3] The Danish Government gave the same reply to the Royal Commission in 1948.

Finland. Capital punishment in abeyance since 1826. No statistics available.

Iceland. Capital punishment abolished, but no statistics available.

Netherlands. Capital punishment abolished in 1870, having been virtually in abeyance since 1850. Conclusion of the Netherlands Government's answer to the Royal Commission's questionnaire:

It is definitely established that the abolition of the death-penalty in the ordinary penal code has not resulted in an increase or a worsening of crime.[4]

Norway. Capital punishment in abeyance since 1875, abolished in 1905. Conclusion of the Norwegian Government's report to the Select Committee:

The experiences gained . . . have strengthened the view that the abolition of capital punishment has not caused any increase in the number of murders.[5]

Conclusion of the Norwegian Government's answer to Royal Commission's questionnaire:

There is no information to indicate that the abolition of the death-penalty has led to any increase in the number of homicides, of crimes of violence in general, or of attacks on prison staff.

Portugal. Capital punishment abolished in 1867. No statistics available.

Sweden. Capital punishment in abeyance since 1910, abolished in 1921. Conclusion of the Swedish report to the Select Committee:

On the basis of the above figures it is obviously impossible to express an opinion on the question whether the abolition of capital punishment has had any effect on the number of murders. It may, however, be stated that the correctness of the view (which appears to have been the principal motive for the abolition of the death-penalty) that the State did not require this penalty for its protection, has hitherto not been contradicted by experience.

In its answer to the Royal Commission questionnaire, the Swedish Government merely refers to the statistical tables in its report without further comment. The tables show that in the five years 1916–20 *prior to* abolition, thirty-eight persons were charged with murder and thirty-two convicted, of whom sixteen were found insane; in the five years 1922–26 *after* abolition, thirty-eight were charged and thirty convicted, of whom seventeen were found insane. Annexed to the report is a memorandum submitted by Ivar Strahl, Professor of Criminal Law, University of Upsala, which concludes:

The general view is that the abolition of the death sentence has not entailed any increase in the number of crimes.

Switzerland. Capital punishment abolished in 1874, but a revision of the federal constitution in 1879 gave each canton liberty to reintroduce it. Fifteen cantons, representing 75% of the total Swiss population, did not reintroduce it, ten cantons did. It was finally abolished in all Switzerland in 1942.

The case of Switzerland is particularly interesting, therefore, for it allows one to compare developments in abolitionist and non-abolitionist parts of the same country. In its memorandum to the Select Committee, the Swiss Government stated:

The Department [of Justice] therefore conclude that Switzerland provides no convincing evidence on the question of the value of capital punishment as a deterrent, but, on the whole, inclines to the view that the virtual abolition of capital punishment has had no perceptible effect on the rate of homicidal crime.

Eighteen years later, in its annex to the Swiss Government's answer to the Royal Commission's questionnaire, J. Graven, Professor of Criminal Law, Geneva University, provided a much more detailed analysis. The relevant passages read as follows:

The abolition of capital punishment in 1874 undoubtedly had the immediate effect of encouraging some criminals because of the disappearance of the supreme form of deterrent. In fact, it was a series of heinous murders committed in several cantons that disturbed public opinion and led to the partial restoration of capital punishment in 1879. . . . But when this first wave of homicide had died down, experience showed that serious crime was no more frequent in those cantons that did not restore capital punishment than in those that did, and that there was no great difficulty in dealing with the murderers who were not executed. . . . During the period 1864–73, when capital punishment existed, there were 11 cases in which the death sentence could have been imposed, in the ten years after capital punishment had been abolished 11 such cases, while in the next ten years there were only 5 such cases.

Such considerations, as well as general feelings of humanity, resulted in the complete abolition of capital punishment in 1942. . . . The complete abolition of the death-penalty and the general reduction in penalties laid down by the new Penal Code have not resulted in an increase in the number of homicides or in the number of crimes in general. A study of the six years before the new Code came into force and the six years following its introduction shows that, in spite of the increase in the number of offences made by the Code, and in spite of the war and the moral results of war, which caused such an alarming increase of crime in some countries, the number of crimes in Switzerland has remained constant and even began to decrease in 1947.

The memorandum concludes:

As a member of the Swiss Parliament said in 1928, "I do not conceive of the State as an executioner; I conceive of it as an educator, seeking to prevent crime, to prevent evil, to correct the offender . . . I cannot see the Switzerland of today, this ancient democracy, setting up the State as an executioner."

The upshot of all this is that seventy-five years ago abolition in certain cantons (incidentally, the most backward ones)[6] was followed by a momentary increase in crime which soon gave way to a decrease; whereas abolition in 1942, *in spite of war-time conditions,* was followed by no increase at all but by a decrease.

Switzerland is the only European country where abolition was followed by a momentary increase in crime—three-quarters of a century ago; yet even in this one case it is not proven that this increase was causally related to abolition, as the following example will show. Professor P. Cornil, of the Free University of Brussels, quoted in the Royal Commission report,[7] describes a remarkable incident that took place in Belgium in 1918:

A series of robberies with murder were committed by gangs of criminals in the open country. The bandits penetrated at night to isolated farms and forced the farmers to tell where their money was hidden by beating them and by burning their feet. . . . When the farmers resisted, they were killed on the spot. One of these gangs was arrested, tried, and the five leaders were sentenced to death. . . . Contrary to the customary rule, the Attorney-General refused in the case of the 26-year-old Pierre N. to recommend the commutation of the sentence . . . and insisted that an example should be made. . . . At that time the Minister of Justice was the socialist Emile Vandervelde. He refused to have the man executed. . . . The sentence *was* commuted. And then, a strange thing occurred. Almost suddenly, that series of robberies died away without any apparent cause. . . .

Whenever I relate this incident, I cannot refrain from pointing out how narrowly we escaped a grave danger. Suppose for a moment that this man, following the Attorney-General's proposal, had been put to death, and then that special kind of crime had disappeared almost immediately. What a victory for the advocates of capital punishment! They certainly would not have hesitated to conclude that this improvement was due to the deterrent effect of capital punishment and it is quite probable that the death-penalty for the common law criminal would have been reinstated and retained for a long time.

Italy. Capital punishment abolished in 1890 (last execution, 1876); restored by Mussolini in 1931, and abolished for the second time in 1944.

The homicide rate (including murder, manslaughter, etc.) gradually declined from an annual average of 10·6 per hundred thousand of the population in 1880 to 3·5 in 1920.[8]

The second abolition coincided with a peak period in murder: 13 per hundred thousand in 1946 (no figures for 1945), but fell rapidly to 8·8 in 1947 and 6·9 in 1948.[9] The first decline was no doubt mainly caused by gradual social progress; the second, by return to normality after war and defeat; whatever the causes were, abolition of the death-penalty did not arrest the fall in the homicide rate.

Western Germany. Capital punishment abolished on May 24th, 1949.

As one would expect, the German statistics are the most thorough and complete. They are so thorough that, in pre-Nazi days, legal executions were included in official murder statistics under the heading "voluntary homicide".[10] The following official figures were published by Dr. Bernhard Duesing, *op. cit.* The first column indicates the monthly average homicide rate before, the second column after abolition of the death-penalty in the various Federal Republics. In some cases the figure in the first column was computed over three, in others over two, years before abolition; the second figure in all cases refers to the two years after abolition. Some Federal Republics included attempted murder and manslaughter, others did not. In one case (Wurtemburg-Hohenzollern) infanticide is included.

No doubt, as in the case of Italy, the downward trend after abolition reflects a return from war and tyranny to more humane standards. Yet it should be noted that both countries embarked on the experiment of abolition in a period of chaos, when the murder-rate

	Average monthly homicide rate before abolition	Average monthly homicide rate after abolition
North-Rhine Westphalia	9·08	5·83
Bavaria	16·4	9·41
Lower Saxonia	17·1	8·16
Hesse	4·12	1·79
Wurtemburg-Baden	5·83	2·95
Palatinate and Rhineland	3·33	3·00
Schleswig-Holstein	3·83	2·12
Hamburg	2·37	1·41
Baden	1·13	0·58
Wurtemburg-Hohenzollern	1·88	3·95 *
Bremen	0·63	0·29
West Berlin	2·25	2·05

* Infanticide included; see above.

was at its peak and when it was easy for the defenders of the death-penalty to argue, as they argue in this country, that "this is not the proper moment for experiments".

Commonwealth Countries and U.S.A. Several states in the U.S.A. and Commonwealth countries abolished the death-penalty and later reintroduced it; others never abolished it; yet others stuck to abolition. The Royal Commission quotes Professor Th. Sellin's exhaustive study in comparing the homicide curves between neighbour-countries or states which are "closely similar in composition of population and social and economic conditions generally, in some of which capital punishment has been abolished and in others not". Of Commonwealth countries, he established comparative tables between:

(*a*) New Zealand—capital punishment in abeyance since 1935, abolished in 1941, reintroduced in 1950.

(*b*) Queensland—in abeyance since 1911, abolished in 1922, not reintroduced, and

(*c*) New South Wales—capital punishment never abolished.

The comparison showed that the fluctuations in the homicide rate of all three countries exhibited "a striking similarity" regardless whether capital punishment was retained, abolished or reintroduced. Similar conclusions were reached in the United States of America.

The following table [11] shows the position in the fifteen states which at one time have abolished the death sentence:

	Date of Abolition	Date of Restoration	Date of Re-abolition
Michigan	1847	—	—
Rhode Island *	1852	—	—
Wisconsin	1853	—	—
Iowa	1872	1878	—
Maine	1876	1883	1887
Kansas	1887	1935	—
Colorado	1897	1901	—
Minnesota	1911	—	—
Washington	1913	1919	—
Oregon	1914	1920	—
North Dakota *	1915	—	—
South Dakota	1915	1939	—
Tennessee †	1915	1917	—
Arizona	1916	1918	—
Missouri	1917	1919	—

* Except for a prisoner serving a life sentence and convicted of the murder of a guard or keeper.

† Capital punishment was retained for rape during these years.

Five of the ten states which restored capital punishment after a period of abolition did so under the impact of the crime wave at the end of World War I, which affected death-penalty and abolition countries alike; just as the subsequent decrease in the crime rate affected both categories in the same way. The reason for reintroduction was, as a member of the Royal Commission put it, "always the same: something happens which arouses popular feeling, probably quite irrationally, and the legislature rush into imposing the death-penalty." [12] Professor Sellin gave the same opinion: "During the demobilisation period . . . it was assumed that it had been a mistake to abolish the penalty and they reintroduced it; yet the homicide rates of later years indicate that there was no relation between the two." [13]

To quote a few examples of an earlier period: Iowa abolished the death-penalty in 1872 and restored it in 1878. During the seven years previous to abolition, the average number of murder and manslaughter convictions was 2·6 and 3·4. During the seven abolition

years the corresponding rates were 8·8 and 5·9. During the seven
years after reintroduction of capital punishment they were 13·1 and
5·6.[14] Colorado abolished in 1897, restored in 1901. The annual averages in the five years before abolition were 15·4 and 2·6; during
the four years of abolition, 18 and 4, and during the five years following reintroduction, 19 and 1·5.[15]

Comparison between groups of states similar in social structure
and economic conditions again led to the same result. Thus Colorado
and Missouri abolished capital punishment only briefly; Kansas
abolished it in 1887 and reintroduced it in 1935. But that did not
make any difference. The murder-rate declined after 1935 in all three
states; but in spite of the novelty of the deterrent in Kansas "the improvement of the murder-rate in Kansas after restoration of capital
punishment was not greater than the improvement in the other
two states".[16] The improvement for the decade 1936–45 over the
decade 1925–34 was in Colorado 40%, in Missouri 47%, in Kansas
44%. At the end of its exhaustive statistical study the Royal Commission endorsed Sellin's view that:

The murder trends are very similar in the states that have abolished
capital punishment and those that have not . . . The only conclusion
which can be drawn from the figures is that whether the death-penalty
is used or not, or whether executions are frequent or not, both death-
penalty states and abolitionist states show rates which suggest that
these rates are conditioned by other factors than the death-penalty. . . .
In spite of some differences in the *level* of the rates of these states,
which is determined by the peculiar social and economic conditions of
each and the composition of their populations, the general picture is the
same, a rise in the rates of the early twenties and a downward trend since
then.

APPENDIX II

PATTERNS OF MURDER

*A Survey of Men and Women Executed
in England, Scotland and Wales during
the Five Years 1949–1953*

THE LIST printed below is a complete record of all murderers executed in the five years 1949–53, with a brief description of their
crime. It is intended to fill a conspicuous gap, for no such record for
any period past or present has hitherto been published by the Home
Office. The only available information of a related kind is a survey,
published in 1905, by Sir John Macdonell, C.B., LL.D., Master of
the Supreme Court, which tabulates the motives of murder during
the preceding twenty years; and a similar tabulation of motives,
published by the Royal Commission for the years 1900–49. These
statistical summaries do not mention individual cases, and provide
no answer to the question: Who are the people whom we hang? The
absence of any concrete information on this fundamental point has
given the debate on capital punishment a somewhat abstract, un-
realistic character and has led to serious misconceptions regarding
the type of murderer who is executed. Whenever the death-penalty
is discussed, one or two famous (and thus *ipso facto* untypical) cases
are quoted, but of the obscure "average murderer," hanged on an
average one a month, very little is known.

The five-year period 1949–53 was singled out for reference in the
Home Secretary's statement in the recent Parliamentary debate on
the second reading of the Abolition Bill on March 12th, 1956. In
that statement the Home Secretary contrasted the type of murderer
who was reprieved with those who were executed. He said, *i.a.*:

"Many hon. Gentlemen in this House are of the opinion that, because
reprieved murderers today are released after nine, eight or seven years,

or whatever it may be, that is what is going to happen if imprisonment takes the place of execution. I can assure the House that that is not so. . . . All the murderers who have been reprieved have been reprieved because of extenuating circumstances—either because of their youth, provocation, or pathetic circumstances of one kind or another.

"If we look at the records of those who have been executed, on the other hand, I can assure the House that there will be no question of release after nine years, and that is a point which has to be clearly understood. . . .

"I have looked into this possibility with a great deal of care, and on a rough assessment—obviously, it can be no more than that—of the murderers executed between 1949 and 1953, something like 60 would have had to be detained for periods of up to 20 years and some 25 for longer, some of them for the whole course of their natural lives. . . . They would have to be kept under conditions of maximum security."—*Hansard*, Vol. 550, No. 115, columns 88 and 89.

The operative phrase in this statement is "if we look at the records of those who have been executed." These records were not available either to Parliament or to the public when the Home Secretary made his statement. An attempt to supply this missing element of information is made below.* Even in this necessarily compressed form it will enable the reader to form an independent opinion on the Home Secretary's statements.

1949

1. MARGARET ALLEN, 43, killed in a quarrel an elderly woman friend. The judge described the act as "senseless, unjustified and purposeless." Defence: insanity. Allen was the twentieth child of a family of twenty-two. At 29 she went to a hospital, afterwards said that she had had an operation which changed her sex, and had worn

---

* Owing to the Home Office's refusal to make the shorthand transcripts of murder trials available to the public, the record had to be compiled from the material available in the Press Association's files. They consist of Press cuttings and (though not in all cases) of the Press Association Special Reporting Service's trial reports. Accordingly, the survey could not be based on official sources, but an effort was made to state objectively the relevant features of each case as far as these could be ascertained from the files. Jury recommendations to mercy are marked [R.M.] and strong recommendations [S.R.M.]. Where the accused had a previous criminal record, and it is mentioned in the files, the fact is stated. The cases are arranged in the chronological order of the executions, *not* in the order of the crime or trial dates.

men's clothes ever since. After her execution Chaplain Walker, of Strangeways, resigned from the prison service. Hanged on January 12th, 1949.

2. GEORGE SEMINI, 24, a Maltese miner, inflicted a fatal knife wound in a fight against three men. One of the three had made an offensive remark about Semini's girl friend as they walked past. He had a previous record of violence. Defence: provocation and "chance medley." In rejecting Semini's appeal the Lord Chief Justice quoted the "test of the reasonable man" on provocation. Hanged on January 27th, 1949.

3. JAMES FARRELL, aged 18, killed his girl friend, aged 14. Defence: insanity. Farrell's mother had been in a mental home for the past three and a half years. Hanged on March 3rd, 1949.

4. KENNETH STRICKSON, aged 21, killed Borstal matron Irene May Phillips, 56, in an alleged brainstorm. Defence: insanity. E.E.G. abnormal; medical officer of Lincoln Prison testified to "abnormal parental and personal psychopathic and epileptic history." Father "a lunatic" (according to counsel, R. Paget), mother went off with another man when Strickson was one; brought up by grandmother and in orphanage. Hanged on March 22nd, 1949.

5. [R.M.] HARRY LEWIS, 21, of no fixed address, a small-time burglar, entered through an open window the flat of cartoonist Michaelson. Surprised by victim, he knocked him down with a steel chair. Lewis was unarmed. Michaelson died the next day. Jury recommendation to mercy. Hanged on April 21st, 1949.

6. BERNARD COOPER, 49, strangled his wife allegedly because she accused him of continuing to carry on improper relations with his daughter, aged 14 (which he admitted, but said he had stopped), and admonished him to let himself be castrated. Hanged on May 18th, 1949.

7. DENNIS NEVILLE, labourer, 22, killed his girl friend of 21 after she told him she was with child by another man. Discharged from the Army with 20 per cent. disability pension because of "anxiety state of psycho-neurosis." After his discharge his father was killed in a brawl and his brother killed in action. Two defence psychiatrists testified to schizophrenia. Hanged on June 2nd, 1949.

8. SIDNEY CHAMBERLAIN, 32, lorry driver, married, had been associating with a girl of 15; when his wife and the girl's parents objected he strangled her, allegedly at her own request, intending to

commit suicide. Twice refused legal aid. Defence: insanity. Medical evidence for defence put his mental age at 11, medical evidence for prosecution put it at 12. Hanged on July 28th, 1949.

9. [*S.R.M.*] REX HARVEY JONES, 22, Rhondda Valley miner, strangled his girl friend of 20 on a Welsh mountain-side after intimacy and seven pints of beer, then called the police and led them to the body. He had an exemplary character. Mr. Justice Croom-Johnson, in summing up: "You have to steel your hearts against good character and steel your hearts in order to see that justice is done, not merely to the individual, but for the good of all citizens." Strong jury recommendation to mercy. Hanged on August 4th, 1949.

10. ROBERT MACKINTOSH, 21, steel worker, strangled his girl friend of 16. Pleaded mental blackout because "since Egypt and Palestine not the same person as before." Hanged on August 4th, 1949.

11. JOHN GEORGE HAIGH, 39, choirboy turned acid-bath murderer. Sir David Maxwell Fyfe, for the defence, quoting the testimony of Dr. Yellowlees, described him as a classic case of paranoia, acting under the delusion that a divine and mystic force drove him to drink the blood of his victims and his own urine. Hanged on August 10th, 1949.

12. WILLIAM J. DAVIES, a waiter, 31, lived with a waitress for four years. After a jealous quarrel he attacked and killed her with a knife in the café where she worked. Hanged on August 16th, 1949.

13. TIMOTHY EVANS, lorry driver, 25, illiterate and mentally defective, charged with murdering his child. Evans's counsel accused prosecution witness Christie of murdering Mrs. Evans and the child. Hanged on November 8th, 1949.

14. [*S.R.M.*] BENJAMIN ROBERTS, a miner, 23, found his girl friend in the arms of another man. Shot her, then shot himself in the head with a double-barrelled sporting gun. Was nursed back to life and hanged on December 14th, 1949. Strong recommendation to mercy.

15. JOHN WILSON, 26, a Durham miner, strangled his girl friend in a cornfield, then confessed immediately to his father. Defence: provocation. Hanged on December 14th, 1949.

16. E. S. COUZINS, 49, a caretaker, shot his woman friend's son-in-

law because the victim "made trouble between them," then cut the victim's throat and his own throat. Defence: insanity. Hanged on December 30th, 1949.

1950

17. JAMES FRANK RIVETT, 21, labourer, strangled a schoolgirl aged 17, with whom he had been intimate for several years, then gave himself up to the police. He was tried at Suffolk Assizes on January 20th, 1950. Counsel for the Crown raised the issue on Rivett's fitness to plead. Dr. Calder, a psychiatrist, and Dr. Basil Tracey, medical officer at Norwich Prison, both said Rivett was certifiably insane. The judge, Mr. Justice Stable, told the jury it was for them to decide; not the doctors.

The jury returned after an hour, saying they had been unable to reach a unanimous decision and asked for further guidance. They retired a second time, then found Rivett "sane and fit to plead." The judge called the jury's findings "a very sensible verdict."

The case was transferred to Norwich Assizes, where a new jury was sworn in. The medical officer of Norwich Prison again testified that Rivett was unfit to plead, and Dr. Matheson, medical officer at Brixton Prison, confirmed that Rivett was certifiably insane and "would not be able to understand fully the proceedings." Rivett, he stated, was suffering from schizophrenia.

The jury retired for seven minutes, then returned to announce that Rivett was sane and fit to plead.

A third jury was now sworn in and Rivett formally charged with murder. Rivett answered the charge with a plea of guilty. His counsel, Sir Charles Doughty, said: "You have heard this man plead guilty to the charge. He does not want to get off. It is an incredible position and a difficult position for counsel. I am pleading against the capital sentence against his will and against his instructions."

Dr. Matheson and Dr. Tracey again testified that Rivett was insane, and a Harley Street specialist, Dr. Louis Rose, testified that Rivett was obsessed with fantasies of self-destruction.

Mr. Justice Stable in his direction to the jury asked them to remember the difference "between mad and bad." The jury found

Rivett guilty, and he was sentenced to death. Mr. Justice Stable, in discharging the jury, said: "I am satisfied the contribution the jury system makes to the administration of criminal law is invaluable."

The Court of Criminal Appeal rejected Rivett's appeal on February 27th. Lord Goddard, in delivering judgment of the Court, said, *i.a.*:

"The evidence that he was unfit to plead was that he was suffering from schizophrenia, which was apparently a modern and perhaps more imposing name for what used to be called *dementia praecox* [*sic*]. . . .

"All the doctors agreed that he knew what he was doing; for the rest, their opinion was that he did not know it was wrong, or that he did not know how wrong it was. But none of them ventured to say that a schizophrenic, or at any rate this schizophrenic, did not know that murder was wrong. . . .

"The second matter of emphasis was that it was for the jury and not for medical men of whatever eminence to determine the issue. Unless and until Parliament ordained that the question was to be determined by a panel of medical men, it was to a jury, after proper direction by a Judge, that by the law of this country the decision was to be entrusted. . . .

"Let it be assumed he suffered from schizophrenia, or whatever doctors might call it; . . . a jury of his country were satisfied that he was responsible, and it was not for the Court of Criminal Appeal to say that he was not."—*Times* Law Report, February 28th, 1950.

Hanged on March 8th, 1950.

18. GEORGE KELLY, 27, and his friend Connolly, 26, were jointly charged with having in the course of a planned robbery in a cinema in Liverpool, killed the manager by revolver shots. In the affray the assistant manager was also shot to death. Kelly had a long criminal record for assault, larceny and receiving stolen property. He denied the charge. The further developments of the case were summed up in a memorandum submitted by the Muir Society, a Scottish lawyers' organisation for penal reform, to the Royal Commission in March, 1950: "Connolly and Kelly were charged jointly with the murder of a man named Thomas. After a trial lasting thirteen days the jury disagreed and separate retrials were ordered. Kelly, after a second trial lasting six days,

was sentenced to death. When Connolly was tried a second time for the murder of Thomas, the prosecution offered no evidence on that charge, and on the direction of the judge the jury returned a formal verdict of not guilty. . . .

"This society desires to express very bluntly the view that a criminal system which permits such procedure is a disgrace to a civilised country. To require an accused person to undergo such an ordeal a second time is unpardonable cruelty; nor can it be overlooked that it may seriously prejudice the fairness of the second trial. It was not improbable that jurors in the second trial would have read accounts, both condensed and misleading, of the first trial, and have formed opinions without seeing witnesses."

Hanged on March 28th, 1950.

19. Piotr Maksimowski, 33, a refuse collector in a Polish settlement camp in Buckinghamshire, had lived for five months with a woman when she confessed that she was married, with two children. They made a suicide pact; he cut her wrists, then cut his own wrists, and went to the police station "dishevelled and obviously distraught and with his shoes on the wrong feet." Victim had no injury except wrist cut, which could only have been inflicted by victim's consent. He refused legal aid, stating that he wanted to die. When sentenced to death he asked through the court interpreter whether he could be shot instead of hanged. Hanged, March 29th, 1950.

20. Water Sharpe, aged 20, apprentice, together with Gordon Lannen, 17, intended to burgle Abraham Harry Levine's watch-repair shop in Leeds. Levine resisted, Lannen hit him on the head with his pistol and Sharpe shot him, alleging it was by accident. Lannen reprieved because under 18. Sharpe hanged on March 30th, 1950.

21. Daniel Raven, 23, advertising agent, brutally murdered his parents-in-law, Leopold and Esther Goodman. He pleaded not guilty, denying the act, but evidence for insanity was published and submitted to the Home Office by his solicitors after the trial. Raven had joined the R.A.F. at 16 and was the only survivor of a plane crash in which the remainder of the crew were killed. Discharged from the R.A.F. because of "severe anxiety neurosis." Dr. M. Mackenzie, who previously treated Raven, made a statutory declaration that he suffered from blackouts and brain-storms. Dr.

Denis Hill, of the London University Institute of Psychology, carried out E.E.G. tests in the presence of Home Office specialists, who reported (according to the solicitors' statement) that the prisoner was suffering from idiopathic epilepsy.

Sixteen thousand signatures on petition for reprieve. Hanged on July 6th, 1950.

22 and 23. ROMAN REDEL and [S.R.M.] ZBIGNIEW GOWER, two Polish labourers, both 40, held up a bank in Bristol. In the subsequent chase Robert Taylor, a judo expert, grappled with Redel, who held a revolver, and was shot to death. Gower was unarmed, but sentenced on grounds of joint responsibility. Strong recommendation to mercy for Gower. Both executed on July 7th, 1950.

24. DONALD DOUGLAS ATWELL, 24, gas worker, battered to death Lily Irene Palmer, 26, unemployed factory hand. She had been on the waiting list for an institution for mental defectives for the past three years. Atwell met her in a cinema, took her next day to the fields, where she allegedly told him she had been "out at midday with another chap. I got up and as I did so she said to me, 'You slimy bastard for bringing me out here for nothing.'" He then went berserk. Defence: insanity. Dr. C. R. Gibson, Bath police surgeon, said Atwell was mentally unstable but not certifiable, and lost control of himself because of the woman's insults.

Atwell never knew his parents, was brought up by his grandparents believing them to be his parents, and his aunts and uncles to be his sisters and brothers. Hanged on July 13th, 1950.

25. JOHN WALKER, 48, labourer, killed Francis Wilson allegedly because Wilson had been consistently cruel to his wife with whom Walker had had an affair for many years, with Wilson's consent. Hanged on July 13th, 1950.

26. [S.R.M.] ALBERT PRICE, 32, painter, murdered his wife, Gladys, with an axe and suffocated their two children in their sleep because "his mind broke down" when after years of financial trouble they received notice of eviction and had nowhere to go. He then tried to commit suicide, but lacked courage.

Plea: guilty but insane. Strong recommendation to mercy. Hanged on August 16th, 1950.

The Howard League for Penal Reform commented that the case raised an important question. The judge had told the jury that a recommendation to mercy would be forwarded. "One does not know whether, if the jury had known their recommendation was to be set aside, they might have taken another line."

27. [*S.R.M.*] Two brothers, PAUL HARRIS, 28, and Claude Harris, 30, fatally injured a man with bottles and kicks in a public-house brawl.

Plea: provocation and self-defence. They were both sentenced to death with strong recommendations to mercy.

The two brothers and their families had been known as "the inseparable Harrises." On October 27th, 1950, Claude and Paul, who shared the same condemned cell, were told that there would be no reprieve. Paul thereupon made a full confession which partially exculpated Claude. Claude's sentence was subsequently commuted; Paul was hanged, three days after the confession, on October 30th, 1950.

28. FRANK GEORGE TURNAGE, 31, ship's engineer, confessed to the sex-murder of Mrs. Julia Beesley, aged 78. Turnage insisted, against the solicitor's advice, on pleading guilty, and was sentenced to death after a trial lasting seven minutes. Hanged on November 14th, 1950.

29. NORMAN GOLDTHORPE, 40, a cook, strangled Emma Elizabeth Howe, a prostitute, 66, in Yarmouth, "to keep faith with the woman he loved."

Dr. Matheson, principal medical officer, Brixton Prison, and Dr. Tracey, medical officer, Norwich Prison, as well as Goldthorpe's Army records, described him as a psychopathic personality "with impulsiveness to self-injury or the injury of others."

Defence: insanity. Hanged on November 24, 1950.

30. JAMES HENRY CORBITT, 37, toolmaker, strangled his girl friend. She was found in the bed of their hotel room with a five-letter word written on her forehead by Corbitt with a ball-pen.

They had had an affair for eighteen months (both married to others). His diary showed that the relation was pathological on both sides. Defence: insanity. Hanged on November 28th, 1950.

31. EDWARD ISAAX WOODFIELD, 49, labourer, strangled a 65-year-old woman shopkeeper. No motive. Described as "timid, mild-mannered man." Defence: insanity. When asked if he had anything to say as to why he should not be sentenced to death he said: "God knows best, sir."

Dr. Gibson, R.U. Hospital, Bath, said he could not find any

definite evidence of present insanity in Woodfield but "I have been more unhappy about this case than about any other in which I was involved." Hanged on December 14th, 1950.

32. JAMES RONALD ROBERTSON, a Glasgow policeman, killed Catherine McCluskey by running her over in a stolen car. His defence was that he knocked her down by accident, then panicked because of stolen car, absence from his beat, and associating with the woman. Majority verdict. Case mentioned in Royal Commission Report, page 322. Hanged on December 16th, 1950.

33. NICHOLAS PERSULIOUS CROSBY, 22, a hawker in Leeds, killed a girl of 19, after raping her. Hanged on December 19, 1950.

1951

34. FRANK GRIFFIN, 40, a labourer, in a state of drunkenness got at the till of the 74-year-old licensee of a public house, and when she protested hit her and knocked her down. The woman, suffering from heart failure, subsequently died. Hanged on January 4th, 1951.

35. NENAD KOVACEVIC, 29, Yugoslav voluntary worker, fought with the partisans during the war in Yugoslavia. His father, two brothers and three sisters were shot by the Germans. His compatriot Radomir Djorovic was stated to have been a quisling fighting with the German Army. In a railway workers' cabin near Ramsbottom, where both sheltered against the rain, Djorovic was said to have taunted Kovacevic because he was crying over his family. In the subsequent fight Kovacevic picked up an axe and killed Djorovic, who was 6 feet 2 inches tall. Defence: provocation. Appeal dismissed. King Peter of Yugoslavia appealed to King George for a reprieve. Reprieve refused. Hanged on January 26th, 1951.

36. WILLIAM ARTHUR WATKINS, 49, an enameller in Birmingham, was accused of murdering his new-born baby by the woman with whom he was living. His defence was that the baby slipped out of his hands into the bath. The couple had made no preparation for the baby's birth and did not report its death.

Mr. Justice Finnemore said that "the jury might feel that, at the very least, Watkins had acted with gross negligence and, in fact, callousness.

"It is an unhappy, sordid story. In most homes the arrival of a child is an event of rejoicing and happiness. But there is the tragedy of the unwanted child, and the prosecution declares that was so in this case."

Jury out for two and a half hours. Watkins hanged on April 3rd, 1951.

37 and 38. JOSEPH BROWN, 30, a dealer, and EDWARD SMITH, 30, a lorry driver, caused the death of a 79-year-old shopkeeper in the course of a robbery. The victim, Frederick William Gosling, 79, found gagged and bound to the foot of his bed, had died from asphyxia due to the gag. Smith and Brown were hanged on April 24th, 1951.

39. JAMES VIRRELS, 56, a labourer of Worthing, murdered his landlady in the course of a violent quarrel. Defence: manslaughter. Dr. Matheson, chief medical officer, Brixton Prison, said that Virrels occasionally saw vivid flashes of red light before his eyes. Hanged on April 26th, 1951.

40. JAMES INGLIS, 30, labourer of no fixed address, strangled a prostitute, aged 50. He told the police: "I went barmy." Dr. Poole, psychiatrist, for the defence said that Inglis was suffering from an epileptic furore at the time of the offence. Dr. J. Walker, medical officer of Leeds Prison, said he could find nothing in Inglis's mental condition to explain the crime. When sentenced to death Inglis said: "All I ask now is for you to get me hanged as quickly as possible."

Hanged on May 8th, 1951.

41. JOHN DAND, 30, press operator, stabbed a 72-year-old pensioner in the heart in a quarrel about a small sum of money. Hanged on June 12th, 1951.

42. DENNIS ALBERT REGINALD MOORE, 23, a labourer of Norwich, strangled his fiancée, Eileen Cullen, 21, fourteen days before they were to have been married, then called the police. Next to the victim's body lay a note written in lipstick: "I love her—good-bye all." The girl's father agreed that they were a "devoted couple." Two psychiatrists for the defence testified that Moore was immature, unstable and liable to outbursts of explosive rage, during which he did not know what he was doing. Hanged on July 19th, 1951.

43. ALFRED GEORGE REYNOLDS, 24, of Dereham, Norfolk, shot through the head his girl friend, 19, who was about to become the mother of his child.

Defence: insanity and suicide pact. Dr. Matheson, chief medical officer of Brixton Prison, expressed the view that Reynolds had never suffered from any disease of the mind, but agreed that he had the emotions of a man of 24 controlled by the mentality of a boy of 12. When sentenced to die Reynolds smiled at the judge and said: "Thank you very much." Hanged on July 19th, 1951.

44. ROBERT DOBIE SMITH, 30, an electrician in Dumfries, was "roaming about the town threatening to shoot everyone" at three o'clock in the morning. A police car was called and when it pulled up Smith shot to death the police sergeant inside it and wounded a second one.

Three days before the crime Smith had been on a trip to Glasgow with the girl whom he was engaged to marry. She bought a crime novel which he took away from her because he "hated crime" and had written essays about its evils. This led to a quarrel and in the evening Smith began drinking. The next day a two-year-old boy, Alan Service, to whom Smith was devoted, was killed in an accident. Smith sent a wreath "to my wee pal," then went back to his drinking. Late at night he woke his brother Andrew and forced him at gun-point to write down for two hours a long and confused statement which began "Today is the 22nd of May, my birthday. When I go out of this door I'll shoot the first policeman I see. . . . I know how to use weapons because I had six years of killing men [this refers to Smith's war-time service]. . . . At the age of thirty I have no further use for this world. . . ." After writing the statement he made Andrew go out with him and ring the police from a telephone box to say "that there was a madman in Holme Avenue." He then left his brother, went to the house of a friend, Kenneth Macdonald, and dictated to him another confused confession, in which the murder he was to commit was put in the past tense.

Two psychiatrists for the defence, including the superintendent of the Gartnavel Mental Hospital, Glasgow, testified that Smith, at the time of his motiveless act, was insane. Hanged on September 15th, 1951.

45. JOHN O'CONNOR, 29, a labourer, partially strangled and

stabbed to death his landlady, aged 84, and gave himself up to the police. Since counsel for the defence had been instructed by O'Connor not to put before the court the medical evidence gathered regarding O'Connor's sanity, he was found guilty without a word on his behalf addressed to the jury. Hanged on October 24th, 1951.

46. HERBERT LEONARD MILLS, a 19-year-old dispatch clerk in Nottingham, strangled a woman of 47, Mabel Tattershaw, allegedly in order to make money out of an article for the *News of the World* describing how he found the body. The article was published by the *News of the World* and Mills a few days later handed a written confession to the *News of the World* crime reporter, allegedly to make more money. Mills had been born with crippled feet and was described by the defence as "a desperately lonely boy, cruel, boastful and vain," who gambled for high stakes and wrote bad poetry. His main motive in committing the "perfect crime" and his subsequent confession was apparently exhibitionism. Hanged on December 11th, 1951.

1952

47. HORACE CARTER, 30, a labourer of Birmingham, assaulted and strangled a girl of 11. Defence: insanity. Hanged on January 1st, 1952.

48. ALFRED BRADLEY, 24, battered to death watchman George Camp, 58, in his hut at Wythenshawe, Manchester. At his trial Bradley picked up the copy of the New Testament with which he had taken the oath, shouted: "I have finished with it," and hurled it across the court room at Mr. Justice Lynskey. The prison medical officer told the judge that Bradley was "in a highly overwrought emotional condition and in his present state not fit to give evidence." The jury were discharged and the trial reopened with a jury from another panel. Hanged on January 15th, 1952.

49. ALFRED MOORE, 36, of Kirkheaton, Huddersfield, was a poultry farmer by day and a burglar by night, who broke into mills and offices. The police having thrown a cordon round the farm, Moore, on his way home, was apprehended, and killed two police officers. Defence: mistaken identity. Hanged on February 6th, 1952.

50. [*S.R.M.*] ROY HERBERT HARRIS, 23, a silk worker, killed his

wife in the course of a violent quarrel. The Home Office pathologist testified that Mrs. Harris's wounds were "consistent with
having been made by a man in a frenzy." Defence: manslaughter.
Strong recommendation to mercy. Hanged on February 26th, 1952.

51. TAHIR ALI, 39, a sailor from Pakistan, stabbed to death his
former girl friend, who had left him for another man. Mr. Justice
Hallett said: "The position could be described as one in which the
woman had got his money and fooled him." Defence: mistaken
identity. Hanged on March 21st, 1952.

52. JAMES SMITH, 21, wounded with a dagger William Loudon
in a dance hall in Glasgow and killed with the same weapon
Martin Maloney, who came to Loudon's aid. Smith pleaded that
the act was done accidentally in self-defence. Appeal lodged on
the grounds that the prosecution failed to reveal in time to the
defence that a second dagger had been found by the police in the
dance hall. Previous record of theft and assault. Hanged on April
12th, 1952.

53 and 54. EDWARD FRANCIS DEVLIN, 22, and ALFRED BURNS,
22, both professional burglars, were convicted of battering to
death Mrs. Beatrice Rimmer, a widow of 52, after breaking into
her home in Liverpool. They took no money or other property.
They pleaded an alibi—another burglary in Manchester at the
time of the murder. After the appeal was dismissed the Home
Secretary ordered a private inquiry on new evidence offered by
the defence. The inquiry found no miscarriage of justice. Both
hanged on April 25th, 1952.

55. [S.R.M.] AJIT SINGH, 27-year-old Sikh pedlar of Bridgend,
Glamorgan, shot his former sweetheart, a widow of 27; a stray
bullet wounded another woman. Mrs. Thomas had decided to stop
seeing Singh. The jury added to its verdict of guilty "the strongest
possible plea for mercy." Appeal dismissed. Hanged on May 7th,
1952.

56. BACKERY MANNEH, 26, a native from Gambia, West Africa,
stabbed to death Joseph Aaku, another West African Negro who
trafficked in marijuana cigarettes. Manneh first denied the act, then
pleaded self-defence. Hanged on May 27th, 1952.

57. PATRICK GALLAGHER DEVENEY, 42-year-old labourer, father
of five children, strangled his wife, Jean, 37, in the course of a
quarrel. Defence: insanity. Dr. H. Miller testified that in 1942,

when he was a psychiatrist in the Army, he had certified Deveney as a psychopathic personality. As a result Deveney was discharged from the Army. Hanged on May 29th, 1952.

58. [*R.M.*] HARRY HUXLEY, 42, a labourer, shot in the street a married woman of 32 after she broke off their affair which had lasted seven years. Huxley's defence was that he merely wished to frighten her and that the gun went off accidentally. An expert of the forensic science laboratory said he tested the shotgun and found the right hammer unstable so that jarring would cause it to fall without touching the trigger. After the gun had gone off Huxley shot himself, but a metal buckle deflected the bullet from his heart. Jury recommendation to mercy. Nursed back to life and hanged on July 8th, 1952.

59. [*S.R.M.*] THOMAS EAMES, 31, a labourer, killed his mistress, Muriel Bent, after she told him that she intended to marry another man, then gave himself up. Jury recommendation to mercy. Hanged on July 15th, 1952.

60. [*S.R.M.*] FRANK BURGESS, 21, a porter, strangled a maid of 23 at a Croydon hotel. Burgess had been a voluntary patient in a mental hospital for two months. When he was born his mother was an inmate of a mental institution and he was brought up in a school for orphans. Dr. J. Matheson, of Brixton Prison, testified that Burgess was a psychopath. Strong recommendation to mercy on medical grounds. Hanged on July 22nd, 1952.

61. [*S.R.M.*] OLIVER GEORGE BUTLER, 24, factory worker, strangled his girl friend of 21. Victim's mother said that the two had been "desperately in love." Butler was a married man; he strangled the girl after she had told him that she would "find another fellow" because his wife would not divorce him. Detective Constable Hebert, who arrested Butler after Butler had given himself up, stated that Butler asked him: "Can't you hang me now? I want to be with her." Strong recommendation to mercy. Hanged on August 12th, 1952.

62. MAHMOOD HUSSEIN MATTAN, 28, a Somali seaman, was convicted of murdering with a razor Miss Volpert, a shopkeeper. More than £100 was missing. He denied the act. His counsel described him as a "half-child of nature, a semi-civilised savage." Hanged on September 3rd, 1952.

63. JOHN HOWARD GODAR, 31, a film cameraman, killed his

fiancée, Maureen Cox, 20, with forty-eight stabs in a taxi. He had been court-martialled for cowardice during the war, was subsequently treated in a psychiatric hospital and discharged from the Army on medical grounds. He stated that the girl "had been on all night about having a date with another fellow on Sunday." When charged he replied: "That's right. I just want to go where she is as quickly as possible and no messing about." Hanged on September 5th, 1952.

64. DENNIS GEORGE MULDOWNEY, 41, a porter at the Reform Club, Pall Mall, stabbed to death Christine Granville, a Polish countess, secret agent and war heroine. Motive: unrequited love. Muldowney insisted on pleading guilty, refused legal aid and was sentenced to death after a trial lasting three minutes. Hanged on September 30th, 1952.

65. [R.M.] RAYMOND JACK CULL, 21, labourer, killed his 17-year-old wife with a bayonet in her father's house, then gave himself up. They had been married a little over a month when his young wife, who had been going out with another man, left him and wrote him a farewell note. Recommended to mercy. Hanged on September 30th, 1952.

66. PETER CYRIL JOHNSON, 24, a coloured street trader of Brixton, killed in a fight his friend Charles Mead. It was intimated that their friendship was of a homosexual nature and that the fight was caused because of Johnson's jealousy of Mead's wife. In the dock Johnson had two fits of violence and after the second wanted to change his plea of self-defence to guilty. Hanged on October 9th, 1952.

67. DONALD NEIL SIMON, 32, a machinist of Slough, became jealous of his wife's friendship with another man, and after some drinking shot both of them as they were returning from a dance. Simon was a heavy drinker, had had a nervous breakdown and spent two months at a hospital for nervous and mental diseases. Hanged on October 23rd, 1952.

68. ERIC NORCLIFFE, 30, former R.A.F. sergeant, stabbed his wife, 23, and then cut his left forearm. Both were taken to hospital, where Mrs. Norcliffe died. They had been married five years and had three children. Dr. G. M. Woddis, psychiatrist for the defence, stated that Norcliffe suffered from two diseases of the mind—melancholia and temporary amnesia—during which he was unaware of what he was doing. Hanged on December 12th, 1952.

69. JOHN KENNETH LIVESEY, 24, a miller, was convicted of having stabbed to death his mother-in-law, presumably in the course of a domestic quarrel, and hanged on December 17th, 1952.

70. LESLIE GREEN, 29, an unemployed chauffeur, was convicted of killing his former employer, Mrs. Wiltshire, who surprised him while he was burgling her house. Green denied the act. Hanged on December 23rd, 1952.

71. HERBERT APPELBY, 20, a sling loader of Grangetown, stabbed to death at a wedding party John David Thomas, 29, a fitter, who had his arm round Appelby's girl friend. Psychiatrist for the defence said that Appelby did not know what he was doing at the time he committed the act because his mind was diseased. Petition for reprieve bore over 12,000 signatures, drawing attention to Appelby's youth, his previous exemplary character, and the medical evidence at the trial. Hanged on December 24th, 1952.

1953

72. JAMES JOHN ALCOTT, 22, railway fireman (former Grenadier Guardsman), stabbed to death the booking clerk of Ash Vale Railway Station, Surrey, with the apparent motive of robbery. He made no effort to cover up his tracks and was arrested the next morning in an Aldershot boarding house. After the trial it became known that Alcott, while stationed in Germany with the Grenadier Guards in 1949, had been sentenced to death by court-martial, but on the advice of the Judge Advocate-General's Department in the War Office the King had quashed the conviction and sentence.

Defence: insanity. Hanged on January 2nd, 1953.

73. GEORGE FRANCIS SHAW, 25, and GEORGE DUNN, 22, both farm labourers, were jointly convicted of having murdered an 80-year-old recluse known as "Old Nick," near Lanark. Dunn, who was stated to have a mental age of eight, was ordered to be detained in a State mental institution; Shaw was hanged on January 26th, 1953.

74. [R.M.] DEREK BENTLEY, 19, Grade 4 mental deficient, was found guilty as an accomplice in the shooting of a policeman by 16-year-old Christopher Craig. Recommended to mercy. Two hundred Members of Parliament, including ten former Ministers, placed a Motion upon the Order Paper:

"That this House respectfully dissents from the opinion of the Home Secretary that there are not sufficient grounds on which to advise the exercise of Her Majesty's mercy in the case of Derek Bentley."

Hanged on January 28th, 1953.

75. MILES WILLIAM GIFFARD, 26, an ex-public school boy and Cornwall county cricketer, murdered both his parents with an iron pipe, then threw their bodies over a cliff, with the apparent motive of getting hold of his father's car and some money to drive to London to see the girl with whom he was in love. He was arrested in front of her house.

One of the jurors, Mrs. Angele Clemence Godfrey, wrote after the trial to the Home Secretary, stating that she had disagreed with the verdict of guilty because she was convinced that Giffard was insane at the time of the murder, and that owing to a misunderstanding the disagreement was not made known to the judge; being of French origin, she did not understand English law procedure.

General George J. Giffard, the murderer's uncle, wrote after the trial to *The Times* (March 7th, 1953):

". . . The accused man had a long history of abnormality and mental illness from the age of four. As this was given fully in evidence at his trial I will not mention details beyond emphasising that the distinguished mental specialist who was called in to examine him at the age of 15, and subsequently treated him for two years, warned his parents then of the possibility of mental breakdown in the future. . . . Very little weight was given at the trial to the long history of abnormality and mental disease, and the attention of the court was focused on the point whether his behaviour on the night of the crime did or did not come within the M'Naghten Rules. . . ."

Hanged on February 25th, 1953.

76. JOHN LAWRENCE TODD, 20, an unemployed labourer, was convicted of having murdered Hugh Walker, the 82-year-old proprietor of a curiosity shop in Liverpool. The murder was apparently motiveless. Hanged on May 19th, 1953.

77. JOHN REGINALD CHRISTIE, 54, murdered at least six women and practised necrophilia after their death. Defence: insanity (gross hysteria). Hanged on July 15th, 1953.

78. PHILIP HENRY, 25, a coloured private, was convicted of assaulting Miss Flora Jane Gilligan and then pushing her unconscious body out of the window of her home in Diamond Street,

York, which resulted in death. Henry denied the crime. Hanged on July 30th, 1953.

79. MRS. LOUISA MERRIFIELD was convicted of having murdered by poisoning with phosphorus her employer, 79-year-old Mrs. Sarah Ann Rickets, for financial gain. Conflicting medical evidence. Professor Webster, Home Office pathologist, testified for the defence that the victim died of necrosis of the liver and not of the phosphorus which had been found in her body. A passage of the judge's summing up was discussed in the House of Commons debate on capital punishment in February, 1955.

Hanged on September 18th, 1953.

80. JOHN OWEN GREENWAY, 27, a machine operator, killed in a quarrel a widowed woman of 68 with whom he lodged. The reason for the quarrel was that "Chris," a second lodger with whom Greenway shared a bed, had left "because he found the food bad." Defence counsel stated that he was not in a position to discuss Greenway's mental state because Greenway insisted on pleading guilty and seemed "to wish to die." Hanged on October 20th, 1953.

81. JOSEPH CHRISTOPHER REYNOLDS, 31, strangled a girl of 12 in a wood in Leicestershire. Previous conviction for attempted murder of the same type. Insisted on pleading guilty and sentenced to death after a trial lasting four minutes. Hanged on November 17th, 1953.

82. STANISLAW JURAS, 43, a Polish railway worker, strangled his landlady. He stated to the police: "I murdered her because I was in love with her and I think she was in love with me." Defence counsel described Juras as illiterate, uneducated, of low mentality and hysterical. Hanged on December 17th, 1953.

83. FRANCIS WILKINSON, 24, a furnaceman, beat to death his landlady's five-year-old daughter, then attempted to make a sexual assault. Wilkinson's mother said that at an early age he suffered a shock when he found a new-born baby torn in half in a dustbin. Later on he broke a mirror because he could not bear the sight of himself. Dr. Desmond Curran and Dr. Matheson gave evidence to the effect that Wilkinson was a psychopath but was not suffering from any mental disease which would bring him within the M'Naghten Rules. The judge ruled that "there was no evidence that Wilkinson was suffering from a disease of the mind which

would bring him within the M'Naghten Rules." Hanged on December 18th, 1953.

84. ALFRED CHARLES WHITEWAY, 22, a labourer of Teddington, assaulted and murdered two girls of 16 and 18 ("Towpath murders"). Hanged on December 22nd, 1953.

85. GEORGE JAMES NEWLAND, 21, a metal toymaker of Walthamstow, battered to death with a hammer a 65-year-old tradesman and also attacked victim's wife, because "he got desperate and wanted money for a new suit. . . . What really got into my mind was the cosh-boy picture I saw the other day." E.E.G. showed "abnormality of unspecific character." Hanged on December 23rd, 1953.

Conclusions

1. The record confirms the statement by Sir John Macdonell, based on the statistics of 1885–1905, and endorsed by the Royal Commission fifty years later, that murder "is not generally the crime of the so-called criminal classes, but is in most cases rather an incident in miserable lives." *

2. *Prima facie,* about seventy cases, i.e., over 80 per cent., seem to belong to the category of *crime passionnel* and/or crimes of the disordered mind. Murders for financial gain *without* a marked trait of mental abnormality (cases 5, 18, 22, 23, 37, 38, 49, 53, 54, 70, 73, 79) number twelve in all, and in most of these cases the psychiatric aspect was not discussed. Even these are almost throughout unpremeditated and committed in an affray or panic to avoid detection or arrest. Of the so-called "cold-blooded premeditated murder for gain" by a sane person, there is only one example, No. 79. The master minds who plot the perfect crime are pathological minds: 11, 46, 77.

3. By far the most prevalent cause of murder is insanity and mental disorder, ranging from the certifiably insane to epileptics, psychopaths, and borderline cases of varying kinds. This point can only be fully appreciated against the statistical background of the period in question. The total number of murderers known to or suspected by the police in 1949–53 (England and Wales only) was 554. Of these, 186, i.e., 34 per cent. of the total, committed

* Royal Commission Report, page 330.

suicide. A further 149 were found insane on arraignment, unfit to plead, guilty but insane, or certified insane after conviction, accounting for another 28 per cent. Among those who were actually executed, about 50 per cent. had a psychiatric history of one kind or another. In some cases medical evidence for the prosecution concurred with the defense that the accused was certifiably insane (17, Rivett) or mentally defective, or otherwise abnormal. In the majority of cases the prosecution did not deny that the accused was mentally abnormal, but denied that he was insane according to the M'Naghten Rules of 1843. The result is this tragic procession to the gallows of psychopaths, epileptics, mental defectives, hysterics, sex maniacs, depressives, and people on the border of paranoia and schizophrenia. If the Government's recent proposals concerning diminished responsibility had been in effect during the period under review a substantial proportion of those executed would have been spared.

4. The record bears out the Royal Commission's statement that "there is no sharp dividing line between sanity and insanity, but that the two extremes of 'sanity' and 'insanity' shade into one another by imperceptible gradations. The degree of individual responsibility varies equally widely; no clear boundary can be drawn between responsibility and irresponsibility." * Likewise, "crimes of passion" shade without a sharp division into crimes due to mental disease. Character and circumstances interact and, by and large, we call "crimes of passion" those in which the emphasis is on the circumstances, and pathological crimes those where the emphasis is on some compulsive trait of character. Accordingly, it seems impossible to make satisfactory statutory distinctions between more or less "heinous" crimes, as proposed in the majority of the amendments to the Abolition Bill. The most odious crimes, such as the strangling of small children, are often committed by the palpably insane, who would be automatically immune against the death-penalty.

The same fluidity prevails, as the record shows, with regard to premeditation, provocation, and malice aforethought. The point may be illustrated by comparing a recent case with the cases on record. On March 15, 1956, Derek Roberts, a medical student of 22, killed a 19-year-old fashion model by a shot in the head,

* Royal Commission Report, page 143.

and immediately afterwards shot himself. The jury at the inquest returned a verdict that he took his life "while the balance of his mind was disturbed." Both the jury and the Press treated the tragedy with compassion and understanding. Yet on the day before committing the murder the student had first acquired a gun licence, then a gun, then the cartridges in a different shop, all proof of careful premeditation. If the shot against his own body had failed to kill him, as in cases 14 and 42, both of whom had been executed (the former against the jury's strong recommendation to mercy), Derek Roberts's act of despair would have fallen into the same category of premeditated murder.

A study of the kaleidoscopic record of five years, with its interlocking patterns of motivation, will further confirm the Royal Commission's statement that "grading according to the degree of responsibility is beyond the capacity and knowledge of either judge or jury. . . . We conclude with regret that the object of our quest is chimerical and that it must be abandoned."

5. Special attention with regard to the deterrence problem should be paid to cases 8, 17, 28, 40, 42, 43, 44, 45, 61, 63, 64, 66, 80 and 81, who either insisted on pleading guilty against the judge's warning about the inevitable outcome, or expressly said that they were in a hurry to be hanged, or words to a similar effect. It seems probable that in these cases the prospect of a quick death had more of a reassuring than a deterrent effect and that the prospect of a long prison sentence would have held for these desperate and despairing men a more effective threat.

6. The Home Secretary said in his statement quoted on page 180 that all reprieved murderers "have been reprieved because of extenuating circumstances" and the next sentence in the statement implies that where reprieve was refused such extenuating circumstances were absent. This is not the case, as the following considerations will show:

(a) Mental abnormality may or may not be regarded as relevant at the trial, but is relevant to the exercise of the prerogative of mercy. In cases 8 and 34 the prison medical officers agreed with the defence that the accused men's mental age was that of a child of 12, and in a number of other cases there was similar agreement about mental abnormality outside the Rules; yet mercy was refused.

(b) The jury made a recommendation to mercy in four cases

(5, 58, 65 and 74), a strong recommendation to mercy in nine cases (9, 14, 23, 26, 27, 50, 59, 60 and 61), and "the strongest possible recommendation to mercy" in case 55. In all these cases mercy was refused. These cases should be compared with case 17, where the prison medical officers testified that the accused was certifiably insane and unfit to plead, yet the jury's finding that he was sane and fit to plead was accepted by the Home Office, and the man was hanged. The Lord Chief Justice, in rejecting the appeal, emphasised that "it was for the jury and not for medical men of whatever eminence to determine the issue" (page 184). The Home Secretary cannot have it both ways. If the jury's voice carries such authority that a man is hanged in spite of the unanimous medical evidence that he is insane, then the jury's recommendations to mercy ought to carry the same authority.

(c) The Royal Commission calls it "a foregone conclusion" that the survivors of genuine suicide pacts are reprieved.* Case 19 (Maksimowski) was not reprieved, though there could be little doubt that the case was one of a genuine suicide pact. Cases 14 and 42, in which the accused killed his girl, then tried to kill himself, and was nursed back to life, are not suicide pacts but genuine tragedies in which extenuating circumstances cannot be said to have been lacking.

(d) The Royal Commission further lists the following types of murder which are "recognized as needing specially close scrutiny to see whether there are such extenuating circumstances as would justify reprieve": "murders committed in some sudden excess of frenzy where the murderer has previously had no evil animus towards his victim" (cases 3, 4, 8, 14, 24, 28, 29, 40, 42, 60, 61, 63, 65, 68, 71 and 82); provocation (cases 2 and 35); "murders committed in a state of drunkenness . . . especially if the murderer is a man of hitherto good character" (cases 9 and 44); murders "committed by two or more people with differing degrees of responsibility" (cases 27 and 74); women (case 1); and, finally, youths (cases 3, 46 and 74). I have quoted against the above headings only the most conspicuous cases where the presence of extenuating circumstances could hardly be denied.

7. Lastly, some comment is called for on the Home Secretary's prediction that "of the murderers executed between 1949 and 1953,

* Royal Commission Report, paragraph 37.

something like sixty would have had to be detained for periods of up to twenty years and some twenty-five for longer, some of them for the whole course of their natural lives"—as opposed to the average sentence served by reprieved murderers, which is between seven and nine years. He further emphatically stated that "if we look at the records of those who have been executed . . . there will be no question of release after nine years, and that is a point which has to be clearly understood."

It is respectfully submitted:

(a) That a number of the more pathetic *crime passionnel* cases on the list seem *prima facie* to belong to the category of murderers who, when reprieved, traditionally become model prisoners, serve part of their sentence in open prisons, are released after less than nine years and successfully reintegrated into society.

(b) That thirty-two of the eighty-five who were executed, i.e., 37 per cent., were under 25 years af age and that eight out of fourteen recommendations to mercy, i.e., more than half, referred to these. To hang someone under 25 every two months, and to defend this routine on the grounds that they are incapable of reform, amounts to a repudiation of modern penology and of common sense.

(c) That the statement of "sixty having to be detained for periods up to twenty years and some twenty-five for longer" stands in such complete contrast to the experience relating to reprieved murderers that it could be plausible only if a corresponding contrast existed between the categories of the reprieved and the hanged. This is not the case; the type of murderer on our list conforms according to the prevalence of mental disorder and *crime passionnel,* scarcity of premeditated murder for gain, extenuating circumstances, etc., to the classic average pattern as known since 1905.

(d) In his pessimistic speculations of what would have happened if nobody had been executed during the five years in question, the Home Secretary seems to have forgotten the statements made by his own Department to the Select Committee and the Royal Commission. To the Select Committee:

". . . *the Home Office witnesses have testified* that, were Capital Punishment abolished, the number who could not be set free after the usual period, on grounds of prison conduct or of danger to society, would be very small. They predict that the greater number of the 300 prisoners convicted of murder . . . would not be likely to give any exceptional trouble to Prison Officers, and that those who could not be safely released in due time would *form a very small proportion of the whole.*" (Select Committee Report, paragraph 246; our italics.)

And the Royal Commission says:

"We agree *with the Home Office* that any convicted murderers whom it would be unsafe ever to release are likely to be in the category *of the mentally abnormal . . . and in it alone.*" (Royal Commission Report, paragraphs 652 and 658; our italics.)

(*e*) In the light of these Home Office statements we can only infer that the Home Secretary's statement in the House about the people "who would have to be detained for twenty years or longer" and who have been executed instead, referred to and defended the execution of mentally abnormal people.

(*f*) The Home Secretary further stated that these people, if reprieved, could not have been sent to Broadmoor because they were not certifiable and therefore would have to be kept in prison. He again seemed to have forgotten that the Royal Commission made detailed recommendations about the secure institutionalisation and treatment of aggressive psychopaths and other mentally abnormal, borderline groups. When Mr. Reginald Paget, M.P., called his attention to the fact that an institution for such people is in the process of being built, the Home Secretary evaded the question by answering:

"I am not talking about that. I am not saying what the position will be in years to come. Anything may happen. Nobody can tell what may happen about the treatment, and so on. . . . I am not arguing with the hon. and learned Gentleman about the future. . . ."

It is respectfully submitted that our concern is with the future and that the execution of the mentally abnormal on the pretext that they do not fit into the traditional classification of insanity contradicts the practice of other civilized countries and is morally indefensible.

April, 1956

AFTERWORD

For more than a quarter-century the House of Commons has, by a small but significant majority, been opposed to the death penalty for murder. In the period between 1930, when it set up a Select Committee, and 1956 when it carried through all its stages a Bill abolishing it completely, there have been five General Elections: there was none between 1935 and 1945. The 1930 House of Commons had no clear majority for any party, though the Labour Party had slightly more members than either the Conservatives or the Liberals. That Parliament was overwhelmed in the world-wide "economic blizzard" of 1931 and between 1931 and 1935 there were barely 50 or so Labour Members: the remainder supported the "National" Government led by Ramsay MacDonald. In the 1935 General Election about 160 Labour Members were elected but the House remained predominantly Conservative until 1945, when the post-war General Election gave the Labour Party a majority as decisive as the Conservatives had had in 1931, though not so large. The elections of 1950 and 1951 left the House of Commons almost equally divided, while that of 1955 gave the Conservatives an adequate though not large working majority. The changing fortunes of the political parties did not affect the parliamentary struggle for this penal reform. Whenever throughout this period the House of Commons had the opportunity of affirming its own view, each member voting according to his own judgment, there was a clear majority in favour of either abolishing or at least suspending for a trial period the penalty of death. There were five such opportunities. Yet capital punishment for murder still remains.

The first of these opportunities occurred in the days of the Labour Government of 1929 to 1931. It was a curiously-composed House of Commons. Though the Labour Party was stronger than it had been in the days of the first Labour Government five years before, it was still a minority Government: still dependent on the precarious support of the Liberals. The Home Secretary was

J. R. Clynes, a much respected Labour leader of the old school who had been Ramsay MacDonald's rival for the leadership. It soon became clear as the debate on 30th October 1929 proceeded that most Labour members were for abolition, most Conservatives for retention and that, as on so many issues in those days, the Liberal vote would be decisive. Their spokesman was Herbert Samuel, who had himself been Home Secretary and was to be Home Secretary again. Nothing in this curious story is more curious than the position of the various Home Secretaries: with one exception unless Herbert Samuel be himself an equivocal further exception, whenever the House of Commons in these 25 years has considered the question the then Home Secretary has been a former abolition-ist advising the House to retain the death penalty while among the leading abolitionists has been a former Home Secretary who in his day had advised the House against abolition. We shall return to this phenomenon later in the story.

On this occasion Samuel adroitly and lucidly produced an atmosphere of considerable confusion in which he easily persuaded the House, which—as the debate makes clear—would otherwise have had little difficulty in reaching a decision for abolition, that they would do well not to reach a decision at all.

In the result, a Select Committee was set up which unanimously reported in favour of suspending the death penalty for murder for an experimental period of five years. But its unanimity was arti-ficial: all the Conservative members absented themselves from the Committee's sessions at which the Report was adopted, refused to vote for it or against it, and declined to make any recommenda-tions of their own. The Government fell within a few months, and no action on the Report was ever taken.

No other opportunity occurred until 17th November 1938. In those days there were more opportunities for non-official Members to initiate discussions and even legislation than have been available since the outbreak of the Second World War. Every Friday was available to private members for Bills, and every Wednesday for Motions. The Motions had no legislative effect but they were useful opportunities for developing and ascertaining opinion. The "Whips" were not on. The Government was not bound by the result. Everyone voted as he saw fit, without the complications and embarrassments of group or party loyalties of any kind.

On that date, a courageous and independent-minded Conservative long interested in penal reform, Mr. Vyvian Adams, moved a Motion along the lines of the Select Committee's Report. The Home Secretary was then Sir Samuel Hoare—later Foreign Secretary in Stanley Baldwin's Government and now Lord Templewood. He was a life-long abolitionist and when the Death Penalty (Abolition) Bill, having passed the Commons, reached the Lords, it was Templewood who proposed it to their Lordships in a most eloquent and persuasive speech.

On the earlier occasion he neither spoke nor voted. The Home Office spokesman was the Under-Secretary, and he advised the House most strongly to reject Mr. Adams' Motion. Among those who advised the House to vote for it was a Labour back-bencher Mr. J. Chuter Ede, later to be Home Secretary in the Labour Governments after the War, and in particular, as we shall see, during the passage of the Criminal Justice Act 1948.

The House, despite its large Conservative majority and the advice of the Conservative Government, adopted Mr. Adams' Motion by a substantial majority: 114 against 89. It was no more than an expression of Parliamentary opinion: as such, it was clear enough.

During war the laws, though not exactly silent, are rarely changed. No further opportunity for an expression of Commons' views, still less for legislative action, occurred until 1948. The post-war Labour Government—the first Labour Government in British history with real parliamentary power—was on a floodtide of legislative reform. The various acts for the nationalisation of basic industries or services, the provision of free medical attention and services for all, the comprehensive national schemes for social insurance accompanied, were indeed an organic part of the effort, not merely to rescue the country from its post-war bankruptcy, but to build the foundations of a juster, more humane society.

Among the new-proposed laws was the Criminal Justice Bill. It was not exactly new. Partly it consolidated the existing law. But it incorporated a good deal of what penal reformers had striven after for the better part of a generation. It must be admitted that now, eight years after its enactment, many who were enthusiastic for some of the changes it made are not so certain they were right. But on the whole it was a valuable, constructive measure of penal reform.

Rather surprisingly, it made no proposal for the abolition of the death penalty. Surprisingly, because it did abolish all forms of corporal punishment, except for offences involving violence by prisoners in gaols: because Parliament had so clearly and frequently expressed its wish for abolition: because the Home Secretary was known himself to be a life-long abolitionist. Moreover, opinion on the Government side was known to be overwhelmingly —though not universally—in favour of abolition.

A compromise was reached. Though the Government would not propose it, would indeed advise against it, it would leave to a "free" vote of the House of Commons the question whether capital punishment for murder should be suspended for an experimental period of five years. The Government promised that it would accept the result, and if the proposal was carried would adopt it.

This proposal, which was identical with that of the 1931 Select Committee, was embodied in a new Clause to be added to the Government's Bill. After a well-informed debate, which covered all the only-too-familiar ground, it was duly carried. The discussion revealed the same curious streak which had characterized all previous, and was to mark all future, discussions of this issue. Mr. Chuter Ede, prominent among those who in 1937 had advised the House against the death penalty, now as Home Secretary advised the House to retain it. Among the Conservatives who voted against the death penalty was Mr. Gwilym Lloyd George, himself in the long struggle of 1956 destined as Home Secretary not merely to advise the House to retain it but to compel the House by making the issue one of confidence in the Government, to reverse the decision it had reached when left to decide for itself.

The Criminal Justice Bill, with its new Clause, went to the House of Lords. The new Clause was rejected by an overwhelming vote. The Lord Chancellor did in fact propose it: it was Government policy. But the Government did not believe in it, and made no secret of its real views. It was attacked most violently by the ex-Lord Chancellor, by the Lord Chief Justice, by the Archbishop of Canterbury. Of the bench of bishops, only 1 voted for it: of the judges, none.

The main criticism was that it went much too far in itself, and was much too far in advance of public opinion. There were so many kinds of murder in respect of which the death penalty must be retained: deliberate premeditated murders, murders by professional criminals, murders of policemen or warders, murders in the course of other foul crimes. It was conceded that there was a case for reform, but not for this wholesale abolition.

The Government was in a difficulty. The House of Commons could re-insert the Clause. If it did, and if after all the exchanges between the two Houses for which the constitution provides, the House of Lords also persisted, the whole Criminal Justice Bill would be lost. True, the Parliament Act provided a means by which the Commons could ultimately prevail. But as the law then stood that would take three years, and meanwhile the valuable reforms which had already been so long delayed, would be held up. Was it not possible to devise a compromise clause that would meet the Lords' objections?

The attempt was made. With full Home Office co-operation a new Clause was drafted. It took into careful scrutiny the Lords' debate, and produced a Clause which, while abolishing the death penalty for murder in general, retained it for certain categories of murder as so many authoritative voices had urged in the Lords' discussions.

The House of Commons adopted it with great reluctance, not really believing in its justice or practicability, but realising that otherwise all progress would be indefinitely postponed. But the House of Lords would have none of it. They ridiculed it without mercy. Their speeches, believers in capital punishment as they were, have remained ever since an inexhaustible treasury out of which abolitionists borrow with respect and gratitude the arguments with which to expose the fallacies of every subsequent attempt at compromise. They rejected the compromise clause with contumely.

The Government, and the House of Commons, surrendered. The Lords had their way and the Government got its Criminal Justice Act without the Death Penalty clause. Instead, the Government set up a Royal Commission to enquire whether compromise was practicable. The Commission was precluded from considering the death penalty itself: that, said Prime Minister Attlee, was a matter for Parliament! Its terms of reference were merely: "to consider and report whether liability . . . to suffer capital punishment for murder should be limited or modified" and other matters incidental to or consequential upon that.

It was a most influential Commission and, after four years of exhaustive enquiry in Great Britain and in many other countries, it produced what is almost certainly the most exhaustive and comprehensive investigation into the subject ever made. As to classifying different categories of murder they reported: "We began our enquiry with the determination to make every effort . . . to succeed where so many have failed, and discover some effective method of classifying murders so as to confine the death penalty to the more heinous. . . . degrees of murder . . . have undoubtedly commended themselves to public opinion, but in our view these advantages are far outweighed by the theoretical and practical objections which we have described. We conclude with regret that the object of our quest is chimerical and that it must be abandoned." After unanimously recommending a system of jury discretion they add: "We recognise that the disadvantages . . . may be thought to outweigh its merits. If this view were to prevail, the conclusion would seem to be inescapable that in this country a stage has been reached where little more can be done effectively to limit the liability to suffer the death penalty, and that the issue is now whether capital punishment should be retained or abolished."

The Royal Commission, appointed in 1949, did not report until 1953. By that time two more General Elections had resulted in a change of Government. Frequently pressed to declare their intentions, they ultimately—in 1955—tabled a Motion to "take note" of the Report, defeated—*not* on a free vote—an amendment in favour of abolition, and made it clear that so far as the major recommendations were concerned, they proposed to take no action at all. Meanwhile, a number of sensational cases had renewed public interest. There was Derek Bentley, a mentally-retarded youth of 18, who had never committed an act of violence in his life, but who had joined in warehouse-wrecking with a boy of 15 who, in resisting arrest fifteen minutes after Bentley had himself been arrested, shot a policeman. Bentley was hanged. There was the Evans-Christie case in which it was established, to the satisfaction of everyone but the authorities, that Evans was executed for a murder committed by the principal witness for the prosecution. There were several cases in which miscarriages of justice were proved and in which, but for the good fortune that the victim did not die, innocent men would certainly have been hanged.

On February 16th, 1956, Mr. Lloyd George moved on behalf of the Government his Motion offering reform of the law of murder but retaining the capital penalty. To this an amendment was moved declaring against the death penalty as being no longer consonant with the needs of a civilized society. He offered a free vote of the Commons and indicated that the Government would "expect to base its policy" on the result. The Motion was defeated. The amendment was carried. When the successful amendment was again put to the House as the substantiur Motion it was not even opposed.

The Government, however, did not introduce a Bill themselves. Instead, they offered time—which they had always previously refused—for the Second Reading and all subsequent stages of the private member's Death Penalty (Abolition) Bill to which the House had already given a First Reading without a vote. It undertook to allow full facilities and a free vote at every stage. In the result, the Second Reading was passed after another full debate and in long and fiercely contested Committee and Report stages every conceivable amendment, exception and modification of the Bill's single principle of total abolition was tabled, discussed and ultimately defeated. The Bill duly passed its Third Reading in the Commons without amendment.

In the Lords, the Government also allowed a free vote: a somewhat incomprehensible manoeuvre, since the Government could not accept the result of a free vote in each House, unless the result was the same. If it was the same, the Bill would become law in any event. If it was not the same the Government would clearly have created for itself a grave constitutional problem. The Lords rejected the Bill outright and the debate was only interesting in that it repeated the pattern of the 1948 discussions precisely as though the Royal Commission had never sat and never reported. But the voting did show interesting changes. All the Bishops except one and half the Judges voted for the Second Reading, as did the two Archbishops, the Archbishop of Canterbury repeating however his 1948 pleas for compromise. Moreover, whereas only 28 peers had voted for abolition in 1948, 95 did so in 1956.

Here was a pretty constitutional tangle! In the British system, Ministers, though they may be members of either House, must enjoy the confidence of the House of Commons. In other words, they must

be able to command a majority of the House of Commons in support of what they do as Ministers. Otherwise, they would govern
without the consent of Parliament, which no British Government
since Charles 1st has attempted. It is by no means necessary that
they should enjoy the confidence of the House of Lords. For if
that were necessary, there could never be any Government in
England save a Tory Government, and that would be a denial of
the whole basis of representative democracy.

The Government was already expressly pledged to base its policy
on the Commons's decision. Even had there been no such pledge, it
would still have been under the plainest constitutional obligation
to do so. For whether the Commons expresses its will in obedience
to Government directive enforced by the party machine or, at the
Government's invitation, by the free judgment of its individual
members, that will is still binding upon Ministers. The Lords,
equally freely, had reached an opposite conclusion, and the Government's difficulties were not reduced by the fact that its own view
was not that of the Commons, but that of the Lords.

The Parliament Act 1911 had provided the means for dealing
with such an impasse. If, after all procedural exchanges between the
two Houses had been exhausted, the deadlock remained, then the
Commons could prevail if it wished. But it must re-enact substantially the same measure in each of the two next following Sessions.
If the Lords accepted it on either occasion, the Bill became law in
the ordinary way. If the Lords rejected it on all these occasions, the
Bill received the Royal Assent and became law in spite of them. By
a subsequent amending Act, the two succeeding occasions were reduced to one. If therefore the Death Penalty (Abolition) Bill were
to pass the Commons again in the 1956–57 Session, it would reach
the Statute Book whatever the Lords decided.

The Government's constitutional duty seemed therefore plain. It
could itself re-introduce the measure into the Commons as a Government Bill. Failing that, it could again provide time and facilities
for its introduction and further stages on the initiative of a private
member. It has taken neither of these courses.

It has refused to introduce the Bill itself. It has refused any
special facilities for it as a private member's Bill. It did indeed offer
not to stand in its way if the luck of the private member's Ballot

for private member's restricted opportunities gave it another chance. The Bill has had no such fortune and its chances of becoming law under the Parliament Act are remote.

Instead, the Government has introduced its own Homicide Bill. So far as the Bill deals directly with the death penalty it is an elaborate contrivance to defeat the Royal Commission, the House of Commons and the Parliament Act itself. The bulk of the measure has no direct reference to the death penalty. It removes a number of anomalies in the law of murder: it purports to abolish the doctrine of "constructive malice", it introduces a new defence based on diminished responsibility, it improves the law as to provocation, and it makes a number of administrative and incidental changes. These are Parts 1, 3, 4 and 5 of the Homicide Bill.

Part 2 changes the law as to the death penalty. It makes another attempt to do what the Royal Commission declared to be impossible, namely, to keep the death penalty for some murders and abolish it for others, in such a way as to confine the death penalty to the more heinous murders. It succeeds no better than other such attempts. Thus it keeps the death penalty for shooting, but not for poisoning: for murders committed in the cause or furtherance of even the pettiest of larcenies, but not of rape: for second murders on different occasions but not on the same occasion. The effect of including Part 2 in the Bill is that, even if all the exceptions were removed—so as to assimilate Part 2 to the Death Penalty (Abolition) Bill—the Parliament Act would not apply, by reason of the inclusion of the other parts. Moreover, no part of the Bill is to be left to a free vote. The whole weight of the Government party machine is to be used in order to compel Members of Parliament to vote for what they have already declared that in heart and conscience they reject.

That Bill is, at the moment of writing, before the House of Commons. By the time these words are read it may even be the law of Britain. Its authors estimate that it will reduce the number of executions from a normal annual average of 12, to an annual average of perhaps 3. Some may wonder whether it was worth while doing so much violence to so many accepted principles in order to ensure three hangings a year. They will wonder even more when they remember that in practice, having regard to the Commons' view, every death sentence in Great Britain has been commuted to life imprisonment since August 1955 and that if ever, as many doubt, there is again an execution for murder in our country it will be in defiance of the declared opinion of the British House of Commons.

SYDNEY SILVERMAN, M.P.

REFERENCES AND SOURCES

Abbreviations

R.C.M.: Royal Commission on Capital Punishment, 1949–53, Minutes of Evidence.
R.C.R.: Royal Commission Report on Capital Punishment, 1949–53.
S.C.M.: Minutes of the Select Committee on Capital Punishment, 1929–30.
S.C.R.: Report of the Select Committee on Capital Punishment, 1929–30.
The numbers refer to *paragraphs*.

Chapter I

1. Charles Duff, *A New Handbook on Hanging* (London, 1954).
2. *The Observer*, July 1st, 1952.
3. R.C.M., 8402.
4. R.C.M., 8405–8410.
5. R.C.M., 8302.
6. R.C.M., 3212.
7. R.C.M., 8468.
8. R.C.M., 3123.
9. R.C.M., 8466–8467.
10. R.C.M., 3112.
11. R.C.M., 3252.
12. R.C.M., 3125.
13. Leon Radzinowicz, *A History of English Criminal Law and Its Administration from 1750,* vol. i (London, 1948), p. 4.
14. Ibid., 5.
15. Hansard 1810, vol. xv, column 366.
16. Hansard, April 1st, 1830, column 1179. Quoted from S.C.R. p. 8.
17. Quoted from Radzinowicz, op. cit., p. 24.
18. W. Andrews, *Bygone Punishments* (London, 1899, p. 39).
19. Ibid., p. 75.
20. B. Williams, *The Whig Supremacy, 1714–1760* (Oxford, 1945).
21. Viscount Templewood, *The Shadows of the Gallows* (London, 1951), p. 21.
22. B. Mandeville, *An Inquiry into the Cause of the Frequent Execu-*

tions at Tyburn (London, 1725), pp. 18–26. Quoted from G. Ryley Scott, *The History of Capital Punishment* (London, 1950), pp. 46–7.

23. Minutes of Evidence of the Select Committee of the House of Lords, 1856, p. 3.

24. E. Cadogan, *The Roots of Evil* (London, 1937), p. 147.

25. G. Ryley Scott, op. cit., p. 55–7.

26. E. Cadogan, op. cit., pp. 147–8.

27. Ibid., p. 139.

28. G. Ryley Scott, op. cit., p. 137.

29. Ibid., pp. 200 ff.

30. E. Cadogan, op. cit., p. 141.

31. Condensed from the *Newgate Calendar*.

32. Radzinowicz, op. cit., p. 12.

33. Ibid., pp. 12 f.

34. Ibid., p. 13.

35. Quoted from R. T. Paget, Sydney Silverman and Christopher Hollis, *Hanged—and Innocent?* (London, 1953), p. 98.

36. Radzinowicz, op. cit., p. 14.

37. G. Gardiner and N. Curtis-Raleigh, "The Judicial Attitude to Penal Reform", *The Law Quarterly Review* (April, 1949), p. 8.

38. Ibid., p. 8.

39. Ibid., p. 8.

40. Radzinowicz, op. cit., pp. 290 f.

41. Ibid., pp. 291 f.

42. Ibid., pp. 293 ff.

43. Ibid., pp. 295 ff.

44. Ibid., pp. 289 f.

45. Ibid., pp. 287 f.

46. Ibid., p. 147.

47. Ibid., p. 148.

48. Trevelyan, *British History in the Nineteenth Century and After* (London, 1943), p. xiv.

49. Quoted from Radzinowicz, op. cit., p. 318.

50. Sir Thomas Fowell Buxton in 1821, quoted by Radzinowicz, p. 36.

51. Quoted by Radzinowicz, op cit., p. 36.

52. *Encyclopaedia Britannica* (1955 edition), article on "Common Law", vol. vi, p. 122.

53. Ibid., p. 122.

54. Ibid., p. 123.

55. Ibid., p. 123.

56. Gardiner and Curtis-Raleigh, op. cit., pp. 2 f.

57. House of Lords Debate, May 30th, 1810.

58. Hansard, April 27th, 1948, column 411; and June 2nd, 1948, column 106.

59. *Encyclopaedia Britannica* (1955), vol. viii, p. 367.

60. Radzinowicz, op. cit., pp. 727 ff.

61. Ibid., p. 527.

62. Ibid., p. 528.

63. *Quarterly Review* (1820–1, vol. xxiv), pp. 232 f. Quoted by Radzinowicz, op. cit., p. 553.

64. Gardiner and Curtis-Raleigh, op. cit., p. 10.

65. Hansard, April 28th, 1948, column 492.

66. Ibid., April 28th, 1948, columns 546–7.

67. Gardiner and Curtis-Raleigh, op. cit., p. 9.

68. Hansard, 1811, Appendix to vol. xix, column 92.

69. Ibid., Appendix, column 109.

70. Quoted from Gardiner and Curtis-Raleigh, op. cit., p. 10.

71. Quoted from Gardiner and Curtis-Raleigh, op. cit., p. 5.

72. Sir Samuel Romilly: *Memoires*, vol. ii, pp. 177–8. Quoted by Radzinowicz, pp. 510 f.

73. Radzinowicz, op. cit., pp. 221 f.

74. Ibid., p. 519.

75. Ibid., p. 519.

76. Gardiner and Curtis-Raleigh, op. cit., p. 15.

77. Ibid., p. 14.

78. Ibid., p. 6.

79. Ibid., pp. 10 f.

80. Ibid., p. 11.

81. Hansard, June 2nd, 1948, column 195.

82. *The Howard Journal*, vol. viii, no. 4 (1953), pp. 227 f.

83. Gardiner and Curtis-Raleigh, op. cit., pp. 18 f.

84. Ibid., p. 19.

85. Ibid., pp. 20 f.

86. Ibid., p. 20.

87. Ibid., p. 21.

88. Ibid., p. 14.

89. *Encyclopaedia Britannica*, vol. iii, p. 687.

90. Radzinowicz, op. cit., p. 257.

91. Ibid., p. 251.

92. Sir James Stephen, *History of the Criminal Law*, vol. 1, p. 479. Quoted by Gardiner and Curtis-Raleigh, op. cit., p. 13.

93. Quoted from Gardiner and Curtis-Raleigh, op. cit., p. 13.

94. Hansard, April 28th, 1948, column 484.

95. Report from the Select Committee of the House of Lords, July, 1856, pp. 35 ff.

96. R.C.R., 61.

97. Ibid., 61.

98. S.C.R., 255–7.

99. Minutes of Proceedings and Evidence of the Joint Committee of the Senate and the House of Commons on Capital and Corporal Punishment and Lotteries, Appendix F, p. 718.

100. Ibid., p. 723.

101. Ibid., pp. 725–7.

102. Ibid., p. 728.

103. Ibid., p. 725.

104. Ibid., p. 735.

Chapter II

1. Templewood, op. cit., p. 76.

2. R.C.R., Appendix 6, p. 5.

3. Ibid., Appendix 6, p. 5.

4. Hansard, June 2nd, 1948, column 115.

5. Ibid., June 2nd, 1948, column 119.

6. R.C.R., Appendix 3, Table 1.

7. Ibid., Appendix 3, Table 2.

8. S.C.R., 29.

9. Ibid., 17.

10. Gardiner and Curtis-Raleigh, op. cit., p. 23.

11. S.C.R., 28.

12. S.C.R., 32.

13. Radzinowicz, op. cit., p. 100 n.

14. E. Roy Calvert, *Capital Punishment in the Twentieth Century* (fifth edition, London, 1936), p. 10.

15. S.C.R., 38.

16. S.C.R., 455.

17. Ch. Phillips, *Vacation Thoughts on Capital Punishment* (fourth edition, London, 1858).

18. Report of the Royal Commission of 1866, Appendix, p. 632.

19. *The Case Against Capital Punishment,* The Howard League (London, 1953), sheet 15; and B. Duesing, *Die Geschichte der Abschaffung der Todesstrafe* (Offenbach/Main, 1952), pp. 232 ff.

20. S.C.R., 453.

21. R.C.R., 790.

22. R.C.R., 61.
23. R.C.R., 65.
24. R.C.R., 64.
25. R.C.R., 66.
26. R.C.R., Appendix 6, p. 54.

Chapter III

1. Paris, 1872.
2. E. P. Evans, *The Criminal Prosecution and Capital Punishment of Animals* (London, 1906), p. 150.
3. Ibid., p. 334.
4. Dr. J. A. Hobson, "Psychiatric Evidence in Murder Trials", *The Howard Journal*, vol. ix, no. 2 (1955).
5. R.C.R., 292.
6. R.C.R., 374.
7. R.C.R., 141.
8. R.C.R., 128.
9. R.C.R., 137.
10. R.C.R., 137.
11. R.C.R., 74.
12. R.C.R., 74.
13. Quoted by Templewood, op. cit., p. 34.

Chapter IV

1. Templewood, op. cit., p. 75.
2. S.C.R., 154.
3. R.C.R., 292.
4. Gardiner and Curtis-Raleigh, op. cit., p. 23.
5. Dr. J. A. Hobson at the Medical Legal Society, 1951.
6. Mercier, *Criminal Responsibility* (1905), p. 169. Quoted from R.C.R., 295.
7. Dr. J. A. Hobson, "Psychiatric Evidence in Murder Trials". *The Howard Journal*, vol. ix, no. 2 (1955).
8. R.C.M., 3219.
9. R.C.M., 3225.
10. R.C.M., 3224.
11. R.C.M., 3220.
12. R.C.M., 3226 and 3228.
13. R.C.M., 3248.
14. R.C.M., 3280.

15. R.C.M., p. 246, paragraph 11.
16. R.C.M., 3244.
17. R.C.M., 3245.
18. R.C.M., 3251.

Chapter VI

1. H. Sidgwick, *Methods of Ethics* (London, 1874).
2. William James, *Psychology: Briefer Course* (1892), p. 237.
3. *Encyclopaedia Britannica* (1955), vol. xix, p. 749.

Chapter VII

1. *Daily News,* March 16th, 1846.
2. St. Augustine's Epistles, nos. CLII and CLIII quoted by S.C.R., 292.
3. R.C.R., 374.
4. R.C.R., 606.
5. R.C.R., 606.
6. R.C.R., 605.
7. R.C.R., 611.
8. R.C.R., 790 (46).
9. R.C.M., 3231.
10. R.C.M., 3153.

Chapter VIII

1. Paley's Works, 1825, vol. ii: *Crimes and Punishments,* p. 388.
2. S.C.R., 219.
3. Letter to Benjamin Vaughan, March 14th, 1785.
4. Statement in the French Chamber of Deputies, August, 1930, quoted by S.C.R., 222.
5. Capital Punishment Commission, 1866, Minutes, 1054–5.
6. Ibid., 1063–74.
7. Ibid., 1060–3.
8. Clifford Sully, *Mistaken Identity* (London, 1925), p. 15.
9. Paget, Silverman and Hollis, *Hanged—and Innocent?* (London, 1953).
10. C. H. Rolph, "Personal Identity", 1956.
11. S.C.M., 4386.
12. *The Times,* September 13th, 1955.

13. Hansard, February 10th, 1955, columns 2085–6.

14. Templewood, op. cit., p. 66.

15. Quoted from Paget, Silverman and Hollis, op. cit., p. 113.

16. Ibid., p. 87.

17. Ibid., p. 101.

18. Oxford, 1933.

19. Ensor, op. cit., pp. 11 f.

20. Ibid., p. 22.

21. Archbold, *Criminal Pleading, Evidence and Practice* (Edinburgh, 1949), p. 325.

22. Hansard, February 10th, 1955, column 2153.

23. Hansard, April 14th, 1948, column 1077.

24. All quotations in this section (pp. 123 to 128) are quoted from Paget, Silverman and Hollis, op. cit., unless a different reference is given.

25. Hansard, February 10th, 1955, column 2090.

26. *The Times,* September 9th, 1955.

27. *The Times,* September 12th, 1955.

28. "Psychiatric Evidence in Murder Trials", *The Howard Journal,* vol. ix, no. 2 (1955).

29. Paget, Silverman and Hollis, op. cit., pp. 42 f.

30. *The Criminal Law Review,* September, 1955.

31. *The Times,* September 7th, 1955.

32. *The Times,* September 15th, 1955.

Chapter IX

1. Letter to *The Lancet* by a medical practitioner, August 20th, 1955.

2. Statement by Miss Margery Fry to the Royal Commission. R.C.M., pages 282 and 283.

3. R.C.M., 8402–10.

4. R.C.M., 8477–80.

5. R.C.M., 8483–6.

6. R.C.R., 732.

7. R.C.R., 714.

8. *Encyclopaedia Britannica,* vol. xi (1955), p. 151.

9. R.C.M., 8412–3, 8417–8 and 8428–31.

10. R.C.M., p. 627.

11. R.C.R., 732.

12. R.C.M., p. 788.

13. R.C.R., 717.

14. Ibid., 720 and 722.

15. Quoted by Calvert, op. cit., p. 32.

16. R.C.R., Appendix 6, p. 4.

17. S.C.R., 237–40.

18. R.C.R., 617.

19. R.C.R., 627. The text says that there were 79 prisoners of the Star Class, but the subsequent figures in the same paragraph seem to indicate that the Commissioners made a mistake in adding up.

20. R.C.R., 650.

21. R.C.R., 650. R.C.R., Appendix 15, pp. 486–7.

22. R.C.R., Appendix 15, pp. 487–8.

23. R.C.R., 651.

24. R.C.R., 652.

25. S.C.R., 246.

26. R.C.R., 658.

27. S.C.R., 244.

28. S.C.M., 844.

29. Calvert, op. cit., p. 194.

30. R.C.R., Appendix III, table XII.

31. R.C.R., 646.

32. R.C.R., 627.

33. R.C.R., 626.

34. R.C.R., 624.

35. Hansard, April 27th, 1948, column 397.

36. R.C.R., Appendix XIV, p. 4.

37. Hansard, April 27th, 1948, columns 397–8.

38. Hansard, April 27th, 1948, columns 454–5.

39. R.C.R., 653.

40. R.C.R., 622.

41. R.C.R., 643.

42. R.C.R., Appendix XV, (i).

43. R.C.R., 658.

44. R.C.R., 659.

45. Hansard, April 28th, 1948, columns 492–3.

46. R.C.M., 3251.

47. R.C.R., 278.

Chapter X

1. Quoted from Duff, op. cit., p. 56.

2. Quoted from *The Manchester Guardian*, July 22nd, 1955.

3. Statement by Sir William Joynson-Hicks in the House of Commons, June 23rd, 1927. Quoted from Howard League, op. cit., Sheet 17.

Appendix I

1. S.C.R., p. 180.
2. R.C.M., p. 798.
3. S.C.M., 5072.
4. R.C.M., p. 829.
5. S.C.M., p. 603.
6. Uri, Obwalden, Zug, St. Gall, Appenzell, Schwyz, Lucerne, Valais, Schaffhausen, Fribourg.
7. Appendix 6, 22.
8. S.C.R., pp. 375–6.
9. R.C.M., p. 826.
10. Calvert, op. cit., p. 146.
11. R.C.R., p. 345.
12. R.C.M., 8896.
13. Ibid., 8896.
14. R.C.R., p. 346.
15. Ibid., p. 347.
16. Ibid., p. 352.

INDEX